City
on a Hill

**William Jessup University
Celebrates 75 Years of History**

BRYCE JESSUP

The Story of William Jessup University

Of the 75 year history of William Jessup University, my tenure is primarily over the last ten years. I enjoyed the preaching, teaching and friendship of Bill, the founder, but only well into his retirement years. My wife and I received marriage counseling from Bryce before he took the role of President. Two sons and one daughter in-law graduated from WJU with others likely to come. I served on Bryce's dream-team and have most recently been honored to be board chair for the past five years.

The beginnings of San Jose Bible College were modest to say the least. Essentially no funds, minimal facilities, a young small barely functioning parent church, and a passionate vision by Bill to start a training center aka Bible College. Clearly not a well funded Silicon Valley start up (or any other type of startup for that matter). A mustard seed at best and a rather sickly looking one at that.

Fast forward to the present. A thriving student body now over 1200, resident upon a spacious Rocklin, CA. property, occupying gleaming award winning facilities, a vibrant Christ centered student body, 20 majors ranging from preaching to political science and physics. Even more significantly the future is bright and powerful as the student body growth is continuing at a strong clip, the first graduate program is soon to launch, on-line and degree completion are rapidly expanding and multi-campus continuous expansion is clearly in front of WJU in the near future.

This is the story that rests between those unlikely book-ends. Days were dark along the way with multiple near death experiences through the journey. Today, many of the Bible Colleges that were born of similar timeframe are now faint memories of an era gone by. Few made it to critical mass and today are thriving and growing as WJU has. Difficult decisions and deep sacrifices were made by many along the journey. Throughout, God has been faithful in protecting the seedling to grow and stabilize. He has clearly closed doors but also kept opening other windows of Spirit led paths on the way. Our enemy has won some battles but has failed to squash the vision and win the war. God has been faithful!

I attended a 250 year old east coast church where the preacher wisely described his tenure of leadership of the church, how it was successful before and will continue being so long after he is gone. Should our Lord tarry for another 75 years, this period of Bryce, John and myself will have a similar view. We had our turn at carrying the torch but God will have written a powerful story long after our turn is ended.

Today the founder Bill Jessup peers over the edge of heaven and joins with our Savior in saying 'well done' to those that have carried the torch over this 75 year journey. Sit back and join with Bill peering into the history of WJU as you read of this journey of vision, sacrifice and ultimately, extraordinary success and global impact.

Dr. Pat Gelsinger
Board Chair William Jessup University
CEO VMware.

CONTENTS

INTRODUCTION

For a number of years I have been thinking about writing a book on the history of William Jessup University and the time has arrived. There is no more appropriate time than the year of the celebration of the 75th anniversary of its beginning in 1939. I was just four years old when Dad pulled together the first student body of San Jose Bible College, now William Jessup University.

It seems only appropriate, but especially exciting to me, that this book would be dedicated to the founder of the college, my Dad, William L. Jessup, or as known to most, simply Brother Bill. He not only started the college, but served as its President for more than twenty years. Mom and Dad gave out of their limited resources $50,000 to start an endowed student scholarship fund near the end of their earthly journey, and the fund continues to this day. Therefore, all the proceeds from this book will be added to the Bill and Carrie Jessup Endowed Scholarship fund so that students for generations yet unborn will be able to attend William Jessup University.

The purpose of this book is to put in print the 75 years of history of the college. Much more could be written about the students, faculty, administration, partners, academics and sports programs than will be found in this book. Some may be disappointed with what is said and what is not said, as everyone likes to remember what was important to them. Therefore, the path that I have taken is not to simply present historical facts, but to present the material conversationally, to let the lives of my Mom and Dad bless us again as they remind us of what motivated them to start the college and to keep it going. I wanted to deal with the challenges and how God led, provided, and preserved His family so that we all could continue the legacy of passionate Christian education that he started. I wanted to write the book to also encourage us in the challenges we face, to not give up, to think big, and to hope for a certain future.

As I wrote this book, there were many times when I had to get out my handkerchief and wipe away the tears of gratitude as I reflected on the lives of Mom and Dad. Their dedication, sacrifice, humility, passion for God and His word, prayer, simplicity, and their compassion for hurting people and the lost, blessed me again and again as I researched and read the documents and his sermons. Their vision to start a Bible College because they saw in people the potential to change the world if given the proper tools, began a legacy that continues to this day. If they were still alive they would be amazed at what God has done. Thanks Mom and Dad for what you taught me. And Veltie, my brother, thanks for your patience with your younger brother "peewee" as we were growing up. You taught me much about baseball, hard work, service in the Kingdom, and life itself.

To my beautiful bride, Jo, I owe you so much more than I deserve. Your sincere love for the Lord and His word has blessed me. Your steadiness, bright smile, and especially your belief in me during the times when I didn't believe in myself, has contributed more to my life than I know how to say. Thanks for the way you loved our children, cared for them, and believed in them. To Jerri and Jeff, Jan and Frank, Jim and Liz, and your kids and grandkids, you are all the best! Jo and I are so proud of you, your love for the Lord and your fruitful service for Him.

There are so many others that I would like to thank who contributed so much to my life and growth, but space does not permit that. However, I would be remiss if I didn't thank Pat and Linda Gelsinger for your friendship, partnership, and mentoring. There were many times when I was ready to throw in the towel but you wouldn't let me. You saw in me things I didn't see in myself which gave me confidence and hope. Little did I know when I performed your wedding 30 years ago how God was going to use that occasion to build His Kingdom in the years which would lie ahead. Thanks for your perseverance, trust, and leadership in my life.

As I stepped down after 26 years as President of the University, it was with joy that I soon welcomed Dr. John Jackson as the sixth president of WJU. It is a delight to work with him both on and off campus, and I know that God has a marvelous future planned for WJU under his leadership.

Most of all, I want to thank my heavenly Father for His refusal to give up on the college and me during the most challenging days of the journey. WJU is in Rocklin because of God's leadership and provision. He provided the vision, the resources, and the courage to be where we are today. As I go about my daily activities these days, most of my prayers have been the continual offering of thanksgiving and praise for what He has done and for what He will be doing in the future. I love to drive around the campus ring road and offer prayers of thanksgiving for the facilities, staff, and for each student as I see them getting in and out of their cars. May God be glorified in all that occurs through the ministry of WJU...may you be blessed by reading His story!

The title of the book *City On A Hill*, is the title that was given to the property by its previous owners, the Herman Miller Office Furniture plant, when they opened for business in 1988. Many of the top executives of the corporation are Christ followers, and thus the name which was taken from Matthew 5. It seems appropriate for the book and especially now for what is happening on the property. The original buildings were designed by the world renown architect, Frank Gehry.

An original description of the buildings and the architectural debate that ensued was given to us upon the purchase of the property. Below is a copy of a portion of the front page document. The square building in the center was taken down after a couple of winters because of water leak problems.

City on a Hill

As principal designer of Herman Miller's new factory, Frank Gehry turned over a piece of the program to his friend Stanley Tigerman. Although such ad-hoc collaborations of big-name architects are now common among status-seeking developers, they raise the inevitable question of *who* will play the leading role. In Rocklin, California, however, the improbable pair achieved surprising harmony: esthetic differences aside, Gehry and Tigerman are true kindred spirits.

CHAPTER ONE

The Birth of San Jose Bible College

San Jose Bible College was launched by my Dad when he was 35 years old. Passionate about the need to prepare preachers who were committed to Christ, Biblical truth and evangelism during a time when the church was drifting away from the authority of scripture to what was called modernism in his day, it was his belief that the best way to change the world was to start a Christian college.

"On September 19ᵗʰ, 1939, our first students enrolled and classes began. There were 14 who enrolled at that time. During the year we almost doubled our enrollment. Our teachers were, Roy and Dorothy Shaw [his sister and brother in-law], Bill and Carrie Jessup and Ruth Bond. The school began in a good old rally and prayer meeting. Every morning that first year we had chapel at 7:00 a.m. The whole student body and faculty spent each morning on their knees in prayer. Thank God for those early days of faith and trust in Him. He blessed abundantly."

Pictured are some of our first year students: Paul Boyer, Dave DeWelt, Earl Chambers, Rodney Reyman, Eldon Melton (bottom right). Jack Kendrick, Ruth Bond, Jean West, Thelma Jane Nester, Maxine Smith, Effie Oliver, Mary Enjaian, Don Jessup (top right).

The college began at 306 South 5th Street in San Jose, in three buildings right across the street from San Jose State College, now San Jose State University. Before buying a home at 844 East Saint John Street, our family lived briefly in the building on the left side of the property, the chapel was in the middle along with a couple of classrooms. The building on the right side was the library and additional classrooms. Upstairs was the women's dorm, affectionately called "No Man's Land".

Our family moved to San Jose from Visalia in the spring of 1939, when I was 4 years old and my brother Veltie was 7. The picture on the left was in front of our home in Visalia and the one on the right was taken in front of the chapel building after we moved to San Jose.

The early years were great years of faith, sacrifice, growth, and anticipation about what God was going to do in the future from this small beginning. Little did our family know at that time what was in store. The financial resources were very limited. I remember a student in the early years who worked at Clapp's Baby Food. He would bring discarded dented cans of baby food to the school and the faculty would take from the box the dented cans of the "tasty food" they needed to help feed their families as there were no salaries. Dad would always let the others dive in first until about all that was left was cans of "fig pudding". It tasted terrible! My brother and I sat at the dinner table with a spoon in one hand and a glass of water in the other to quickly wash the "fig pudding" down as we consumed it. I would say to my Dad, "this is horrible" and he would say, "eat it, think of all the poor starving children in China", and I would say, "box it all up and send it to them." The company went out of existence and deserved to from my point of view as a child consumer! As I look back, we were poor in those days, but I never knew it for we were wealthy in the things that count and in those things which money can't buy... love, joy, peace, hope, acceptance, grace, etc.

God faithfully supplied for our needs and through much prayer and a strong conviction that He was leading, there soon was the establishment of San Jose Bible College. Shortly before the start of the college in Fall of 1939, we moved to a small, two bedroom home at 844 East Saint John Street. It was about two miles North East of the college. Mom and Dad bought it for $2,500. This is where I grew up until I was a Junior in High School at which time mom and Dad purchased a home on Rosemar Avenue in East San Jose. Here are a couple pictures of where we lived on Saint John Street. The first picture is of our car, my brother Veltie, and me with our family dog, as Dad watches us from the front porch. The second one is as the house looks today.

God Prepares A Leader

God began to prepare Dad at an early age for his special role in God's Kingdom someday. He was born on August

29, 1905, in Artesia, California, and moved to Ceres with his family when he was just two years old to live on a farm. He grew up in a strong Christian home, as the last of six children in the family. Grandpa Calvin and Grandma Matilda were committed to Christ and served as leaders in the Ceres Christian Church. Calvin never knew his own father, Calvin, Sr., as he had been killed in a Civil War uprising before Calvin, Jr. was born. At age 26, Calvin Jr. married an 18 year old named Matilda Sensenig Breitigam on November 8, 1891 in Saratoga, Wyoming. Dad's parents taught him the way of the Lord, giving him a godly example. Dad gave his heart to Christ on April 29, 1916, and was baptized. When he was only 17 years old, his Dad, Calvin went on to glory. The story was told at his memorial service how his horses had gotten out one day and they could not locate them. After an all day search for them they ended up discovering them at the church where Calvin had gone for an elders meeting that evening. Hearing the story, I am told that someone stated, "If you live out your commitment to Christ correctly in the home, even your horses will want to go to church." My Dad said of his father:

> *"My Dad was an elder in the church of Ceres. In fact his mother was among the early converts of New Testament Christianity when the Restoration Movement swept through Missouri about the time of the Civil War. So I have a long background in that religious tradition."*

Well, Grandma Matilda had plans for Dad when he was just a small boy. She used to introduce him to people and say, "This is Willy and he is our preacher boy." Dad told me a number of times how that used to irritate him because he felt preachers were sissies. His mom wanted him to go to Eugene Bible University and study to be a preacher, but Dad wanted to play baseball and become a coach. However, he reluctantly went to Eugene, Oregon, to study due to his mother's insistence at Eugene Bible University, now Northwest Christian University. He only lasted one year and dropped out. When he returned to Ceres he went to work carrying 75 lb. chunks of ice to people's homes for their ice boxes. This was before the invention of modern day refrigerators. He took with him for the rest of his life a slightly drooping right shoulder which he said was due to the weight of the ice, and a daily reminder of his spiritual journey. In addition, he worked at a second job for a cement contractor pushing wheelbarrows of cement. He put it this way:

> *"After breaking my Mother's heart in quitting Bible college, it took 6 months of working for a cement contractor and pushing hundreds of wheelbarrow loads of wet cement to convince me that maybe Mother was right. So I went back to Bible college and on one rainy winter night, under a large fir tree in the hills west of Eugene, I spent a night in prayer and really committed my life to Christ. From that time on, my course was set and I settled down to preparing myself for ministry."*

I have heard Dad tell the story many times with additional comments on how he was fighting with the devil about God's call upon his life. He struggled in prayer in the cemetery near the college to seek God's call and future for him. And pray he did, most of the night, until he fell on his face before the Lord and said, "I will be whatever you want me to be and I will do whatever you want me to do." It was at that moment that he sensed the call of God to become a preacher …and from that moment he never looked back or questioned God's call on his life. His mother had it right! It was somewhere in this cemetery that Dad made his commitment.

Calvin and Matilda Jessup   *Ruth, Calvin, Abe, Dorothy, Bill, Bob, Matilda and Helen*

Marriage and Early Days of Ministry

While in college Dad met and then married a charming young lady by the name of Carrie Esther Elliot at her home church in El Monte, California, on September 2, 1928. She was a beautiful lady, dedicated to the Lord, energetic, gifted in music, loved people and wanted to minister to them. Her Dad died at an early age and so she was raised in a single parent home by her mother. By the time mom got to college her mother had invested all of their resources in gold mines that never produced, and went broke. Finances were thus a struggle for mom, but being the hard worker that she was, she funded her own college education through hard work in the community.

Bill and Carrie Jessup

It was always interesting to hear Dad tell of how they met. Dad was from California and so too was a young lady named Carrie Elliott who had come to college from El Monte. From time to time students from a particular state would get together for a party and both mom and Dad discovered they were on the dishwashing committee at that meeting. Apparently washing and drying dishes together is a great indicator of future marital harmony. Within a year, they pledged their lives and love to one another and for almost 64 years that vow was undimmed. Here is how Dad put it:

> *"How thankful I am for that meeting. For almost 64 years Carrie has stood by my side through thick and thin and has been supportive of all the work the Lord called us to do. Her life has not always been easy, but praise God, she always remained sweet and willing to help. Whatever success has been achieved has been because of her faithfulness."*

Well, Dad took to preaching almost immediately after his encounter with God in the cemetery, and mom was his personal coach as she was taking homiletics from the same teachers as he had. She was not an aggressive lady, but when it came to evaluating his sermons, if it was a quiet ride home in the car, he knew that he was in for it. Arriving home she would attempt to tactfully help him to understand ways in which he could improve. One of his favorite homiletics professors was Veltie Pruitt, the preacher of a church in Franklin, Oregon. He was just what Dad needed and he became Dad's preaching mentor. Veltie invited Dad to preach at his church and Dad was very nervous. In fact, so nervous that he had a very short ten minute sermon, but he was not judged or humiliated by Veltie but encouraged and inspired to keep learning and growing. Veltie took him under his wing, spent time with him and even gave him a love for fly fishing for trout. They fished many times together on the McKinsey river near Eugene, Oregon, and fly fishing became his summer delight until his homegoing. It was from Veltie that Dad got the fly pattern, the Strawberry Rohn, which to this day is the favorite with all of our family fishermen and the only fly which I make. Veltie made such an impact on Dad's life that he named his first son, my brother, after him.

With Dad's love for the Lord, his passion for preaching, and his desire to speak the "good news" of the gospel into people's lives, when Veltie Pruitt stepped down to devote full time to teaching, Dad became a "shoe in" as the preacher for the Franklin church mentioned above. As a 21 year old student, he would spend his weekends with mom at Franklin ministering to the people there. The final two years of his schooling he spent preaching for a church in Carlton, Oregon, while he finished his Bachelor of Divinity degree in 1932. Here are six of the 20 graduates that were in his class. That's Dad on the upper the left. Look at that hairdo...mom said many times that before they were married she couldn't wait to get her hands on his head of hair to get it under control!

Following graduation in May 1932, mom and Dad moved to Visalia, California, to begin their first full time ministry in August. However, after preaching for four years at the church, he was told by the district leaders of the Disciples of Christ Churches that he would no longer be the minister there for Dad wanted the church to pull out from the denomination. So as he stood on the front steps of the church receiving this information on a Sunday morning, he invited those interested in starting another church to follow him to the park down the street. So he went down the street with most of the congregation to the park and started another congregation and called it the Visalia Church of Christ. They met temporarily in the Woman's Club House and seven months later they found the church building below and purchased it for $1,500. The new congregation raised $750 through a sacrifice offering and Dad's brother, Bob Jessup, who had an auto repair and farming business in Keys, California, assumed half of the loan at $750 for the purchase of the church.

Building in 1936

11

Building in 2012

Week's Prize News Item

YOUNG CHURCH BUYS HOUSE OF WORSHIP

The seventh-month-old congregation at Visalia, Calif., with which William L. Jessup is minister, recently purchased a small house of worship from the Full Gospel people for $1,500. A sacrifice offering on the part of the members provided for half of the payment and the remainder was borrowed, to be paid in two years.

The building is in a fine residential section on a main boulevard.

The work has been growing steadily under the leadership of Brother Jessup, the elders—Fred Ward, A. E. Hicks, C. J. Boyd and Roy Oberholtzer — and the deacons — Ray Wimer, Dale Funderburk, A. J. Corwell, J. E. Hurley and W. E. Frost.

New House of Worship at Visalia, Calif.

May 2 - 1936

Page Fourteen (425)

W. L. Jessup, minister with the church at Visalia, Calif., began a meeting, October 29, with Lewis Mick and the church at Pomona.

A Preacher Training Institute in Visalia

The congregation grew rapidly and so did Dad's burden to see Northern California and beyond reached for Christ, but he knew he couldn't do it by himself, it was going to take an army of prepared, Christ-filled leaders to make an impact. He didn't know of any preacher training centers in Northern California at that time that weren't denominationally affiliated. He believed in the autonomy of the local congregation, free from any denominational relationship or control. Therefore, only a year after the church moved into its new facilities he started a preacher training institute at the church for any men or women who wanted to explore the possibility of becoming preachers. The curriculum was focused on Bible and theology, prayer, evangelism, leadership, and preaching. During the next two years Dad poured his life into 10 people as they studied for the ministry at the Visalia Church of Christ.

The church was an independent Church of Christ within the Restoration Movement. It was not affiliated with the acapella Churches of Christ, but was a part of the independent Christian Church movement in America which had its roots in the Stone/Campbell movement of the early 1800s. There was no district superintendent, or denominational control of any kind. He strongly believed in the restoration principle of "We are not the only Christians, but Christians only." Dad liked that! Though he was conservative, and by his own admission legalistic in the early years of ministry, he believed in the freedom of the local congregation, preached and practiced unity, and was frequently upset by the sectarianism of many within the local church and the broader church community during his early ministry days. The church grew and Dad started churches in the neighboring communities of Ivanhoe and Woodlake and later merged them into the Visalia Church of Christ.

In the midst of a thriving church ministry and a promising Bible Institute in the Fall of 1938, Dad received a phone call from his brother Bob, an elder in Dad's home church in Ceres asking him if he would consider going to San Jose to take over the presidency of a Christian college that had never gotten off the ground, though it had some buildings. The call excited him and frightened him at the same time. Excited because his passion was to see a strong Bible College in Northern California to stem the tide of liberalism and his passion was growing for training preachers as a result of the institute he had started in Visalia; frightened, because resources were lean due to the Great Depression of the 1930s! How could something like this work during such a lean time in our country and within the Christian community?

Eugene Sanderson Moves To San Jose

The original dream for a Christian College in the San Jose area was the dream of Eugene C. Sanderson. He was a great man of God with a big vision and had previously started a number of Christian Colleges, including Christian Workers University in 1927, now Manhattan Christian College in Manhattan, Kansas, Minnesota Bible College, Spokane University which ultimately merged with Eugene Divinity School, and Eugene Divinity School in 1895, now Northwest Christian University in Eugene, Oregon.

In 1932, Eugene C. Sanderson, in his early 80's, moved to the San Francisco Bay area with the intent of starting another Christian College. He purchased two houses at 5th and San Carlos streets from the Walters, a strong Christian family in Salinas and shortly after built a chapel building between them. The buildings were across the street from San Jose State College. It was his conviction that a private Christian College should be next door to a public college so that students could take their Bible and theology courses at the Christian College and the other subjects at the public college or university. He felt the duplication of teaching material was needless and most importantly it provided for the student a place to share his/her faith in addition to having it challenged for better integration of faith and learning.

"In 1932 [Eugene Sanderson] gathered around him a few men and women and formed a corporation named, Christian Evangels of God...On April 4, 1934 he secured from Bro. and Sister Walters of Salinas two

houses at 306 and 312 South Fifth street with nothing down and an agreement that he would pay $14,000 in 5 years time and at 6% interest payable annually... With these two old houses he contracted with Emmett Farnham of Campbell (a brother to Grace Farnham missionary to Japan) to build a chapel between the two buildings. This Emmett did with the promise that he would be paid for the materials and the work. To back his promise Brother Sanderson gave him several boxes of rare books and Bibles that he valued into the thousands of dollars. This chapel was completed and dedicated on June 30, 1936."

Following this Brother Sanderson faced some very difficult times. He rented the buildings to a group of Plymouth Brethren to try and help pay the bills. However, nothing had been paid to Bro. and Sister Walters, not even interest on the money. The taxes had not been paid for four years and another year and the buildings would have been taken over by the city of San Jose.

My Dad recounted it this way:

"He borrowed money from a few friends who had compassion for him. Had it not been for Wayland Phillips, Balfour Bigelow and Bob Jessup, he would have gone hungry many times. At the end of 1938 he knew that he was nearing the end of a dead end street and that something had to be done. Bill Baird was preaching in Modesto and he was asked to take over the work. Bill was not interested. He contacted James Merle Applegate of Los Angeles and others of his Eugene Bible University days and none wanted anything to do with what he thought he had. On Thanksgiving day November 24, 1938, my brother Bob and his wife had him over for the weekend. Bob told him how I was interested in training young people for the

ministry. He told him about the mini Bible College we had in the Visalia Church for our own young people. We had classes on Tuesday and Thursday nights from 7-9pm. I had 10 students who were in their second year of study in this home spun Bible College (later when S.J.B.C. began 5 of these were among our first students). Bob told him these things and said that he might call me and see if I would be interested. On that same day I received a phone call from him asking me if I would come and take over the work."

Aunt Edna and Uncle Bob in later years, and now with the Lord!

I doubt that WJU would exist today were it not for the encouragement, prayer support, and financial resources that Aunt Edna and Uncle Bob provided during the early days of SJBC. Uncle Bob promised Dad that he would be his partner and help fund the college as he was able. I remember on many occasions my Dad calling his brother and asking, "Bob, how are your crops doing? We are getting a bit hungry over this way." He would send money and the church would send food. The church canned fruit as a ministry and I can remember receiving frequent jars of peaches and pears...they were delicious! So you can see the generous heart of Uncle Bob, here is a story as told by one of our graduates about Uncle Bob.

Bob Jessup
By Stan Faddis

In 1969, when I was 12 years old I attended First Church of Christ in my hometown, Ceres, California. I started going there after being invited by my friends Ron Megee and Wayne Dunbar. One Sunday I heard some of the other kids in our youth group talking about the upcoming summer camp at a place called Heavenly Hills Christian Camp which was somewhere in the Sierras. My interest was piqued so I began asking them questions about what camp was. It was explained that camp was a week where kids would go, live in cabins, play games, swim in the river, sing around a campfire and study the Bible.

I was smitten with the thought and wanted badly to go. Only problem, I was a kid from a single parent family whose mother struggled to house and feed four children. It cost $25.00 to go to Heavenly Hills and I knew that there was no way my Mom could pay such a high price. When asked if I was planning to go, I mentioned this huge obstacle. Someone told me that a man in the church would sometimes pay a kid's way if the kid asked him personally. His name was Bob Jessup and he was one of the church elders.

I really wanted to go to camp but I was mortified to ask for such a large sum of money from anyone, let alone a total stranger. It seemed a shameful thing to do. However, I really wanted to go because it sounded like such a great week. So, one Sunday morning I asked someone to point out Mr. Jessup to me. Then, I followed him all around the building in an effort to get him alone so I could ask him. I would have died if anyone heard me asking him for such an extravagant amount of money,

Finally, I saw my chance. He had gone into the restroom and I prayed as I entered the door behind him that no one else was in that bathroom. I was so relieved to see only the two of us in there! As he stood at the urinal, I made my pitch saying I had heard that if I asked you to pay the fee for me, I would be able to go to camp. He did not seem upset that I had asked him this, despite the surroundings or the task he was presently performing. He smiled and said, "What is your name?" I said, "Stanley Faddis." He replied, "Well, Stanley, you're going to camp." I cannot describe how happy I was. It was the greatest thing that had ever happened to me.

I look back on that event as one that set in motion another event that has forever changed my life. Several weeks later, our youth group went to Heavenly Hills Christian Camp in a caravan of vehicles. Camp was every bit as exciting as I had been told it was. Sitting around the campfire that week with everyone, I listened to a missionary to Africa talk about Jesus Christ in a way I had never heard. I went forward to answer that missionary's altar call to accept Jesus as my Lord and Savior. The following day I was baptized in the swimming hole at the river. Six years later, when I was 19 years of age, I moved away from Ceres to attend San Jose Bible College where that missionary man was now the president of the college. His name was Woodrow Phillips.

I am now 55 years old and to this day I credit both Bob Jessup and Woody Phillips for my life change. Woody's preaching was made available to me by Bob's generosity which sent this poor kid to camp. I have said many times that if I were not a follower of Christ, I would be in one of three places – sitting on a bar stool in a tavern, living in prison or lying in a grave.

Well, Dad gave a positive response to the opportunity and almost immediately on that Thanksgiving weekend, November, 1938, he called the elders of the Visalia Church of Christ together and told them the story, emphasizing the need and asking for their support for him to go to San Jose the first of the year to start a church in the buildings. Dad knew that if he was to become President of the Bible College, he was going to have to find a way to fund it, and the local church was the only answer for him as he strongly believed in the partnership of the local church with the college. So the elders sent him north to San Jose agreeing to pay him $75 a month as wages for six months so that mom and Dad would have some income. We owe a great debt of gratitude to the Visalia church for its vision and its Kingdom commitment...it would have been much easier for them to have done otherwise.

Then on December 29, 1938, his brother-in-law Roy Shaw, brought him to San Jose, where Dad felt himself an outsider to this big city. He later wrote, "I was a total stranger in what I thought was a large city of 61,000 people. But I knew the Lord and I knew He would stand by me and lead me. I will always remember that first night in San Jose, most of it was spent in prayer. It was a blessed experience."

On Sunday, January 1, 1939, around 20 people came to the services at 5th and San Carlos streets for the first service for what would eventually become Central Christian Church in San Jose. This was the first service of a three week evangelistic meeting which was held every night except Monday for the next three weeks. Four people came to Christ and were baptized. This church became the founding church for SJBC and the strongest supporting church in the history of the college and continues to be so to the present day. WJU exists today because of the early generosity, vision and commitment of this partner church, where I also had the personal privilege of serving as Pastor for 12 years before I became President of SJBC in 1984. Dad commuted back and forth to Visalia until May of 1939, when it was time to make the break and move the family to San Jose. Below is a copy of the printed invitation cards that were printed and distributed throughout the neighborhood inviting people to the newly formed church.

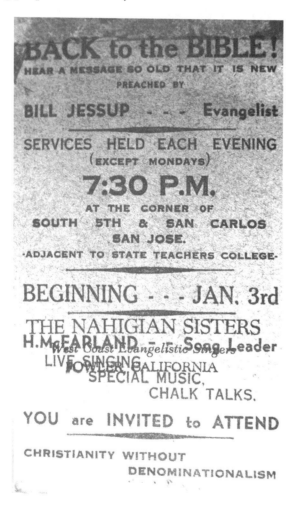

BACK to the BIBLE!
HEAR A MESSAGE SO OLD THAT IT IS NEW
PREACHED BY

BILL JESSUP - - - Evangelist

SERVICES HELD EACH EVENING
(EXCEPT MONDAYS)

7:30 P.M.
AT THE CORNER OF
SOUTH 5TH & SAN CARLOS
SAN JOSE.
·ADJACENT TO STATE TEACHERS COLLEGE·

BEGINNING - - - JAN. 3rd

THE NAHIGIAN SISTERS
H. McFARLAND - - - Song Leader
West Coast Evangelistic Singers
LIVE SINGING
FOWLER, CALIFORNIA
SPECIAL MUSIC,
CHALK TALKS.

YOU are INVITED to ATTEND

CHRISTIANITY WITHOUT
DENOMINATIONALISM

Our Family Moves to San Jose

Dad's first priority when we moved to San Jose was to find a way for the college to survive. He dug into building the church and to exploring ways for the college to take care of its debt.

"My first priority was to see about all the unpaid bills. I visited many individuals and business houses during those days and explained the situation and what we were trying to do. The personal friends who had loaned money cancelled their notes. Emmett Farnham, a fine Christian man, decided to keep the old books and cancel his bill. I never did hear how he came out on the selling of the so called rare books. Roger Darling had buried Mrs. Sanderson as this bill had not been paid, again a few old books were left. Mr. Darling realized this was not a responsibility of ours, cancelled the funeral bill and kept the old books. Many more such calls were made, some cancelled the debts, others were assured that they would be paid, and praise God they all were paid. We ended up with $17,000 debt on the buildings plus back taxes. Most of this was money owed the Walters. Again we praise God that all of these bills were finally paid. We didn't have much to live on, yet we were happy in doing the Lord's work and in the many doors that were opening for us."

It became obvious to Dad and to others that God wanted the college in San Jose and He would provide the way for it to happen. However, as he was studying the legal documents he was stunned with what he found. He discovered that he was the President of Evangel University and President of the Board of Directors of Christian Evangels of God. He found out that this was a world order, having district, state, national and international offices around the world. It was to have Apostles and Prophets who would be located in the different areas to supervise the world program. This was so contrary to the things he had learned from Eugene Sanderson in college, that Dad surmised that Sanderson had been unduly influenced by those he had drawn together to form the first Board, or else he was very confused mentally. By this time, Brother Sanderson was a sick man. He packed up his few possessions and went to stay with some friends in Los Angeles in February of 1939, where he died a year later on February 16, 1940. Interesting that Sanderson was then buried in the same cemetery in Eugene where Dad had struggled with his call to ministry some 15 years earlier! Below are the State of California documents granting certification to Christian Evangels of God in 1933, and a picture of Sanderson's tombstone.

FRANK C. JORDAN
SECRETARY OF STATE

ROBERT V. JORDAN
ASSISTANT SECRETARY OF STATE

FRANK H. CORY
CHARLES J. HAGERTY
DEPUTIES

STATE OF CALIFORNIA
Department of State

I, FRANK C. JORDAN, *Secretary of State of the State of California,*
do hereby certify that I have carefully compared the transcript, to which this
certificate is attached, with the record on file in my office of which it purports
to be a copy, and that the same is a full, true and correct copy thereof. I further
certify that this authentication is in due form and by the proper officer.

IN WITNESS WHEREOF, *I have hereunto set my hand and have caused*
the Great Seal of the State of California to be affixed hereto
this 19 th day of October 1933

Frank C. Jordan
Secretary of State

By Frank H. Cory
Deputy

1106 2-35 10M
CALIFORNIA STATE PRINTING OFFICE

Therefore, on May 29, 1939, Dad called some of the current board together that he could locate, plus some local ministers. They were as shocked as he was when he read to them the Articles of Incorporation for the Christian Evangels of God. Thus, he officially resigned as the President of Christian Evangels of God and the board voted to disband the organization. On that same day, San Jose Bible College was born. Those present, ministers and businessmen, became the Board of the new college and papers were later filed with the state of California. The first Board of directors were Roy Shaw, Lewis C. Mick, V.K. Allison, Wayland Phillips, Bob Jessup, Hal Martin, Wesley Tottingham and Jim Alley. Plans were established to open the college in the fall.

The next day, May 30, 1939, Dad preached a sermon to the church he started five months earlier on Building a Bible College in Remembrance of Christ. I'm confident that the meeting the day before fired him up. Some of the things he stated revealed his heart and passion:

> *The task we have is to build a training center (call it a Bible College if you desire) that will by its life, teaching and purpose present Christ to the world. We are not building to please man, but our only desire is to be pleasing to God. We will present the purity, humility, and spirit of Christ. His purpose was to seek and to save the lost. A Bible College must instill in the lives of young people that passion for souls. God pity us and may we as a school die if after one or two years her young people lose their fire for Christ. The world is lost, in terrible condition. Christ is the only hope! We need to be charged with that statement. If we build after the life, teaching, and purpose of Christ, then we will have a Bible College in remembrance of Christ…which to me should be just the church, the bride of Christ training young people to serve Christ.*

During the summer of 1939, Dad visited the nine churches that were friendly toward the college. He met with ministers, elders, youth groups, etc., and told of the plans for the Bible College. God began to open doors, send students, and school was officially opened on September 19, 1939 with 14 students. San Jose Bible College was up and running and Dad's vision was finally beginning to roll forward! Here is a copy of the bulletin of the Christian Rally which was the official day of beginning for San Jose Bible College. An interesting family side note is that Ting Champie, who is my wife Jo's uncle, delivered one of the afternoon sermons.

SAN JOSE
BIBLE COLLEGE OPENING
AND
CHRISTIAN RALLY

September 19, 1939
SAN JOSE BIBLE COLLEGE
306 South Fifth Street

* * * *

Morning Prayer Service 10:30

Song Service .... James Alley, San Luis, Obispo.
Devotional .... Melvin Sparks, Napa.
Special Music
Special *prayer* meeting for God's Guidance as school begins.

Afternoon service 1:30

Song Service .... Bob Jessup, Keyes.
Prayer.
Special Music .... Ruth Bond, Merced.
Sermon ...."*The Witness Of The Old Testament.*"
       O. V. Wilkison, Santa Rosa.

Announcements
Song
Special Music .... Roy Shaw, San Jose.
Sermon .... "*The Glorious Gospel.*" Ting Champie, Ceres.
Invitation

Picnic Dinner 5 P.M.

Evening Service 7:30

Song Service .... V. K. Allison. Santa Cruz.
Prayer
Special Music .... Santa Cruz Church.
Announcements
Special Music .... Charles Philips, Los Gatos.
Sermon ...."*Why San Jose Bible College?*"
       W. L. Jessup, San Jose.

Invitation

Pianist, Frederick Gabriel Hitt, Los Gatos

San Jose Bible College begins its school year with this rally.

"GO YE INTO ALL THE WORLD". "PREACH THE WORD!.
COME! COME!

The First Teachers at San Jose Bible College

The first faculty that Dad invited to teach at SJBC in September, 1939, included three women and two men, mostly Jessup family members.

Front left is Aunt Dorothy Shaw, Ruth Bond, and my mom, Carrie Jessup. Second row is Uncle Roy Shaw and my Dad Bill Jessup, or as he was affectionately called by most, Brother Bill!

Uncle Roy was the preacher at the Lindsay Church of Christ, from 1930 - 1939. Mom and Dad had frequent contact with them, shared together in evangelistic meetings, pulpit exchanges, and many family gatherings in their early years of ministry. So it seemed natural for Dad to invite his sister, Dorothy, and Uncle Roy to move to San Jose from Lindsay and share in the starting of the Bible College.

"While ministering in Visalia I had talked many times with my brother-in-law, Roy Shaw, about a college in the Bay area. I had used him some as a teacher in our mini Bible College. I knew we would need help in the Fall so I challenged him to come and join us. I couldn't promise a thing. I told him that God would take care of them as He has been with us. So Roy and Dot resigned at Lindsay and moved to San Jose in August 1939."

Aunt Dorothy expressed her thoughts in saying, "We came to San Jose the first of September. Really, it's a most thrilling story when you think of it. We (Roy and Dorothy) came in without anything. Do you realize that when Roy and I landed in San Jose, we had exactly $125.00. It was put in the pot we shared. Whatever came into the church or school was all in one pot. Roy had been called to a revival meeting down in San Luis Obispo for the first of September. James Alley was the preacher. Roy dumped me and all the furniture…Bill had rented us a house right across the street from him at 845 E. St. John St. Roy got a train immediately and went to San Luis Obispo, and they, bless their hearts, gave him another hundred dollars for a two weeks meeting. We…the Jessup family and us..had used up the $125.00. Roy came back with another hundred dollars and that lasted until school started. Really, the story reads almost like the book of Acts, as far as that goes. Do you realize that except for that little church with twenty people in it that Bill had started, there wasn't anything here? There wasn't any other church except Santa Cruz over the hill."

Uncle Roy taught Bible and Theology, and Aunt Dorothy taught speech and oratory. Dad taught Bible, homiletics and practical ministry, and Mom taught voice and song leading. Ruth Bond taught piano and music, and that was the faculty for the 14 students who showed up for classes when the school opened.

I loved Uncle Roy and Aunt Dorothy. So many memories of them. They were fun to be with! Since they lived right across the street from us, I spent a lot of time at their house as a kid growing up. One time he was teasing me, calling me all kinds of silly names as I was leaving and going across the street. Not having many words in my young vocabulary I remember hearing something flying overhead. I looked up and then said to Uncle Roy, "...you...you... BLIMP!" He laughed and reminded me of that many times through the years. When I was about six or seven years old our family traveled with theirs for a weekend preaching assignment. My Dad told me that I would have to sleep with Uncle Roy that night as that was all that was available. Now Uncle Roy walked with a limp because of having polio in earlier years, and I told Dad I was afraid to sleep with him because I might catch what he had. Dad assured me that would not happen. However, the next morning when I got out of bed my leg had gone to sleep and I had trouble walking. I cried to my Dad and said, "See, I told you this would happen!" Fond memories of my Uncle Roy!

It is interesting how Ruth Bond, the only non-family member, connected with the opportunity to teach at SJBC. From childhood forward, she was highly gifted in music and had become well known to Dad and Uncle Roy as a high school student in Merced. Before her graduation from high school in June 1939, she went to San Luis Obispo during Spring break with her mother to visit her mother's sister, Rae Alley. Her husband, James Matthew Alley, was the minister at the San Luis Obispo Church of Christ, the same one mentioned above that Uncle Roy held a meeting for later in the year. My Dad was there holding an evangelistic meeting during Spring break. When he heard and saw her musical gifts and spirit again, he along with the encouragement of James Alley, invited her to come to San Jose at the age of 18 to be the music teacher at

SJBC. This was a tough call for her, as she was pretty much on her own due to the deteriorating health conditions of both her mom and her Dad, but she felt called to do it and believed that God would somehow provide.

The first student to enroll at SJBC was Don Jessup. He was not a relative, though his last name gives that impression. He was from Lindsay and knew Uncle Roy and Dad well. He had attended Pacific Bible Seminary, now Hope International University, for a year. When he returned home in summer of 1939, Uncle Roy and Dad convinced Don that he should come to SJBC as it was opening in the Fall, and so he decided to come North to San Jose. The story was told to me by Graydon Jessup, Don's son, that when he saw Ruth Bond signing up students for her classes on Labor Day weekend, he knew right away that he needed to take piano from her. So he signed up for the class but, as he told Graydon, he only attended one class but got what he was really looking for...a date! He took her along with my Uncle Roy Shaw, to go watch his brother, (not my Dad) Bill Jessup, playing in a football game for the University of Santa Clara. The relationship of Ruth and Don grew rapidly and in the Spring of 1940 when school was out, they were married in the old Gilroy church building and Dad did the ceremony! Don was one of the many students who immediately started a church when he started as a student at SJBC college. The November 25, 1939, Christian Standard reported:

> **Los Gatos,**--Meeting led by W.L. and Don Jessup, of San Jose Bible College, closed with 14 responses –2 by primary obedience, 10 by fellowship and 2 reconsecrations. Students helped with calling and special music. New congregation has been planted, with Don Jessup as minister."

Why San Jose Bible College...
First Chapel Message...Sept. 19, 1939

A number of years ago, Dad gave me his notes from that first chapel message. With special glasses I am almost able to read them. I thought you might enjoy seeing the original copy of the first page of his eight pages of notes. I am not only impressed with the content, but I am impressed with the amount of work he put into preaching it before only14 students and four faculty members. I have an idea he put a lot of work into it because he knew it would set the tone for the ministry for many years to come, including today.

I am encouraged with these foundational values of SJBC and reminded by them of our history and legacy of truth and vision. These values reflect his heart and convictions. Though many of the delivery systems have changed through the years as culture has changed, the message, vision, and passion of SJBC has remained throughout its history.

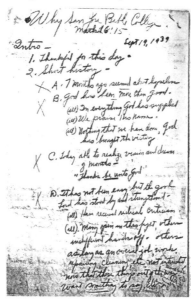

First Sermon 1939

In his chapel series of messages March 31-April 6, 1948, he re-preaches the message above in its entirety, this time typed so we have an accurate statement of what he said. He introduces it by giving a message first on some of the facts concerning San Jose Bible College in 1948.

1. Its position.
   A. It is non-sectarian. Young people of all churches may enroll.
   B. It stands for:
      The complete inspiration of the Bible.
      The Deity of Christ.
      The Church revealed in the scriptures.
      The unity of believers on the Word of God.
      The work and operation of the Holy Spirit.
      Salvation by obedience through the Blood of Christ.
      Prayer.
      Holiness.
      And all other Bible Doctrines.
   C. It stands against:
      Modernism.
      Sectarianism.
      Ecclesiasticism.
      All Sin.
2. Its purpose.
      To prepare young men and women for the Gospel ministry who will stand with firm conviction for the simple things of God and renounce sin in all of its forms, both in the church and out.
   Things for which San Jose Bible College stands…1948

1. A complete separation from the things of the world, or worldly pleasures. I Jn 2:15-16.

2. The restoration of the ideal New Testament Church in Teaching, Ordinances and life. Acts 2:42: Eph. 5:1-21

3. The Inspiration of the Scriptures, the Lordship and Deity of Jesus Christ, His bodily Resurrection and His Second Coming.

4. The Unity of God's people on the New Testament program of Unity.

5. The School takes a definite stand against the following:

   Smoking or use of tobacco in any form.
   The use of alcoholic beverages.
   Dancing, card playing, movies and other forms of worldliness.

   We believe this stand to be in harmony with the program of the New Testament Church as revealed in God's Holy Word. It is our purpose to send forth workers fully consecrated to the task of teaching and preaching the Word.

6. The school is free from all ecclesiastical over-lordships and stands free in Christ. It is non-denominational. We believe that denominationalism is wrong.

I find it interesting the things he includes in his definition of worldliness. The evangelical community of that day was fighting against the evils of a growing Hollywood film industry and a strong reaction to the "modernism" of the day. I remember when television sets began to appear in homes around this time and many from the evangelical Christian community were labeling it as the "pot bellied devil that sits in the corner." I remember trying to reconcile this with riding my bike on Thursday evenings at 7:30 p.m. to the furniture store around the corner to watch "The Lone Ranger" on their large 10 inch black and white TV in the display window. I think I was in about the 5th or 6th grade at the time. Shortly after, my buddy's parents got a 2 inch Pilot TV. It had a 5 inch magnifying glass which sat in front of the set and three of us kids would sit close together and watch the TV programs to avoid the visual distortion when you were unable to be the one sitting in the middle. How times have changed!

As a part of the chapel series in 1948, Dad preached the sermon from the opening chapel on September 19, 1939. He did this to remind the students of the core values and commitments of SJBC. Here is Dad's typed message of that first sermon...this time in legible form!

Why San Jose Bible College
(William L. Jessup...opening chapel Sept. 19, 1939)

Introduction:

"Seven months ago the work seemed hopeless. God has been more than good to us.

In everything He has supplied our every need and we praise His name. Today we are able to realize the vision and dream of many months. It has not been easy, but the good Lord has stood by and strengthened. We have received much ridicule and criticism. Many have been open in this fight while others have been indifferent. Others as long as it was an overall job with cleaning, work and repairing they were not interested, but now that things are out of the way, they would like to help. As we look over the past we can say with Paul, "Forgetting the things which are behind, and stretching forward to things which are before, I press on toward the goal unto the prize of the high calling of God in Christ Jesus." Phil 3:13-14. To forget the past and press on under Christ is the mission of this Bible College. Many people wonder why we have a Bible College here. Some say, we have enough already, others, the leadership is not representative enough. We desire from the beginning to let people know why and where we stand.

I. San Jose Bible College is here because men are lost. Luke 19:10

Many people in this area will be saved because of San Jose Bible College. If only one soul should be saved the college will be worthwhile.

Allow me to digress as I preach this sermon and return to today, March 1948. During this past month 65 were baptized into Christ through the efforts of the Bible College family. So the work has been worthwhile.

Now back to 1939. Men are lost and they need a personal **Conversion**. Matt. 18:3. Many are not preaching and teaching a personal conversion. Men need a complete personal conversion bringing about a change in thoughts, habits and desire. Luke 13:3, 5. San Jose Bible College is going to teach repentance and what it means.

Men are lost and they need a personal **Confession.** Matt. 10:32. Personal confession of guilt to Christ and a personal confession of His name before men. I Tim. 6:12

Men are lost and they need a personal **Concealment.** Col. 3:1-3. A Bible College must instill in its students a passion for souls. Meet Him in baptism.
Rom. 6:3-4: Gal. 3:27
Men are lost and they need a personal **Consecration.** Rom. 12:1-2: Heb. 12:14. This includes a consecration of time. Eph. 5:15-16. A consecration of reading. I Tim. 4:13. A consecration of gifts. Acts 2:42: Matt. 6:2-4. The tithe has always been the minimum in giving. We do not give until we exceed the tithe. Matt. 5:20. A consecration of the whole includes mind, tongue, hands, feet, eyes, ears, habits, etc. San Jose Bible College is going to teach consecration.

II. San Jose Bible College is here because workers are needed in the Lord's vineyard. Jn. 4:35
Many workers are needed and the Bible colleges are few. It is better to have many

small colleges than a few large ones. Some are out preaching as a profession, others money crazy and others without conviction. San Jose Bible College hopes to help supply this need by training young people who will stand with personal conviction. There is a great lack of conviction among preachers. In a certain area recently I was told how many of the preachers attended Sunday big league ball games and movies. This is the professional type. Then others go out to preach loyalty to an institution. Some schools drill into the students that loyalty to Christ and to their school are synonymous. Others instill a conviction of the importance of themselves.

We desire to instill a conviction that the Church of Jesus Christ is supreme. Eph. 1:22-23. We must preach Christ as the hope of the present divided condition. There is a need for a new restoration movement. The old has mired down in the mud of indifference, ecclesiasticism and sectarianism. We need to restore His church, free in Christ, wearing His name and teaching and living His Word.

Worldly pleasures, dancing, cards, movies, etc., need to be examined in the light of the word. Ungodly habits, lusts, drinking, smoking, etc., need to be seen as tools of the devil. We are to leave all the world alone. We may be called fools but thanks be unto Him

we can be called fools for Christ's sake.
I Cor. 4:10

In closing, let me say we stand humbly upon
the Word of God and it alone. Looking
to ourselves first, lest we fall short, then
standing without compromise, seeking to
do His will. We are not trying to represent
"Our Brotherhood", we try only to represent
Christ; seeking only to please Him. May God
give us the power to do so.

The series of messages outlines many of the core values and commitments of San Jose Bible College as it was launched. To summarize his last message in chapel during the 1948 series of messages, he spoke of the life of the school radiating the purity of Christ, the humility of Christ, the Spirit of Christ, and the teachings of Christ. He concluded by reminding the student body "that Christ is the only hope and that students need to go out with bleeding and burning hearts to snatch souls from the fires of sin. We must see Christ as the Lamb of God and apart from His shed blood there is no remission of sins. We need to keep alive the hope of His coming again. We need to work and watch. Work like it is our personal task to convert the whole world to Christ and live a life so close to the Lord that we would be ready for His coming at any moment. Titus. 2:13"

In the Christian Standard of October 4, 1939, Dad reported on the impact of the opening rally on September 19.

"San Jose (College).—Thirteen additions by transfer during past two weeks. Services well attended.

Good group of young people enrolled at Bible College. Large number of visitors at Christian Rally, Sept. 19. Roy B. Shaw and W.L. Jessup are ministers."

Church rallies were held each month by San Jose Bible College in churches throughout Northern California. These were done to strengthen the newly planted churches, give students the opportunity to teach and preach, recruit students, and build the Kingdom of God. The excitement ran high at these meetings as the students brought their enthusiasm and vision casting into the churches. Many of these students who preached at these rallies became preachers, church planters, and leaders in the Christian community in Northern California. There was a strong passion for Christ and His church in the early years of SJBC and a conviction that God is on our side and "the gates of hades shall not prevail against it." Witnessing to students on other college campuses was encouraged. It is recorded in Christian Standard just four months after the start of SJBC.

> **"San Jose (College),**--Meeting in college chapel, led by Roy B. Shaw, professor in College, has resulted to date in 7 re-consecrations and dedication of life by young men of neighboring State Teachers College, to gospel ministry; will enroll in this school. W.L. Jessup is minister."

Below is a picture of students and faculty of SJBC at one of the early rallies which was held at Santa Cruz Church of Christ. V.K. Allison was the minister, and later became part of the faculty. I'm the little guy in the suit standing on the left in front of mom and Dad.

Students & Faculty San Jose B.C.

Year Two of San Jose Bible College

The early years of SJBC were years of rapid change and growth. The word got out about the new college, World War II was in full swing and many students wanted to fight a much bigger battle than the one in Europe or Japan. Some became aware that if they chose to study for the ministry they were exempt from the draft as our government realized their "fighting the good fight" was a more needed war than the one our military was engaged in. The student body increased in its size and impact.

> *"The second year, 1940-41, opened with forty-five students and closed with sixty. The student population increased every year until the end of World War II when it became crowded with more than two hundred students."*

Dad and others wore many hats during those days as the needs were many. Therefore, he knew he had to bathe his life and ministry in much prayer and dedication if the new college was going to survive and move forward.

"Jessup was a teaching president; combining administration and academics required long hours of work and preparation. He arose each morning at 4 a.m. to prepare his lessons before the students arrived. He recalled, 'I used to get tickets for overnight parking when I'd go down there at 4 a.m.' At least one time he was delayed by a San Jose state security patrol when he was walking across that campus at 5 a.m. on his way to work."

I remember Dad telling the story that the reason he was confronted by the security guard was because San Jose State College was having a football game against Fresno State that evening and they were sure Dad was there in the early morning hours to deface some buildings or to sabotage the campus in some way. The security guard was about to cut off all of Dad's hair to teach him a lesson, but the guard reluctantly let him go when Dad finally convinced him that he was indeed the President of San Jose Bible College and that he was going across the street to pray. Students found out about Dad's praying in the early morning hours at the college, and some of them would try to get there earlier than Dad to join him in prayer, but they rarely got there before him. From the very beginning, prayer was the foundation block upon which the college was launched and built. Dad and others had to literally "pray in" the resources as they had nowhere else to turn in the early years of the school. My brother and I had to be in bed and quiet each night by 9:00 p.m. so Dad could get his rest in order to rise at 4:00 a.m. Little did he know that we used to get up around 9:30 p.m. and quietly play games in our room!

Classes were held on Tuesday through Friday of each week. No classes were held on Mondays because Dad wanted all the students out serving churches on weekends. Many of them drove considerable distances on Saturdays to get there, and then with services on Sunday evening in addition to Sunday mornings, they would drive back to San Jose on Mondays to be ready for their classes on Tuesdays.

When students received honorariums for their weekend service, they were taught to tithe it back to SJBC so that needs could be met at the new college, for finances were always a challenge. One incident concerning money I will always remember as it relates to SJBC. As mentioned previously, the church on campus was now up and running strong, with good attendance on Sundays. Dad, Uncle Roy, and a few of the older students shared the pulpit from week to week. Students were out in the community working and sharing their faith. After one of the morning worship services Uncle Roy and another man were counting the offering and I heard Uncle Roy shout out, "That is not a hundred dollar bill, that's a thousand dollar bill." They suspected it came from Herm Link. He was the assistant manager of Sears and Roebuck in San Jose, and he and his wife Wilma were invited to the church while a student was in their home doing house work. She left tracts around on some of the tables, and they began a spiritual pilgrimage that led them to Christ and as excited new Christians they wanted to see the church and the college thrive! Herm served on the College Board and as Chair for a number of years. What a blessing Herm and Wilma were to the Christian community until their homegoing.

The College Grew Rapidly During the Forties

1941-42

As word continued to get out about this rapidly growing, independent preacher training center, more and more students came to San Jose to enroll. The staff and student body were on fire for the Lord. Some of the students were just out of high school, many were further along on their journey, but all shared a unified passion for Christ who saved them and gave them new life, and they were passionate about lifting Him up in a culture that was desperate, having come through the financial depression of the 30's and entering into WWII. Most of them had no formal education when they enrolled in SJBC. There was no accreditation of any kind, and if your heart was beating and you wanted to tell others about Jesus, you met the admission standards!

And tell the story they did. The students would go door to door to witness. There would be street meetings. I remember students standing on the street corner at First and Santa Clara Streets sharing their faith. This was the best known intersection in the heart of San Jose. Some of the students played accordions, violins, and other instruments, and they would sing on the street corner to draw a crowd; then testimonies would be shared and the Word would be preached by Dad, staff or students depending on the occasion. Many came to Christ through these street meetings.

"We have had several street meetings this year in San Jose and Los Gatos. These meetings serve as a good source of advertisement for the school and also give the students a splendid opportunity to testify for Christ. But far more important is the fact that it gives some individuals an opportunity to hear of their Savior. These meetings have been held in the section of town where there are theaters or saloons. We sing a few songs to open the services and then have several short sermons and a few testimonies. Both the students and the hearers are inflicted with new zeal to serve Christ as a result of these meetings."

As the students were challenged to go forth on weekends and plant churches, it is amazing to look back and see how well they did. In the decade of the forties, approximately 30 churches were started in Northern California by the students and staff of San Jose Bible. Many of them are still thriving, Bible believing churches today. I remember many Sunday nights when we got home from a long weekend of preaching that Dad would carry me from the car, into the house and lay me on my bed in the wee hours of the morning.

In the 1940-41 school year a number of churches were started as recorded in the school annual named the **Christian Victor 1941**: Elmhurst, Bob Newberg; Allendale, Don DeWelt; South San Francisco, Rodney Reyman; Vallejo, Earl

Chambers; Redwood City, John McClure; Los Gatos, Don Jessup; Morgan Hill, Jack Kendrick; Ceres, Paul Boyer.

Earl Chambers started at SJBC second semester in January 1940, having given his heart to Christ, and was baptized just two months earlier in November of 1939 in Brookings, South Dakota. He immediately felt the call of God on his life to be a preacher, and Elston Knight and Walter Stram encouraged him to attend SJBC. By fall of his first year in college he was preaching every Sunday at a church in Vallejo. He shared with me in a recent visit: "I enjoyed the classes although they were difficult, as I did not have the educational background I needed. Also, I had many personal challenges. One of the biggest I had to face was my timidity which, with the Lord's help, I overcame. Roy B. Shaw and Bill Jessup were my two favorite professors and the semester passed quickly." In September 1940, Shirley Wilson came from Lindsay to SJBC. She caught his eye, and they were married on September 26, 1941. He started preaching for a church in Yuba City on his honeymoon. As I collected information for this book, I had the privilege of visiting in their home and talking about the early days at SJBC. I was thrilled to find a couple who are now both 92 years old, and they have been married for 72 years. They are in good health, have great spirits, and have superb memories about their fruitful and fulfilling journey in ministry. Earl is still preaching frequently. I heard him recently and brushed away a tear as I listened to him preach about how Christ saves us from the "guttermost" to the "uttermost". It was a powerful message! I took their picture as I left their home in Greenwood, near Sacramento. They are an amazing couple, the oldest couple still alive from the first year of SJBC.

Early Ministry Days   *Today in Greenwood, California*

It wasn't long until the college buildings were bursting at the seams, with 100, then 200 students and beyond within the first decade of the college. The students continued to be passionate about their mission and calling. Music groups were formed, preaching clubs, and teams were chosen to represent the Lord and SJBC in churches, camps, and conventions. Churches continued to be planted and it became obvious that there needed to be another ministry formed to embrace and multiply the church planting movement so that the college could focus its time on equipping the needed leaders for the church. At the 1954 SJBC Conference on Evangelism the program of working together through an organization to be called the Northern California Evangelistic Association (NCEA) was presented to over 200 people at a banquet. An overwhelming vote of approval was received. Therefore, the Northern California Evangelistic Association was formed to provide full time focus on the church planting ministry, and SJBC would focus on equipping and providing the needed leadership for the achievement of its shared mission.

NCEA thus began in 1954 with the first project of paying the salary of Wayne Thomas, an SJBC graduate, at Town and Country Church of Christ in Carmichael, California, so they could build the needed buildings. This church had been started by Chaplain Hal Martin while he was stationed at McClellan Air Force Base in North Highlands, California. The impact of NCEA flourished under the leadership of men such as Franklin Gage, John Sinclair, Jack Boal, Bruce Cushing, Bill Jessup, Byron Moats, Dan Scates, Dean Pense, and Marc Bigelow, all who served as leaders or Directors of NCEA at some point during its more than 50 year history. Scores of churches were planted. Under Marc Bigelow's visionary leadership, on March 3, 2003, NCEA expanded to become a national ministry which was named **STADIA** and continues to this present day in planting churches across America as a part of **Provision** Ministry team.

Early Graduating Classes of San Jose Bible College

1942 OUR FIRST GRADUATES

VERNON BEEKS
From Washington State

PAUL BOYER
From Oakland, CA

GLEN JOHNSTON
From Ashland, OR

ELDON MELDON
From Visalia, CA

DON DeWELT
From Portland, OR

ELSIE PRINTZ
Pomona, CA

LOU MOORE
San Bernardino, CA

Some from outside the region would come to the campus to see what was going on as they had heard of this "startup" Bible College on the West Coast. Edwin R. Errett, editor of the Christian Standard magazine, which is the primary communication tool among the Independent Christian

1949

1949 GRADUATES

Arthur Gott, William Gates, Burl Shoemake, Wayne Bigelow, Charles Richards, Wilbur Garlick, Joe Vaughn, James Caulley, Bonnie Green, Helen Rice, Claudine Waddell, Glenna Wiseman, Frances Sprague, Walter Minkler and Gordon Thompson

Churches, visited the campus. Following his visit he wrote a front page article on November 9, 1940 entitled "This New School Is Unique". Here are some of his comments:

> *I have been in many colleges, and frequently during vacation periods. Always I seem to sense a special atmosphere, but never have I sensed just what I felt here as V.K. Allison, of Santa Cruz, guided me through the offices, classrooms, chapel and library.*

> *Probably it was the effect of what he told me of the method by which the faculty and students share their income upon a tithing basis. That fact stamped the school with the word 'consecration,' and my mind could not*

let go of that thought. Then, too, there was the success of the students and teachers in the evangelistic pioneering in this northern part of California, and the fact that in humble quarters they carry forward this newest school of the prophets.

Perhaps the most significant feature of their work is that every student and teacher tithes whatever he receives for his preaching service or other activity, and puts the tithe into the school treasury. These tithes are added to the gifts from churches and individuals. Out of this fund the current bills are kept paid up to date, and, at the end of each month, the teachers, Brethren Jessup and Shaw, receive for their services what remains after those bills are paid. (A shoe box was passed around to the faculty with the remaining cash in it and they were invited to take out what they needed each month for their families. This was done for about the first three to four years of the college's existence as there were no salaries at that time)

The outstanding characteristic of the school is evangelistic passion. They see an area inhabited by over a million and a half people, where nothing really adequate is being done, and they have inclined the spirits of the youth they have assembled, so that new churches have been launched and dead churches brought alive.

There were twenty-seven students last year, and the latest report I have is forty-five students at the opening this fall. I suspect there are more now.

Brother Jessup and Brother Shaw I did not get to see, because they were busy in evangelistic meetings, as were a number of youth from the student body. But I think I caught their spirit. And it did me good, as it will do good to the whole brotherhood.

As the college continued to grow, most of the students came from California and a few from Oregon. The word was getting out about this being a Bible college that trains Christian workers, especially preachers, and sends them forth into fields that are ripe unto harvest. A weekly radio program was started in 1942 on radio station KLX in Oakland, entitled "The Church of the New Testament on the Air". The theme song was "A Bible Christian I shall be". It reached as far away as Alaska in the evenings. Dad was the main speaker on this program and he received many letters of inquiry about the school and the program and it became a source of recruitment for the college. In addition to Dad's preaching, the college choir would sing and students would give their testimony. The program moved in July of 1943 to KQW in San Jose, and finally for a number of years the program was broadcast from KSJO, also a radio station in San Jose.

KLX Radio Team!

Dialogs...Debates...Divisions

Though there was a huge wave of spiritual vitality that gripped the students and staff in the early years, it was not long until controversy developed over differing views of scripture and its present day applications. The increasing polarization of the left, right, and centrist views usually gained their greatest focus when it had to do with Biblical interpretation and practical application.

I remember as a small child an evangelistic meeting on campus and the evangelist was preaching against sin in all of its forms. He mentioned the usual five cardinal sins of that day which were smoking, drinking, gambling, card playing, and the movies. Then he went off on a tangent to talk about the loose women who are attending our churches. He spoke of their sins of wearing "make up and open toed shoes", and how we needed to be on guard lest we be drawn in and destroyed by their immorality. What was confusing to me was that the only two women in the audience were my aunt Dorothy and my mother! So these were interesting days of highly focused views and interpretations. This kind of interpretation and application of scripture became a wedge between my Dad and some of the early leaders of the Restoration Movement on the West Coast, for though he was very conservative by today's standards, he did not go along with some of the lifestyle extremes of his day. And so a division emerged in the movement and a number of students were drawn into this perspective and went forth to serve with a rigid and judgmental perspective about Dad and his views.

One of the controversies which stirred up the campus student body was the emergence of differing views on the ministry of the Holy Spirit. Two of our teachers held very different views. Both teachers were loved and highly respected, but as students would go to one class they would hear one view, and then to the other where the previous view was countered.

T.R. Appleberry held the view that we receive the Holy Spirit only as we read His writings, the Bible. The more we read and study the Bible, the more of the Holy Spirit we receive and to be filled up with the Holy Spirit only occurs when we fill up our minds with scripture. He used verses like 1 Thessalonians 1:5 (NIV) "because our gospel came to you not simply with words, but also with power, with the Holy Spirit and with deep conviction. You know how we lived among you for your sake." He believed there is no personal indwelling of the person of the Holy Spirit, only the impact of His Spirit through His word. Therefore, it is supremely important that we ingest, saturate, and meditate on His Word so that we will have the Holy Spirit in the fullness that He desires. Few hold this view today, but it became well known in the 1940s.

Don DeWelt held an opposing view. He believed and taught that we receive the person of the Holy Spirit when we are converted to Christ. He comes in to inhabit God's people, to strengthen, encourage, and empower us to live like Christ lived. Don taught that every believer receives the Holy Spirit when he receives Christ. He used verses like Acts 2:38 (NIV) to make his point: "Peter replied, repent and be baptized, every one of you, in the name of Jesus Christ for the forgiveness of your sins. And you will receive the gift of the Holy Spirit." Most people within the Christian community today hold the view of the indwelling presence of the Holy Spirit within the life of the believer and follower of Jesus Christ. T.R. Appleberry believed that the gift of the Holy Spirit was eternal life and had nothing to do with His personal presence.

As the conflicting perspectives gained increased momentum in 1951, a three day conference was held on campus concerning the Holy Spirit. The focus was a debate by T.R. Appleberry and Don DeWelt concerning the Holy Spirit's role in our lives. As Dad served as the moderator of the Conference he gave this conclusion:

There were differences of opinion, yet the unity of the Spirit was kept in the bond of peace. It is good for us to study the different viewpoints of different people on important subjects. I am glad for the differences of opinion expressed...and trust it will cause each of us to study anew this theme. Thank God we can differ and yet have perfect unity through Christ.

The interesting thing about the debate was how Dad handled it. As the moderator of the debate and because his heart was for people and unity, he tried after every session to wrap it up with pointing out the positive value of both perspectives. He was not successful in reconciling the differing views, but he was successful in keeping the SJBC family together and moving forward. T.R. Appleberry and Don DeWelt both continued to teach at SJBC up into the middle 1950s and it always made for interesting corridor conversation by the students as they took classes from both teachers.

One of the values of the differing views was that it challenged the students to do their own research to see where they stood on the issue, which is one of the cardinal principles of education. With the Bible as the foundation of truth, students are not taught what to think but how to think so that their conclusions are not borrowed from someone else, but their own.

In Dad's chapel series of messages on March 31 – April 6, 1948, he concludes by stating:

We have never forced anyone to accept any teaching contrary to his conviction. The student can accept or reject as desired. He has the right to disagree but not to criticize. Whether or not people think we are off the beam is their privilege. We seek to please no one or follow after anyone but Christ.

We have always granted the teachers the freedom

to teach as desired and freedom to express their own opinions. We have always had differences of opinion and will continue to have as long as we are human. I doubt if any two teachers agree on every little detail concerning the scripture. Thank God we are free men and can think accordingly. If all agreed on every minor detail further growth would never be attained. Every student has the right to differ as may be desired. Thank the Lord on fundamentals the faculty stands together as a great wall contending earnestly for the faith once for all delivered unto the saints.

This series has been presented to show that we still stand where we stood in 1939 and by the grace of God will continue to stand. Here are a few additional interesting facts as an outgrowth of this series. Since 1939, 82 have been graduated, representing 64 men and 18 women. Students are ministering in 12 states, Alaska, Canada, Hawaii, China, and Mexico. This year 20 more students graduate.

Faculty in 1946 at SJBC

Front Row left: Bonnie McQuistian, Audrey West, Bill Jessup, Carrie Jessup, Dot Shaw
Back Row left: Harold Rea, Willard Vanderford, Don DeWelt, T.R. Appleberry,
V.K. Allison, Roy Shaw

Unity Meetings

One of Dad's core values and thus of SJBC was unity! At a very early stage in his ministry in Visalia, California, he became burdened with the division which existed in the Restoration Movement. Commonly called the Stone/Campbell movement of the early 1800's, it began as a unity movement with people from the Presbyterian, Baptist, and other denominations, wanting to drop all denominational names and simply be Christians. However it soon became divided into three separate fellowships, representing the usual left, center, and right wings of most movements. The three wings of the movement, Disciples of Christ, Independent Christian Churches, and the a capella Churches of Christ, had little fellowship with each other and little good to say about one another.

Before he moved to San Jose, Dad had connected with a judge from the Church of Christ, Earnest Beam. Dad and Earnest Beam held a number of unity meetings in Visalia at the convention center and more than 1,000 people participated, mostly from the Independent Christian Churches and the Churches of Christ of the Restoration Movement. Dad continued this unity emphasis throughout his time as President, bringing in such men as Carl Ketcherside alongside Earnest Beam to speak in chapel and hold unity rallies on campus.

He expanded these meetings into yearly conferences and named it The Conference on Evangelism. Every January from 1945 until 1990, people from all over the west coast came together for preaching, fellowship, and the acknowledgement of our unity in Christ. In the early years, some of the conferences were attended by more than 1200 people who met at the Montgomery Theater in the San Jose Convention Center,

MUSIC . . .

. . . . HAS ALWAYS BEEN AN IMPORTANT PART OF LIFE AT SJBC.

REMEMBER THE LAMPLIGHTERS? Don Meyer, Tenor; George Ingraham, Baritone; Rex Wallace, Bass; Anna Fern Myers, Contralto.

December 18 1949, 3:30 PM, from radio station KSJO,1590 on your dial . . . the LAMPLIGHTERS were "ON THE AIR"!

George "Rusty" Ingraham leading songs at 1948 Conference.

Marvin Rickard, Tenor; John Morrison, Lead; Bob Day, Baritone; Jerry McCornack, Bass. Quartet traveled for SJBC in the spring of 1950

Double Quartet at Conference on Evangelism, January 7-9, 1948

and then ultimately on the campus of SJBC. They were powerful times of teaching, encouragement, and fellowship. For many years, it was recognized as one of the finest Christian Conferences in Northern California. However, with the development of TV, the internet, DVD's, and the increasing availability of local conferences and church seminars, attendance slowly waned until the need no longer existed for the conferences.

One student in 1946 by the name of Gordon Thompson became an important person in my life because of what our relationship taught me about my walk with God. Gordon was going to have to drop out of college because of finances. My Dad came to me and said, "Son, we have a student at the college who is going to have to quit because he has no money to continue. He wants to become a missionary. Would you be willing to give him your bike so that he can deliver newspapers to earn money to stay in school?" That was a tough call for me because as an eleven year old boy who didn't have much, my bike was very important to me. I decided to give him my bike. He finished college and went to Puerto Rico where he and Vivian, his wife, spent forty years as missionaries. They returned a few years ago to Oregon and recently went on to glory. I ran across this picture of Gordon in our archives and wondered if that might be a picture of my bike with him.

Gordon Thompson outside Fuller Dorm

God taught me an important lesson on that day through my Dad. *People are more valuable than things!*

One of the strong qualities my Dad possessed was his skill at balancing the need to be serious with a sense of humor. "Fighting the good fight" and having biblical values, with a sense of humor and playfulness, ministered to our family and those who knew him. I recall Dad giving to my mother a "smoked bloat" on one of their wedding anniversary days. A "smoked bloat" is a partially cooked, ugly fish, about 18 inches long. He purchased it at the local market. The worst part of it was not its looks, but its smell! It stunk up the house. Dad thought this was so funny and, of course, Mom just shook her head in disbelief! I love this picture of them that I have sitting on my desk in an obviously playful mood in San Jose in the early days. I smile each time I look at it. By the way, I'm confident that is not a cigarette in Dad's mouth, but probably a pencil or large tooth pick as he was a stickler in practicing what he preached! Dad's ability to balance commitment and hard work with humor and lightheartedness served as a great ministry model to me through the years.

Mom and Dad in San Jose during the early years of their ministry

About the same time Dad invited me to give up my bike to Gordon, mom had her own private agenda perhaps motivated by what Dad was asking. My baseball glove was stolen at Horseman Elementary School where I was a student. I remember always coming in the front door of our home after school, but when I came in the back door, mom knew something was wrong. I loved baseball and my glove, and my young heart was broken as, in tears, I told my story to Mom. She cried with me, but little did I know what she was secretly planning. Each week following this, she took a couple dollars of her grocery money and hid it in a kitchen cup until she had $15 saved up. Then she surprised me one day after school. Dad drove the three of us to Gordon Sports Shop on San Fernando Street and there I purchased a new, lefthanded, first basemen's glove. I could not believe my eyes! It was a handmade glove by Hemis, one of the finest of its kind in those days. I was the envy of every kid on the playground and I guarded it like a hawk! For days, I couldn't believe what mom had done. I loved the glove and couldn't wait to use it day after day. Larry Stilgebower, a childhood friend and partner in ministry through the years, my brother Velt, and I with my new Hemis handmade first baseman's glove went off to play a little baseball!

As I have reflected on that experience through the years, I am aware of the profound impact that had on my young life. It modeled much more than the sincere love of a mother for her son, it spoke volumes to me about her willingness to sacrifice her personal needs in order to meet the needs of those she loved. I watched that kind of love expressed by both Mom and Dad as a small child and through my growing up years. I became aware that their love had its source in God and reached

out not just to family, but to everyone. I didn't go through a period of rebellion against my parents for I saw no need to! They loved God, each other, and me deeply, and they would do anything to help me find God's best, and I knew it. Their spirit of love, grace, and unselfish generosity would forever impact my life.

Dad's favorite place to go for our summer family vacation was Touloumne Meadows, in the high country of Yosemite National Park. We would get up early in the morning to hike and fly fish the mountain streams. Dad taught my brother Veltie and me how to fly fish and, of course, we have taught our children how to do it also! It was fun and we love flyfishing to this day. Before I was able to catch them on my own, he would take a fish that he had caught and hook it to my fly and I would play it in the water until it was exhausted and would go "belly up." As people would walk by I would pull the limp fish out of the water so they could admire my achievement. Dad would have me get on his back to cross the fast moving streams from time to time. One time, he hit a slick rock and down we went. We went bumping along on the rocks for about ten feet until he was able to get us stabilized. By that time most of the fish had come out of his creel and were floating downstream. We were laughing and trying to pick up the half dead fish, some swimming away as a God thing in their delightful rescue and others floating upside down. We got a few of them back, but Dad was such a great fisherman it didn't take long for him to fill up his creel again with a fresh batch of new fish.

I remember saying to myself, I want to be like that man! He is so much fun, he lives with so much joy and love. If the God that he serves has grown him into the person I see, then I want His God to be my God.

Dad loved to play games of course, so in the picture on the left he is actually standing back from the fish and acting like he is holding the stringer so that the fish would look bigger than they really are. However, to his credit, the two Rainbow trout on the right measured 19 inches each, which is not too shabby for a dry fly fisherman on a mountain stream in Yosemite!

CHAPTER TWO

The Relocation of the Campus

As growth came rapidly to SJBC, conversation began early in the development of the college about finding a site to accommodate the growth and prepare for the future. With the attendance pushing upward toward 200 students in the middle 1940s, it was obvious that something needed to be done, or growth could not continue. The location across the street from San Jose State was a plus for students being able to take classes there and have a place to share their faith, but the size of the site limited the future growth of the college. Plus, San Jose State wanted our campus.

The search for a new campus led to Alum Rock Avenue near King Road. 17 acres of bare land, the property would put the college into a growing area of the region, had easy access for public transportation as Alum Rock Avenue was one of the main arteries across the region, and gave SJBC high visibility. An architect was hired, who along with Jean West, one of SJBC's early graduates who was gifted in art and creative crafts, designed the facilities and made a model of what it would look like.

San Jose Mercury Herald

SAN JOSE, CALIFORNIA, SATURDAY MORNING, NOVEMBER 24, 1945   Second Section

17-Acre Campus Site Purchased By San Jose Bible College

First Building To Be Occupied Next September

$60,000 Initial Unit Is T-Shaped Site For Classrooms

The San Jose Mercury Herald on November 24, 1945, carried this front page article of the second section announcing the plans for the relocation and the building plans. The main building would be two stories with a full basement, 12 classrooms, six music rooms, auditorium seating for 500, and a recreation room. The estimated cost for the building was $60,000, and the plan was to have it ready by the opening of school in September, 1946. In addition, a men's dorm and a women's dorm were to be built, leaving room for athletic facilities including a gym, a library, and faculty homes. Below is a picture of the first unit that was to be built, with some information concerning construction.

The Proposed New Home of the San Jose Bible College!

We are happy to present this picture of the future home of San Jose Bible College. The plans were drawn by O. A. Tolliver and the model building was made by Miss Jeane West and Victor LaMar of the LaMar Printing Company.

The building is two stories high with a full basement and is 150 feet by 100 feet. Floor plans and additional facts will be shown month by month in the Broadcaster.

In addition to the main building there will be two large dormitories and a dining hall. Other buildings will be constructed as needed.

Actual construction of the dining hall and dormitories will begin at once, with the construction of the main building to begin soon after the first of the year. These buildings are essential and must be built to meet the growing requirements of the school. The Lord has promised to supply every need. We believe this to be a definite necessity and ask all our friends to join with us in prayer that God will supply every need. It all involves a great expense, but God is able to do abundantly more than we ask or think. We believe that God is able to supply the necessary funds and that such a venture can be completed and dedicated free of debt. It all depends upon us. If we faithfully live for Him and pray a true prayer of faith, God will so grant our requests. Will you not join with us in such a prayer of faith?

In an article later that year the San Jose Mercury Herald reported that San Jose State purchased the 306 South 5th Street property for $25,000 and then allowed the college to rent it back for $50 a month until the new facilities were ready for occupancy. State officials long had eyed the property in their expansion plans, and The State Allocations Board was asked to survey the property for acquisition. It stated that W.L. Jessup, head of the Bible College, listed the asking price on the property at $30,000. Well, SJBC didn't quite get their asking price, but they did get it in cash. The story is told in the following two San Jose Mercury News articles.

The interesting twist in the story is that by the time San Jose State purchased the 306 South 5th Street property, the Bible College had sold the Alum Rock property to a developer. I remember Dad telling the story of how a developer came to him after construction had started on the Alum Rock property and made him an offer that he couldn't refuse. The foundation had been poured for the new building pictured above, construction was continuing, but it seems the developer

State Files Suit To Get Land Of Bible College

The San Jose Bible College at Fifth and E. San Carlos Sts. was threatened with an ouster yesterday to make way for expansion of the San Jose State College classroom facilities.

The State of California filed suit in Superior Court to condemn the Bible College's land and the southeast corner of the intersection.

8—Santa Cruz Sentinel-News

San Jose School Buildings Bought For State College

Sacramento, July 2 (P) — The state board of public works has approved a resolution to settle acquisition of San Jose school buildings and property near San Jose State college for $675,000.

Robert Reed, deputy attorney general, recommended the settlement on that basis. A condemnation suit has been pending in court on the property.

"Those buildings are in terrible condition but I think things could be done to make them useable," Reed commented in making his recommendation for settlement out of court.

Chairman of the board, James Dean, remarked during the discussion that the state was actually having to "pay for the privilege of tearing down" the school buildings when it eventually makes use of them.

The board also approved the making of appraisal surveys on the San Jose Bible college property adjacent to the State college for possible future purchase. The State budget has $25,000 earmarked for this purchase if approved.

State College May Buy Bible School

Another step in the expansion of San Jose State College's campus was revealed today when H. C. Vincent Jr., executive secretary of the State Allocations Board in Sacramento, said the board has been asked to consider acquisition of the building and property occupied by the San Jose Bible College at Fifth and San Carlos Streets.

Purchase of the property has been contemplated for several years by the State College, and last year the State allocated $25,000, most of which will be used for purchase of the property.

The Bible College several years ago purchased property on the north side of Alum Rock Ave. west of the old Ice Bowl and planned to build a new college there. Since then plans for building have been canceled and part of the property has been sold, leaving 15 acres off Alum Rock Ave. which the Bible College hopes to sell, according to W. L. Jessup, president of the college.

Jessup said the Bible College is looking for a new site near its present location. He said he did not know the State College was interested in purchasing the Bible College property until appraisers from the State came to inspect the property several weeks ago. Jessup said the Bible College is seeking $30,000 for the building and 90-foot lot.

The State College plan to buy the Bible College property is part of its move to expand the campus to meet the increased growth of enrollment. Property on the east side of the campus from Seventh St. back to Ninth St. is being purchased, and the State has already purchased 36 acres near Spartan Stadium.

The Bible College property is the only piece across San Carlos St. the State contemplates purchasing, according to Edward S. Thompson, college business chief.

really wanted the property and he was willing to make a surprising offer. He offered Dad double the amount Dad had paid for the property. After consulting with others, the offer was accepted and construction ceased. The search resumed for a suitable place to relocate the campus of San Jose Bible College, but this time with a good chunk of change in hand. I will always remember the time that Dad had one of the large checks in his possession. It must have been given to him after the bank's closing time. He walked around the house showing it to us all, thanking the Lord for His provision, and then he put the check between the mattresses of his bed and he and mom slept on it all night to keep it safe. I remember how crazy that seemed to my childhood mind!

We learn from the March 1946 Broadcaster that the search for property continued with $25,000 from the sale of the 306 S. 5th Street property, and $21,442.10 from the sale of the Alum Rock property for a total of $46,442.10. They found a number of properties of interest and the Broadcaster states that they felt it would be best to be closer to down town and still near San Jose State College. Little did Dad and the SJBC team know what they were in for, as the zoning issues of the city were much more limiting than those of the county. The Alum Rock campus was in the county and they had no difficulty in getting approvals for construction there.

An apartment complex just three blocks from the old campus on 8th Street near San Jose State was considered at $31,500, but it was not large enough to accommodate anticipated future growth. However, another property in the region was on Williams Street close to Coyote Creek in San Jose. It was only two acres of land, but it would be adequate to build a much larger college than the one they had at 306 S. 5th Street. The application was reviewed by the Planning Commission and here are some selected portions of what the San Jose Evening News recorded on May 11, 1949, in a front page article entitled:

SAN JOSE NEWS

Leased Wires from the Associated Press, United Press and International News Service, Wirephoto

Vol. 184, No. 93, 66th Year   SAN JOSE, CALIFORNIA, WEDNESDAY, MAY 11, 1949

Spat Over S. J. Bible Campus Grows Hotter

The Rev. W.L. Jessup, president of San Jose Bible College, this morning vigorously attacked as unfair a decision made yesterday by City Planning Commission, denying his institution

PRESIDENT OF COLLEGE HITS RULING

The Rev. W. L. Jessup, president of San Jose Bible College, this morning vigorously attacked as unfair a decision made yesterday by City Planning Commission, denying his institution permission to create a campus on the north side of William St. at Coyote River.

Mr. Jessup also denounced the City Zoning Ordinance under which the decision was made.

The ordinance, he declared, is unfair...

permission to create a campus on the North side of William
St. at Coyote River...

Mr. Jessup also denounced the City Zoning Ordinance
under which the decision was made. The ordinance,
he declared, is so over-restrictive as to prohibit the
establishment of a school or philanthropic institution
anywhere in San Jose, without permission of the City
Planning Commission...

The Planning Commission's denial of the adjustment
sought by the Bible College came yesterday after 35 residents
of the area protested..."We can be stopped from building
on any property we might buy in San Jose." Jessup said
today, "We were told by the Planning Commission to look
for property out of town or at the edge of the city. It would
be just as easy to move to a city that would let us build."

San Jose Bible College's present location at the Southeast
corner of Fifth and San Carlos Sts., has been condemned
by the State for expansion of San Jose State College. The
Bible College, a private institution with 211 students,
must vacate by February, 1951.

In applying for permission to build on the William St.
site two weeks ago, Bible College officials announced they
intended to develop a two acre campus. It would include
classroom building, a chapel seating 400, a library, and
a cafeteria.

There were 35 neighbors who showed up at the meeting
to protest the possibility of SJBC being given permission to
build on the property. For two weeks following the ruling by
the Planning Commission, there were articles in the San Jose
newspapers by citizens of the community supporting and others
opposing the granting permission for SJBC to build on the
property; even the editors got involved in writing conflicting

articles about the issue! Examples were given of other colleges like College of the Pacific who wanted to expand years ago in San Jose and were denied. Thus they moved to Stockton where it became a flourishing university which contributed resources and quality upgrading to the community.

Bible College Asks Approval Of New Site

12th St. Location Would Require Change in Zoning

San Jose Bible College, denied a zone adjustment to allow construction of a new campus at E. William St. and Coyote River two weeks ago, returned to the City Planning Commission yesterday with a proposal to build at a different site.

The new site, a six-acre tract on the east side of 12th St. between Virginia St. and Orvis Ave., would also require a zone change. The area is presently zoned for one-family residences only. Planning Commission must approve construction of school buildings in all residential areas and most commercial areas.

Bruce Griswold, counsel for the Bible college, informed the commissioners that the site takes up practically all the property between 12th St. and Coyote River. He urged the commission to approve the site. He said his client has an option to purchase the property.

With only three of the five commissioners present, the planners voted to take the request under advisement.

The commission also:

1. Approved a plan to widen Lincoln Ave. between Minnesota and Brace Aves.

2. Approved subdivision maps for (a) property of F. Merrell, San Pedro and Old Taylor Sts. (b) DiSalvo lands, Stevens Creek Road and Bellrose Dr., and (c) Ensor Park No. 2, on Beverly Blvd.

3. Approved tentative zoning for Orchard No. 6 tract, when no protests were received.

4. Granted minor zoning adjustments for property at 965 Garden Dr. and 1866 Beverly Blvd.

Bible College To Get Site Hearing Soon

City Planners Agree To Hasten Meeting; Neighbors Opposed

City Planning Commission yesterday asked San Jose Bible College officials to bring in a plan of the proposed home of their institution. Commissioners promised a special meeting, if necessary, any time in the next two weeks to take action.

The college wants permission for a campus on six acres east of S. 12th St. between Orvis Ave. and Virginia St. Property owners have opposed the move because they claim it will "create too much noise and be a safety hazard."

Because the Bible College's options are due to expire shortly, the commission voiced readiness to cooperate by a special meeting, if required, to look over the plans.

Students of the college and nine property owners, who had a petition signed by 63 others, attended the commission hearing.

The commission also denied a requested change for rezoning 2155 The Alameda from R-3 residential to C-2 commercial, proposed by Frank Beckman; set a hearing in two weeks on plan lines on Alum Rock and East Gate Aves.; adjusted a rear yard on lot 30, tract 582, St. James St., and gave an outside sewer permit to Frank W. Handley, 1763 Cottle Ave.

Bible College Still Without Building Site

The San Jose Bible College's attempts to find a home ran on to another snag this morning when the City Planning Commission deferred for another two weeks a decision on a proposed site for the institution.

The college is attempting to gain commission approval of a six-acre tract on the east side of S. 12th St. between Orvis and Virginia Aves.

A group of 75 Bible College students all but swamped the small offices of the planning commission at today's hearing. In company with W. L. Jessup, the college's president, and Bruce Griswold, attorney for Bible institution, the delegation urged that the commission approve the site.

Nine property owners from the area appeared in opposition to the location of the college in their area. They presented a petition signed by 63 area property owners who also are opposed to granting approval of the site.

Chief reason for the opposition seemed to be "it will create too much noise and will be a safety hazard." The commissioners agreed to study the views of both sides and deferred a decision on any action until two weeks from today.

The Orvis Ave. site is the second home which has been proposed by college officials. Earlier, the planning commission denied a request which would have located the college on the north side of William St. at the Coyote River. Residents in the area opposed the location because it would have "created a traffic hazard," they said.

At this morning's meeting the commission also:

Because of the community resistance to the college being on Williams Street, a continued search was made for another piece of property which might receive less neighborhood resistance. A much larger piece of property was found at 12th and Virginia Streets so they decided to let the other piece go.

They were about to enter another fight as neighbors opposed this move also.

The Planning Commission revisited their land use policy documents and chose to reinterpret the policies, deciding that SJBC would not be in violation if given permission to occupy the property at 12th and Virginia Streets. Therefore they recommended to the City Council that approval be granted for the relocation of SJBC to the 12th and Virginia Street property. A number of local residents were present at the Planning Commission meeting and a few days later went before the City Council to speak against the proposal. However, after a number of meetings where opinions were expressed on all sides of the issue, the City Council granted permission for SJBC to establish a college on the property the second week of June 1949.

What a tremendous victory had been gained and the school moved forward rapidly to develop its architectural plans for city approval. It is amazing to see how similar the journey of the college has been through the years whenever it has attempted to relocate its campus. It is obvious that God had His hand on the college and wanted to see it succeed, as there have been a number of Christian colleges in Northern California that ceased operations since 1950 for various reasons. The story of the successful move through the wilderness and into the promised land of a new and larger campus in the early 1950's added to our belief that God would do it again when we were facing seemingly insurmountable relocation problems in the early 2000s.

Architectural plans were drawn up and approved, and construction on the new campus at 12th and Virginia Streets began in February 1950. The ground breaking event attended by students and friends of San Jose Bible College was a great day of rejoicing and grateful acknowledgement of God's faithfulness and future for the college.

William Jessup, director of the San Jose Bible College, breaks ground for the first unit of the $100,000 project to provide classroom facilities, teachers' quarters and an auditorium for the school on a site on the northeast corner of 12th and Virginia Sts. Pictured around Jessup are Samuel Barth, extreme left, contractor for the project, Orville P. Shier, to right of Jessup, and Roy Shaw. Shier drew plans for the project.

Part of the land was used for a nursery, which had to be taken down and the ground prepared for the foundations. As a 15 year old, I remember Dad getting my brother and me, along with numerous SJBC students, out there on a Saturday to help tear down the old nursery buildings. My clearest memory is of us hitting a bee hive with our weapons of destruction and sending bees everywhere, including up our pant legs. Velt and I ran as fast as we could to the back of the property and jumped in Coyote Creek to escape them. It worked! The bees scattered and after we pulled out a few stingers we returned to another part of the property to continue tearing down the old nursery buildings. After it was all over, my Dad thought it was pretty funny watching us trying to outrun the bees and he loved to tell the story in churches as a part of his usual college update presentations.

The April 1950 Broadcaster had this picture of the property with the foundations poured. The four palm trees on the left were affectionately called, Matthew, Mark, Luke, and John!

Soon the buildings began to take shape. The building program was on the fast track as the signed agreement said that San Jose State would take possession of the 306 S. 5th Street campus by February 1, 1951. By today's building standards, the projected quality of the buildings would be below average, but for that time in the building industry, it was quite adequate and would be rated by some as above average. In the September, 1950 Broadcaster Dad wrote these words of encouragement concerning the new campus at 12th and Virginia Streets: "Praise God From Whom All Blessings Flow. We are so thankful to our Heavenly Father that at last we are settled in our first unit of our new buildings. We have looked forward to this day for many months. We are so thankful to you, our friends in Christ, who have stood by us in prayer and who have so wonderfully blessed us with your tithes and offerings. It has only been through the blessings of our Heavenly Father that this unit can now be dedicated to the Lord, free of debt. The construction is well underway on our next unit which will house our offices, auditorium and music rooms. We have borrowed $30,000 to complete this unit. We ask for your continued interest in your prayers that the Lord will supply the necessary funds to retire this indebtedness and to furnish these buildings with necessary equipment. School will soon be underway. The opening rally is on Tuesday, September 12th. A large enrollment is anticipated. Pray for us as we begin this another school year. "

The following picture appeared in the San Jose Evening News sometime during late summer of 1950.

First Bible College Unit Near Completion

NEW COLLEGE QUARTERS —First unit of new home of San Jose Bible College on 5-acre site at S. 12th and Virginia Sts. is nearly complete. School's 185 students will move in Sept. 12. Second unit, about to be started, will be ready in November. Buildings shown contain classrooms and library; second unit will have auditorium, music rooms and offices. W. L. Jessup, college president, is planning open house early in September. Former site of school at Fifth and San Carlos Sts. was purchased by San Jose State College for campus expansion.

The college operated for the Fall semester at both locations, with most of the classes at the new campus at 12th and Virginia, with chapel and the offices still at the 5th Street location. The properties being separated by one mile, it only took about 10 minutes to go from one campus to the other. However, by the end of January 1951, the offices, auditorium, and music rooms were completed at the new campus and the full move from 5th Street to 12th and Virginia Streets took place on February 1, 1951, with most of the student body helping to move the furniture, chairs, offices, and pulpit.

The dedication of the new campus was combined with graduation on Thursday, May 31, 1951. It was indeed a great day of joy, celebration, and gratitude for all that God had provided in making the new campus a reality.

The campus at 12th and Virginia Streets would be the home for San Jose Bible College/San Jose Christian College until moving to the current campus in Rocklin, California in 2004. Additional buildings were added to this campus in San Jose during its 51 years of ministry including dorms, cafeteria, and library. A number of homes were purchased adjacent to the campus and were used for married student housing and additional office space.

This campus served as a meeting place to transform many young people into powerful world changers, many who continue to serve our Lord around the world!

CHAPTER THREE

Life on the New Campus at 12th Street *(1951-1960)*

What makes a college a Christian College is the Christian commitment of the administration, faculty, staff, and board. These are the Christian leaders in transferring the truth, grace, passion, and vision of our Lord to the next generation; the keepers and protectors of the legacy of the institution. They are our mentors in helping the students to integrate Biblical truth with every subject that is taught, both inside and outside the classroom. Christian Colleges go down the slippery slope when its leaders are no longer Christ-centered and their commitment to Biblical truth becomes compromised. From the very beginning of SJBC, its administration, faculty, staff, and board were committed Christ-followers and that continues today at WJU. If a shift should begin to occur where we no longer put as our number one priority that our leaders are to all be committed Christ-followers, then the process of beginning the slide down the slippery slope occurs, and within a short period of time it will be a secular rather than sacred campus.

The heart of any college is measured by the character and giftedness of the people who have wholeheartedly pledged

79

themselves to fulfill the mission of the institution, and lead by example. They impact the lives of those they teach in ways that multiply the students' gifts, lives and ministries for the rest of their journey on planet earth. Anyone who has attended college understands this; there are always those teachers or staff who invested in them their best, and it made a huge difference in their future. Bob Sargent was a student at SJBC in the early 1950's, and later served as VP of Academics under Presidents Al Tiffin, Woody Phillips and Chuck Boatman. He reflects on his memory of his time as a student at SJBC.

Bob Sargent - Student, 1950   *Bob Sargent - Academic Dean, 1970*

"Most of what I remember are the people who contributed to my life and thinking. The professors who helped me were V.K. Allison, Roy Shaw, Don DeWelt, and T.R. Applebury. V.K. Allison was a colorful preacher and teacher who used many personal and graphic illustrations to impress the Old Testament scriptures. I had a course

that included a verse by verse study of Job and Ecclesiastes. I remember he had a bushy mustache that fascinated me as he articulated every word in his own colorful style. I deeply appreciated V.K. as one who showed his love for the scriptures and to me as a person. Roy Shaw was a person with a limp and an energetic Irish personality. He communicated his concern for students by his profound moral convictions and contagious sense of humor. His wife, Dorothy, served the college for many years as a house parent and was greatly respected by everyone, especially the students in the dorms. How indebted I am to Don DeWelt. He made the book of Acts come alive. He made me feel as if I was on the missionary journeys. His wonderful spontaneous smile was contagious as he used maps and charts. I was thrilled when he asked me to help him illustrate his personal evangelism booklet called, "Ten Timely Truths" and some greeting cards. He was a model of effective teaching techniques which I built on in my future education. T.R. Applebury contributed to my education in another way. He taught me to be careful and thorough in studying and teaching the scriptures. I learned how to use the koine greek and got an introduction to the Hebrew language, which helped me in graduate school. To these teachers, I owe much of my faith, my spiritual growth and my biblical knowledge. There were others who influenced my life such as Bill Jessup. He was a role model in so many ways. He used the chapel services to give practical advice for Christian living, which he presented in a simple and well-illustrated manner. He seemed to know what Christian college students needed. Later, when I had been hired as academic dean of SJBC, he was on campus often. I played golf with him. He was a good golfer and I felt honored that he would play golf with me.

I also admired Bill, as he was called by everyone, because he worked with a group of seniors called "Senior Saints" and used his influence to try to bring about harmony with other people in the Restoration Movement. I can't mention many others to whom I owe a debt of gratitude, but I must mention Dot Isbell, whose dedication and service to SJBC was far beyond the call of duty."

I would be remiss if I didn't say some things about Dot Isbell also. She and her husband came to SJBC in the early 1940's, and shortly after her husband was involved in a fatal automobile accident. Dot had two small children to now care for on her own, but she had a conquering spirit, kept her eye on the Lord, and chose to serve the Lord in whatever way He would lead. And lead He did! Dot was invited by Dad to work in the office at SJBC, which she did for more than 50 years, and then came back to the school in the 90's to do volunteer work. Almost everyone who attended SJBC/SJCC knew Dot,

her friendly greetings, and her willingness to serve and help wherever needed.

The culture of the new campus began to shift shortly after the move. During the 40's, many of the students were 20-35 years old, but in the 50's, a much higher percentage of the students came to SJBC right out of high school. The war years were over, though the Korean war began during the early 50's, it did not affect the student body like WWII.

With a larger campus, and now with a track record of more than 10 years of training people for ministry, the campus culture became more defined, systematic and dependable. A couple hundred graduates had gone forth to serve in church ministries locally and globally. San Jose Bible College was now on the map and had proven itself to be a credible training center for those exploring a life in ministry for our Lord. Students continued to serve in churches as youth leaders, preachers, Christian Education workers, teachers, and musicians.

Music continued to play a large part in the life of the school. Choirs, trios, and quartets were formed to engage our students, inspire our college community, and bring joy and hope to our supporting churches and beyond as they told the story of God's love through music. Most of these groups made recordings, and we still have many of them in our college archives. As Dad or faculty would go out to preach in the churches and for SJBC days, a singing group would frequently accompany him to inspire the people and give the congregations a chance to get acquainted with some of our students. Many of the groups did summer tours, sang in camps and at youth rallies and conventions. Pictured below are some of the singing groups from the 50's.

The Challengers - 1952

"THE CHALLENGERS"

Heaven's Harmonaires - 1953

Dr. Jack Morrison, Director

"HEAVEN'S HARMONAIRES"

Jim Sinclair   Mike Pierce   Jim Moore   Ted Gibson

The Loyal Lordsmen - 1955

George Caldwell Richard Moore Dick Palmer Larry Keene

These were my buddies at SJBC, George Caldwell, Richard Moore, Dick Palmer, and Larry Keene in 1955. We all became students after graduation from high school and enrolled in SJBC in the fall of 1953. We had classes together, ran around together, and most of us had known each other from camps and youth rallies before enrolling at SJBC. We were looking forward to being together and our friendship has continued through the years.

I remember when Jack Morrison wanted to form a quartet out of the five of us. I was certainly aware that one of us was going to be cut, and I had heard the other four sing so I fully understood that I would probably be the one to go. It didn't take long and I was right. He called us in one by one for the personal tryout. When it came my turn, he sat me down on the piano bench with him and started playing the notes he wanted me to sing. As he went up and down the keyboard

I was to follow him in my best of voice. After about five minutes, he scooted back a bit, pulled down the lid over the keys, put his elbow on it, looked me straight in the eyes and said with a smile, "Have you ever considered preaching?" Well, that became my clarion call to the preaching ministry and I haven't looked back since!

Becoming a minister and attending San Jose Bible College were on my radar screen from a very young age. How could they not be? They were the center of our family activities throughout all my growing up years. Along with my family, many of the students in the early years had influenced me, played sports with me, challenged me, loved me, and talked about my becoming a student one day at SJBC. In addition, I loved Aunt Dorothy and Uncle Roy who lived right across the street from us, and it just seemed right that I should attend SJBC and prepare for the ministry.

In high school, I was not a very good student. In fact, if I were to apply today to William Jessup University with my high school transcripts, I would not be admitted without taking some remedial work first. My English grades were low, and my math grades insufficient and terrible. In fact, had it not been for the Vice Principal pulling me out of an algebra class as a senior in high school and requiring me to take a Student Body Officer class, I would have flunked the algebra class. I am convinced today that he did that to rescue me as the class was created for Student Body Officers in the middle of the semester.

Heading into my senior year of high school, I remember Dad preaching at a high school youth camp in the summer of 1952. I don't remember much of what he said, but what I do remember is that I felt the call of God on my life to dedicate it to becoming a preacher. I loved God and people and felt a pull to want to help others to know Him, live for Him, and do my part to build His Kingdom. I had seen good preaching modeled for me through the years, had seen its powerful impact, and I felt God could use me to declare His truth from the pulpit and beyond. Many of my friends were going forward to commit or recommit their lives to Christ. But that was not my issue at that time. I had grown up in a loving and genuine Christian home, and though it was not perfect and neither was I, I never felt the need to throw it all over and experiment with some of the world's alternate lifestyles. So around the camp fire at Mission Springs camp in the Santa Cruz mountains, I went forward on a Friday evening to dedicate my life to "full time Christian ministry", which was what we did in those days when we felt "the call". On the way home in the car that evening, I will always cherish my memory of the conversation I had with Dad. I remember him asking me why I made the decision I did. I remember saying to him something along the lines that I had seen so many small struggling churches in my growing up years, that if God could use me, I would love to grow a large and powerful church for God. The reason is so that the community would be aware that something important is happening at the church, and would come and want to check it out. Dad affirmed my decision, said he was proud of the decision I had made, and offered to be available to help in whatever way he could.

My senior year of high school was a year of athletic and leadership service in the student body. I had been co-captain of both the varsity football and baseball teams, won some awards, and continued to feel the call of God on my life to preach. One of my teachers who was a Christian encouraged me to take some speech classes if I was serious about ministry. In addition, he told me I needed to enter the area Lions Club public speaking contest. Therefore, I developed a speech on the assigned subject, "Man's Search For Freedom". I presented it to a number of classes so I could practice it, then I gave it before a panel at my high school where three of us gave our speeches so that one could be selected to represent James Lick High School in the region. I came in third! I had heard the other two speeches and I thought they were lousy by comparison to mine. I was discouraged. Why should I consider being a preacher if I can't even prepare and deliver a meaningful speech to my peers in high school? I told the story to my Dad. His response has helped me throughout my years of ministry. He said, "Do you want to get married someday?" I replied, "Of course I do." He asked, "Do you think you will have any trouble telling your bride-to-be that you love her?" I stated, "That will be easy." Then he said, "That is what preaching is all about. Just tell people how much you love Jesus and what He means to you, and people will get the message." That was just what I needed as I was focusing on what I could or could not do rather than on the One who saved me and gave me life...if I just lifted Him up...people would get the message for they would hear more than what I said because God is in it! (My word will not return void of its intended purpose. Isaiah 55:11)

During my Senior year of high school, Walt McPherson, baseball coach from San Jose State wanted me to come and play baseball for him at SJS upon graduation. He went with my high school baseball coach, John Mason, over to talk with my Dad for they were convinced that Dad was putting pressure on me to go to SJBC. Dad explained that I could make my own choice as to where I would go to college, so they backed off, though they checked it out again with me to make sure that SJBC was what I really wanted to do. Then a scout from the old Saint Louis Browns made me an offer to play professional baseball with one of their Class C farm teams. I can't say that I really entertained the thought with much seriousness for my heart was set on ministry. God's call on my life seemed clear! After graduating from James Lick, I played a couple of summers on a local semi-pro baseball team, the Willey Road Oilers, while I was a student at SJBC, but ministry continued to be my passion.

In a senior Problems class at James Lick High School, I wrote a paper on "The vocation I have chosen for my life's work". In it I stated: "I chose the ministry not because of money or outside influences but solemnly because I am interested in people, and their spiritual life. I had an offer from Walt Williams (San Jose State Baseball Coach) to go to San Jose State to play baseball, but I turned it down. I know of students and faculty members who thought me crazy for not going to State, but I know my conscience would hurt me if I did. My desire for the ministry is something down inside of me that is hard to explain." Later in the assignment I wrote…"If, because of various reasons I would not be able to make a success out of the ministry I would probably go into the field of television service man." I loved electronics and became an Advanced Class license holder in Amateur Radio, or "ham radio" during my junior year in high school and have been active in the hobby all of my life, talking to people all over the world during my leisure time.

During my first and second year at SJBC, I dated a fun loving gal by the name of Shirley-Jo Hulburt. Her parents and my parents were college friends at Eugene Bible College in the 1920's. I would date different ladies but it seemed I kept coming back to Jo. She was a bright, lighthearted, steady, beautiful and gifted musician who loved the Lord. Mom loved her and said frequently when I would date others, "Jo is certainly a wonderful young lady and would make a wonderful wife." In frustration over hearing it a number of times I said to her, "Mom if I want to marry Jo I will…if I don't want to marry Jo I won't…now back off!" I married Jo on September 2, 1955 at the University Christian Church in Los Angeles! Dad and Al Tiffin officiated at the wedding. That was an interesting connection for Al Tiffin became the man to follow my Dad to become the President of SJBC in 1962. They enjoyed an energetic friendship which continued on through the years until the passing of my Dad in 1992.

Wedding September 2, 1955
Bryce and Jo Jessup

The decade of the 50's was an interesting one in the history of SJBC. It was a period of stabilization and change at the same time. We were now on a piece of property which allowed us to grow a larger student body and build additional buildings, while at the same time upgrade and broaden the curriculum, shift the focus to a younger student body, develop athletic programs, and implement new strategies to train church leaders and recruit new students. The size of the student body during the 1950s stabilized to around 150-200 students.

Required chapel was held daily at 7:30 a.m. in the morning. It was a time of singing, prayer, fellowship, and preaching. In addition to speaking into our lives, there were many outstanding speakers from across the USA, and missionaries from foreign lands who shared with us their journeys and challenged us to deepen our lives. I still have notes on some of the messages and have used them myself down through the years of ministry.

The Church of Christ which gave birth to SJBC at 306 S. 5th Street, continued on at the new location at 12th and Virginia Streets. Dad and Uncle Roy continued on as the preachers until the first full time minister, Harold Gallagher, was called to be the minister for the congregation in 1956. I had the privilege of serving as his youth minister at the church during my last two years of Bible College, 1957-58. The congregation ran around 200 in attendance under Harold's leadership. He was a good preacher with a genuine heart for the people, a steadfast faith, and a vision to impact the region for Christ.

Chapel and Church Auditorium

The faculty during the 50's included some new people. Who can ever forget Ruben Ratzlaff, his excellent teachings, homemade ice cream in his home, the dry humor and his frequent forgetfulness? He was an outstanding Old Testament scholar and impacted hundreds of lives. He came to the school in 1958 and I will always remember his "trial sermon" in chapel before he was hired. He spoke of the cross in a way I had never heard, but have repeated many times in the course of my own ministry. He spoke of the "X" as standing for the cross in a number of ancient cultures. Thus the cross is used by baseball players as they come to bat. With the bat they put an "X" in front of home plate because the cross is a sign of hope! When

a man sends a love letter to his special lady he signs it with a lot of "O's" and "X's" for the cross is a sign of love. When you make a mistake on your typewriter you backspace and type over them with "X's" for the cross is a sign of forgiveness. It was a refreshing and powerful message.

But what students remember most about Ruben was his forgetfulness, missing appointments, looking for his glasses when they were on his head, and showing up for class at the wrong time. One popular story about him that circulates to this day was the day he started his lecture and a student reminded him that he had announced in the previous class session that

(Front): H. Douglas, J.Stith, F. Kedall, C. Bowman, P .Buss, (Second Row) R. Ratzlaff, coach, T. Kent, R. Gibson, D. Stockham, E. Payton, J. Ottinger, K. Ratslaff

they would have a test. As he slapped his bald head he replied, "oh, that is right…I will go back to my office and get it." Well, the class waited for about 10 minutes and he didn't come out of his office. Wondering if he was all right a student went to his office at the back of the room only to find him sitting in his chair reading a book, he had forgotten he had a class! Here are three of my favorite pictures of Ruben. He coached the basketball team in the late 1960's…obviously a specialist in shooting free throws!

Lester Wells, Herman Martin, John Sinclair, Dale Chaffin,
Veltie Jessup, Richard Boon, Keith Knepper, Clarence Creamer,
John Bigham, James Kennedy, Tim Eckle, Roger Strachan

1955

Front, left to right: G. Caldwell, S. Nishakawa, B. Blanchard, Jr. Ball,
Back: D. Ruder, B. Jessup, A. Watson (coach), D. Palmer, B. Jennings

CHEERLEADERS:
Barbara Woodward, Jack Taylor and Jan Alexander

COACH:
Art Watson

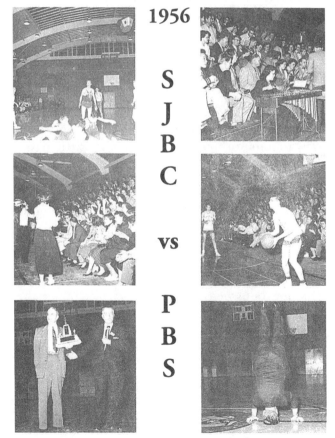

1956

S
J
B
C

vs

P
B
S

Pacific Bible College (PBC) President, Kenneth Stewart (now Hope International) and Bill Jessup.
SJBC lost and so the losing President had to stand on his head. That's Dad doing the head stand!

Another very special teacher was George Alder from Klamath Falls, Ore., who was hired in 1954. He was a favorite of many students for many years until his retirement in 1983. He was a brilliant scholar with a compassionate heart. He read from the original Koine Greek language of the New Testament so easily that some may have wondered if it were his first language.

His classes were stimulating intellectually, but what I remember most was his soft heart and tears as he would tell a touching story. I will never forget the time when he popped out of his office and stopped me in the hallway with a book in his hand that he was reading. It was a book about some phase of third century Christianity and one of its leaders. As he read a paragraph to me and tried to explain what it meant, he teared up and couldn't go on. I couldn't get my mind around seeing what he saw, I wanted to share a tear of excitement and insight with him, wishing my allergies would kick in so that he wouldn't think I was stoic and unappreciative, but I was unable. Obviously, there was great content and insight from the section he read and though I was unable to grasp it, I was impacted by his love for learning and passion for God's truth. His classes on Romans were treasured by his students, and much of what he thought and said is still in print. He also loved backpacking and a number of us were privileged to go with him in the High Sierras on backpack trips. So many sweet memories of a Godly man who contributed so much to our lives including a lot of laughs from his quick wit!

My time as a student at SJBC was from 1953-1958. It was a time of growth and preparation for the future. I worked as a TV repairman in those days for Sears and Roebuck. It became known by the faculty that I repaired TV sets, and

George Alder

many students felt the only way I made it through college with passing grades was because of this! I always knew when George Alder's TV was no longer working for his son Brian would come up behind me in church and kick me, and that was my signal that their TV wasn't working. Interesting years!

While a student at SJBC, I also served as a youth minister on weekends throughout my five years of study. I served at Christian Churches with Walter Minkler at Healdsburg, Rex Wallace at Merced, and Harold Gallagher at the Church of Christ on campus. I owe much to these three men for their friendship and powerful mentoring of a student who received far more than he was able to give. Those were deeply formative experiences and became a strong source of encouragement that I could do ministry, though I had much yet to learn. My wife continued on as a student following our marriage, working at California Supply as an office assistant until we had our first child, Jerri, during our second year of marriage.

I learned much from my days on campus as a student, and all of my life I have drawn frequently from the things God taught me while a student there. There is no way to measure the full impact of what a Christian campus does in the hearts of those who are a part of it. It is a caring community of believers, each at a different place in their journey, but all desiring to help one another climb the hill that God has placed before them. The relationships developed there have continued to be some of the strongest relationships I have maintained throughout my entire life and ministry. Many of them have gone on to be with the Lord, but they live on in our lives because of what they taught us about life.

Having Dad as the President of the college I was attending was a special plus and I never felt uncomfortable being a student there, for I knew his heart. I had the privilege of seeing how he led in the home and church, and now I had the privilege of seeing how he led as president at SJBC. I discovered that much of his leadership style was no different at the college than I knew at home. He was the same person in both places. There was integrity in his and Mom's lives which built trust in the relationships for those who knew them. He was strong in his convictions about Biblical truth, but full of relational grace. He was for the "down and outer"; he wanted to see them succeed and would do what he could to help them. His passion in loving God and people was sincere and all consuming. His love for God's word, prayer, hurting people, and building a community of "world changers" impacted my life forever and the hearts of those who knew him. I was privileged to sit under his feet and learn from him at SJBC as a student.

Having graduated from SJBC in 1958, we accepted a call to become the youth ministers under Alger Fitch at the Milwaukie Church of Christ in Oregon that summer. It was a blessed experience to serve under him for a year and then to serve under Ted Hurlburt our second year there. Alger was a great preacher! His discipline in study through reading and research was amazing. He would write out his sermons word for word and then memorize them. I will always be grateful for what he taught me about preaching. Ted, I had known while he was a student at SJBC in the 1940s, and had observed his ministries since that time. He was a great lover of God and people. He had a smile that went ear to ear, and his presence would lighten up any gathering. Phillips Brooks, a great preacher from the last century, once said, "Preaching is truth through personality." That was Ted. When he finished preaching, you knew him and his God, for both were presented to you in an inspiring way. I will always be grateful to him for what he taught me about letting your heart be known and seen in ministry.

While in Milwaukie, God blessed us with two years of youth ministry and many experiences which helped shape our lives into greater usefulness in the Kingdom. The church was a loving church and we developed a number of relationships which we have maintained all of our lives. In addition, we had a second child, Janice, in December of 1959. As helpful as was everything I described, we constantly felt the need for additional education so that we could continue to deepen our lives in order to broaden our impact in the future. Therefore, we decided to head off to Pepperdine University for graduate study in June of 1960. Little did we know what was in store for us on the way. Here is the story as it was written by my wife Jo in the Guideposts magazine six years later. The story line at the top read: *"Have you ever had a sudden, startling urge to pray for someone, though you had no special reason why? That prayer may be more important than you dream. Such a prayer was for us on the most terrible night of our lives."* She then entitled the article...

"Out of the Depths"
Shirley-Jo Jessup

The day had started out so happily, for it was the day, six years ago, that we were heading for Los Angeles. There my husband, Bryce, was to go back to school for his master's degree in religion. We were sorry to leave the church in Oregon where he'd been minister for two years, but he wanted the extra education.

Our plan was to leave after supper that night, when we could put our two little girls to bed on a mattress in the back seat, and to drive straight through to Bryce's parents' place in San Jose, California. It was 700 miles of straight driving but easier, we thought, than dragging three-year-old Jerri and six-month-old Janni in and out of restaurants and motels. Besides, we told ourselves, it was July, driving at night would be cooler.

We didn't know then, how fatigue can numb the brain and slow the muscles. All through that hot summer day we carried things from the parsonage to the big U-Haul trailer we had rented. It was happy work. Our belongings were like a resume of our five wonderful years of marriage: my wedding dress, Bryce's theological library collected book by book, dishes, furniture, albums of precious photos. Many of our wedding gifts had never left their boxes, waiting for that dreamed-of day when we would have a 'permanent home'.

By 6 p.m., car and trailer were loaded. After supper at a friend's house and a dozen goodbyes, we tucked Jerri and Janni into their back-seat bed and started out.

The heat and the hauling and emotion of leaving good friends had taken their toll. From the start it was a struggle to stay awake. Because of the trailer, Bryce didn't want me to drive. It was my job to keep him alert. But as the miles passed my head would snap up with a jerk and I would know I had been asleep.

At four a.m. we pulled into a gas station in Klamath Falls, Oregon, and bought soft drinks, then walked back to check the trailer. In the gray, pre-dawn light the little red rocking chair looked strangely comforting strapped to the top of the load. It had been my mother's as a little girl and then mine, and now it was Jerri's.

Through the rear window we peeked in at our sleeping children. To find a motel at this time of night and get out bags and baby food and all the rest seemed almost harder than to keep going.

And yet we knew that just ahead lay the hardest driving on the trip: the treacherous straight stretch of road south of Klamath Falls, with a deep ditch running along the right-hand side and on the left a main irrigation canal 12 feet deep and 15 feet wide. But by now the cold drink was reviving us. We climbed back into the car. Fatefully, we made the decision to keep going...

Ten minutes later and 400 miles farther south, Bryce's father sat up in bed. 'The children are here', he said to his wife. Bryce's mother squinted at her watch. 'They can't be', she said. 'They weren't going to leave till after dark. They couldn't get here till mid-morning at the earliest.'

But Bryce's father was already on his way to the front door. When his wife joined him he was standing outside, staring into the empty night. At last, reluctantly, he went back inside. 'You dreamed it', she said. 'It wasn't a dream,' he insisted. 'It was something much stronger.' Back in bed, they both offered silent prayers, not really knowing what they were praying for or why. But both felt a compulsion to pray.

At the moment that Bryce's father awoke, I, too, was startled from sleep. I must have dozed off almost the minute we left the gas station. Now I was wakened by a cry from Bryce: 'Hang on!' He was wrestling with the wheel. The car was rocking sickeningly on the rim of the steep ditch at our right. For a horrid moment we swayed there. Then at last the headlights swung left and we felt pavement beneath the tires again.

Now Bryce spun the wheel the other way. But the car continued a slow, relentless arc to the left. We were heading straight for the deep water canal on the other side. Bryce threw all his strength against the wheel. But the heavily-loaded trailer, jackknifed behind us, was forcing us off the road. We were crossing the shoulder. And then we plunged down the incline into the canal. For an unbelievable moment the car floated there in the early morning darkness, then sank.

'Roll down your window!' Bryce yelled. I heard the handle crank on his side as icy water gushed over us. Bryce was leaning into the back seat. I saw him drag Jerri forward and then, like figures in an underwater ballet, float out the window. It had happened so fast that only then did I rouse myself from my stupor. I seized the window handle on my side, but it was jammed. I threw my shoulder against the door but the water outside pressed it shut. The window's open on Bryce's side. That was the thought I held in my mind as I groped for Janni in a floating debris of diapers, bottles and blankets. The water was cold and thick with slimy moss. There was a pain in my back and my lungs were straining against my chest. The mattress had floated to the ceiling but I couldn't find our baby.

I found a tiny air pocket at the top of the car and pressed my face into it, but soon the oxygen grew short and my lungs seemed to be on fire. For the first time I realized I was screaming. All that seemed to matter was to keep the slimy water from touching my face. 'Dear God,' I prayed, 'let me faint first. Don't let me be alive when the water covers me.'

I felt a hand take mine. It was Bryce. At least I would die holding his hand, I thought. But he was pulling at me, dragging me away from the roof. I struggled to get free. He was pulling me; I was swallowing the slimy water. He wouldn't let go. And then suddenly, unbelievably, fresh air was in my face. My lungs were swelling, filling with it. My hand touched something solid and I held on.

'Janni!' Bryce was screaming at me. 'Where's Janni?' While I coughed, unable to speak, he dove back beneath the dark water. From somewhere I heard crying. Then in the gray light I saw Jerri standing on the bank, shivering in her drenched little nightie. I saw that my hand had closed on the rocking chair.

Bryce's head appeared a few feet away. He was treading water, gasping, too winded to speak. Then he disappeared again. This time he was gone a long, long time. When he came up he was holding Janni. I didn't want to look at that tiny limp form. His feet found the roof of our car and he stood on it, water up to his chest, our baby in his hands. Her head fell back and I knew she was dead.

From the bank came an anxious little cry, 'Don't drop Janni, daddy! Don't drop Janni!' Bryce lifted Janni's face to his own and blew into her mouth. He took a breath, then blew again, and then again and again. At last, her chest shuddered and she let out a tiny wail. 'She's breathing!' Bryce shouted. He splashed with her to the bank while I followed. Jerri threw herself into my arms, and a few minutes later an early motorist found us.

At the hospital in Klamath Falls doctors assured us there was no damage to Janni's brain. X-rays showed three crushed vertebrae in my spine which would quickly heal: the only injury to any of us. From the admitting room Bryce put through a call to his parents. For the first time the wonder of our being alive and well swept over me. How had Bryce ever gotten us all from that car; How had a man who was exhausted, who was only a novice swimmer, who knew nothing about mouth-to-mouth breathing – how had he done all the right things at the right times?

'Hello, Pop,' I heard him say into the telephone. 'What's wrong, Bryce? Are you all right?' his father interrupted. 'Don't be alarmed-we've had an accident but everyone's fine.' 'Thank God,' said his father. Then he asked, 'Was it at four o'clock this morning?' Bryce stared at the phone in surprise. 'How did you know?' Did someone tell you?' There was a little pause at the other end. 'Yes, somebody told me,' said his father.

As one would expect, few experiences have shaped my life more than this one as my family is alive and well today as a result of the prayers of my Mom and Dad, who were burdened to pray for us even though they didn't know the depth of the need. As I stood on the bank of the canal in the afternoon retrieving a few of our things such as Jo's wedding dress floating down stream, and a few of my sunken books, I became aware that the most important thing in life is to always be ready to meet your Creator, for you never know when that moment will come. In addition, do all that you can to help prepare those closest to you and beyond to meet the Lord. Now that the experience is more than 50 years behind me, I would think that it would have faded away in its impact, but I still brush away a tear of gratitude every time I retell the story. How can I not be faithful to His every desire for my life when He has given me abundant life forever, and delivered me from certain death on more than one occasion? **Sometimes God rescues people so that they can continue a legacy!**

Below is a picture of us in front of the Milwaukie Church of Christ and one of Jerri and Janice shortly before our accident in front of the car that went into the canal in 1960.

CHAPTER FOUR

President Transitions *(1960-1968)*

In the years following the move of San Jose Bible College to the 12th Street campus, the culture of the campus shifted from the post-war years when many students were older and attended on the GI Bill military scholarship, to a much younger student body fresh out of high school. Church planting by students was not as much as it had been, plus the church planting ministry had been given over to the Northern California Evangelistic Association (NCEA) so that SJBC could focus more on education and preparation for ministry. Many of our younger students served as youth ministers, associate ministers, and volunteers in music and children's ministries in the churches in Northern California.

As Dad continued to lead the college in the late 1950s, there was a growing awareness in his heart that perhaps his season of leadership at SJBC was coming to a close. The student body was hovering around 100 students, not as large as it had been in earlier days and he was feeling in his spirit that perhaps fresh leadership was needed; in addition, he was feeling the pull to return to ministry within the local church.

Therefore, in the Spring of 1960, Dad submitted his letter of resignation as president of SJBC. The college publication *The Gospel Broadcaster* said of Dad in the July-August 1960 edition:

> *During Brother Jessup's presidency SJBC has become known across the country as a school dedicated to training young people for Christian service and for Christian living. He is known for his constant emphasis on the centrality of the Bible as the key to all spiritual knowledge and for his example and leading in the life of prayer.*

For a number of years, Dad had been in close contact with Ernest Beam, a judge and minister of the Lakewood Church of Christ. They had held many seminars and unity meetings together up and down the west coast of California. The church reflected unity in Christ by having worship on Sunday mornings without the piano, and with the piano on Sunday evenings. This appealed to Dad because of his passion to see the church united in worship, and so he accepted a call to become its minister beginning October 16, 1960. He served for several years there, but soon became restless for a broader ministry and one that served leaders in the churches on the West Coast.

Dad had been a regular contributor to Standard Publishing Company, a Christian company given to producing materials for the Restoration Movement, and in 1964 he was invited to become the West Coast Representative for the company. In this new role he traveled to the churches for leadership training, unity meetings, preaching, and VBS seminars. Both he and Mom would make presentations to help encourage, strengthen, and provide materials for helping churches grow and reproduce themselves in Christ. During this time they became a part of Central Christian Church in Lancaster where I preached for eight years following graduate school at Pepperdine University in 1962. Dad taught classes, made calls, organized a Seniors Ministry, and served in many capacities within the church when he was not traveling for Standard Publishing.

Following this Dad and mom started churches in Bishop and in Grass Valley in the late 1960s. His last fulltime church assignment was to become the Pastor of the Southside Church of Christ in South Sacramento. He retired from fulltime ministry and moved to San Jose in the middle 1970s, and became the Senior Saints minister for Central Christian Church where I was preaching. He not only ministered to the Seniors of CCC, but he mobilized around 500 Seniors in Northern California, drew them together for an annual convention at SJBC, did a number of service projects with them, and also took a couple trips to the Holy Land with over 100 of them. I had the privilege of helping to host one of them on a rather challenging but rewarding trip. As a result of his work among the Seniors of the region, he was crowned Seniors King of the Santa Clara County Fair in 1987 at an elaborate program with marching bands, confetti, balloons, and a host of special speakers giving recognition for his achievements.

Mom and Dad with his Seniors King Trophy, 1987 Santa Clara County Fair

When Dad stepped down as President of SJBC, Al Tiffin was selected by the Board of Trustees to become the second president of SJBC, followed by Woodrow Phillips in 1969. I asked Dr. Gary Tiffin, Al's son, to write the major portion of this chapter of the book as he taught at SJBC during his Dad's presidency. The decade of the 60's was the only decade when I was not living in San Jose, although I served on the Board of Trustees for part of that time. The remainder of the chapter has been written by Gary. I am grateful for his input concerning his Dad's presidency and the first four years of Woodrow Phillip's presidency.

Al Tiffin

1960 had some impressive looking men.

THE TIFFIN PRESIDENCY OF SJBC
By Dr. Gary Tiffin
1960 -1968: Years of Consolidation and Transition

The Last Two Years "Brother Bill" Was President

Since I was enrolled in only one class per semester, I didn't experience William "Bill" Jessup as much as full-time students. Yet, living with SJBC students, I fully participated outside the classroom as if I were a full-time student. We knew that Brother Jessup arose very early to pray in his office each morning – which was a powerful example and incentive for us to develop our own prayer life. Paul Clark remembers that he and other students usually met with Brother Jessup at 7 a.m. for prayer time before classes began at 7:30 a.m. He was always warm, outgoing, and friendly as he passed by or even stopped to talk for a while. He was often gone from campus visiting churches, holding meetings, and travelling with athletic teams and music groups. Students were not very aware of his founding involvement with the college, save that he was the first and only president. Even when away from campus, his presence and influence was obvious, honored, and appreciated.

Some of us decided to "camp out" one spring Friday evening between the classroom and administration-chapel buildings. We thought we were quite clever in our stealth-like set up. We were quite surprised to be awakened quite early the next morning, a bit chagrined to learn that the president evidently sometimes spent early Saturday mornings on campus also. He was not enthralled with our adventurous overnight prank, although I do not recall why!! He likely stated he would pray for us, and we surely knew he would, even though we would have been a bit anxious about the content of that prayer.

In the fall of 1958, at the end of Orientation Week, we new students hiked down the slope at the undeveloped back property of the campus, crossed Coyote Creek, and took our places (awkwardly on the uneven bank) to sit, sing and listen. We were treated to our first Brother Bill talk. While I do not recall exactly what was said, I clearly recall that he communicated with powerful passion not only about the college and its purpose but, more importantly, about the mission of Christ and a world needing the gospel. We more clearly understood what San Jose Bible College was all about!

The daily schedule for the college in these years began at 7:30 a.m. with five 50-minute class periods lasting until 12:20, after which everyone ate lunch. Most full-time faculty taught straight through the morning, with only a break for daily chapel at 9:30, with classes resuming at 10:30. This left afternoons open for students to work and for faculty to grade, prepare, attend meetings and, yes, play golf or ping pong. The college did not move to afternoon classes until the early 70's when student body growth required an expanded schedule. A few classes were offered in the evenings, sometimes attracting local church members or working adults.

Although the student body had been born mostly near the beginning of World War II, it did not dawn on us how recently that event had reshaped the 1950s during which we had moved through junior high and high school. We were now a student body of 100 traditional college age students, with a rapidly decreasing percentage of returning World War II veterans enjoying the benefits of the GI Bill to help pay for college. Japan had just reopened, Germany was rebuilding, the Cold War was heating up, the French had recently been expelled from Vietnam, Sputnik had been launched just ten months earlier, Queen Elizabeth had only been on her throne six years, and Nikita Krushchev had replaced Stalin in Russia.

We were only a few short years from four agonizing assassinations (two Kennedys, Malcolm X and Martin Luther King Jr.), Haight-Ashbury, a divisive Vietnam War, a questioning generation of youth, the Jesus People, and the election of the first Catholic president. These were among the many rapid changes in our country that would shape the trajectory of our lives, ministries, marriages and careers. How could we have known that we would directly minister in post-colonial Africa, Mongolia, former Soviet States, Cambodia and Southeast Asia, China and other places so far removed from the possibilities we could have possibly envisioned that evening?

For these last two years of his ministry at SJBC, Brother Bill led our small college of less than 100 students (93 in 1958-9 and 89 in 1959-60 with 12 and 15 graduates respectively) that still carried his imprint, but more importantly continued the original vision of the ministry of the college. We students believed it was special, and it was!

Before He Was President

Al Tiffin was born (youngest of 8 children) in 1917 to a devout Seventh Day Adventist mother (herself a twin) and an English immigrant father. Having survived the 1906 San Francisco earthquake, the family eventually settled into the Visalia-Lindsay area of California's central San Joaquin valley. Al's father died when he was 16. He eventually graduated from Strathmore High School near Visalia, where his 4th grade teacher at Strathmore was the future Mrs. Archie Word, long before she married Archie. More than 35 years later I graduated in the same Washington High School (Portland) class of 1958 with Archie Jr., the Words' youngest son.

While working at a canning factory in Fresno, Dad was hospitalized due to a conveyer belt accident, which led to his meeting Emory Snyder, minister of Eastside Christian Church who would later marry Mom and Dad. Dad eventually became a member there and later enrolled at Northwest Christian College in the fall of 1936, several years after Bill Jessup had graduated from Eugene Divinity School, the predecessor institution to Northwest Christian College.

Elsie Lichti's father Otto was a Yale University Ph.D. minister of Reedley Mennonite Church, a post he lost because he would not support Germany and Kaiser Wilhelm during World War I. Sadly, both of Elsie's parents died before she turned 5, leaving Elsie and her five siblings, ranging from age 5 to 12, to be raised by an aunt and uncle in their 50's, who had no children of their own. Surviving a rather difficult childhood, Elsie moved to Bakersfield, California, where she became a member of First Christian Church, from where she enrolled at Northwest Christian College in the fall of 1936. Al and Elsie first met when a carload of NCC students from Bakersfield, including Elsie, picked up Al on the way to Eugene. Within months they were dating and later married in Fresno in the fall of 1938, a marriage which would last 58 and one-half years until Al died in 1997.

Mom (1939) and Dad (1940) both graduated from NCC, during which time Dad took his first full-time ministry at Dayton, Oregon, where I was born in late 1940. From that ministry in Dayton until Dad assumed the presidency of SJBC in 1960, he and Mother served congregations in Montana, Oregon, Indiana and California and welcomed three daughters into the family. After two graduate degrees from Butler University and School of Religion (1947-52), Dad became minister of University Christian Church (this was the home congregation of Jo Jessup who was a senior in high school at that time) near the University of Southern California and the Los Angeles Coliseum in 1952, where he served for three and one-half years. Eldred Illingworth of that congregation served for several years as a board member at SJBC. Dad also taught homiletics at then Pacific Bible Seminary during those years. While minister at University Church, Dad served as a member of the San Jose Bible College Board of Directors from 1954-1956.

In January 1956, Dad became minister of Central Christian Church in Portland, at which point we four "kids" ranged from 12 to 16 years of age. Central was the largest Christian Church in the state at that time, which meant mom and Dad were always hosting travelling preachers, missionaries, and other amazing Christian workers as guests in our home. From that congregation would come SBJC board members Gay Stavney, Art Simonson, and Sherman Holmes. Dad also served on the SJBC Board of Directors during the last two years of the Jessup presidency, so he was well acquainted with the college when he became president. By this time he was also serving on the North American Christian Convention Continuation Committee that planned the annual national preaching and teaching convention, which was held in Portland in 1958 and Long Beach in 1963.

My oldest sister Becky (15 months younger than me) and I had already graduated from Washington High in Portland by the fall of 1960, where Nancy (a junior) and Sharon (a senior) were still both very active in a wide range of school activities and groups. So when Dad accepted the call to become president of SJBC, there was anguish before and after that decision regarding the impact on them, uprooted from a high school where they were well known and active, to a much larger high school where they were unknown. That transition indeed was difficult but, to this day, they are able to appreciate that it was about more than them. Sharon would spend two years as a student at SBJC before she married, Nancy one year before entering nursing school in Portland, whereas Becky had already spent a year at Puget Sound College of the Bible. So with family in place, Becky married, and me a junior at SJBC, the Tiffin presidency began November 1, 1960, just before the November presidential election when John Kennedy defeated Richard Nixon.

The Beginning Months

As already noted Dad was ministering in Portland and serving on the SJBC Board as the Jessup presidency came to a close. Board minutes from the September 7 & 8, 1960, Board meeting indicate that Don Meyer, minister at Park Avenue Christian Church in Montebello (where both Bryce Jessup and I would later serve as youth minister, and also where I met Pat) and chair of the "Special Presidential Committee," reported that 27 names had been submitted to follow Bill Jessup as the next president of SJBC. Then he proceeded to place Dad's name in nomination to become president. He was voted in by voice acclamation.

My parents had always lived in parsonages as was common in the years of their church ministries. So their purchase of a modest home on Anna Drive in West San Jose marked a new venture for them. After two years they moved into a new home in northeast San Jose on Camino Del Rey Avenue, where they hosted many faculty, students, and visitors for the next six years. Mom became secretary to the principal at San Jose High School, a role she held all during the San Jose years. That did not stop her from accompanying Dad and singing groups on weekends visiting congregations to represent the college.

Many would have been surprised at the schedule she kept, which has marked her long 95 years of life. In the tradition of all SJBC presidents and spouses, long dedicated and sacrificial hours were required for the task taken and lived out as a calling.

Dad was well aware of the challenges of following a beloved founding president. He was also very aware of continuing enrollment, financial, and physical space issues. More than that, he clearly understood that he was not alone in this task. At the end of his first calendar year as president, on January 29, 1962, he delivered a hand-typed 9-page double-spaced report to the Board, which began as follows: *It was just one year ago that I stood before you for the first time in this capacity [president]. At that time I had been at this challenging task only three months. I will admit that I stood here with considerable misgivings and concern for this was truly a most exacting task and an important work. I stand here this evening with the same sense of concern and inadequacy, not because my fear and anxieties have been confirmed, but because I am desperately aware that this job still lies ahead of us. I still need God's grace and your prayerful help to be His instrument in operating our school. I am sure that if I am permitted to serve another five, ten years or more, this feeling of need and fellowship of labor will never leave.*

In the details of the report that followed, he addressed the needs for construction of additional buildings, financial solvency (especially concerned about meeting payroll on time), public relations, his positive view of the faculty and students, and the future as he envisioned it. He raised the question about whether and how to educate students beyond the preaching ministry, including women students, concern for the advantages of accreditation, and then challenged each Board member to fully support the college in prayer, finances, and public relations.

He closed his report by stating: *I believe in the Bible College here enough to invest my life in it. The same is true for every member of our faculty and staff. You men believe in it also or you would not be here at this meeting. I believe that what we are trying to do together is within God's will. If we get busy, plan, decide and work, only success can come. On this I stake my life and witness.*

His next seven years were testimony to the commitment and resolve stated in that first (of many) reports to the Board. He was very concerned that the college was so far behind in paying faculty salaries that faculty had to take personal loans from banks or other sources just to live. With the knowledge of few Board members, he proceeded to arrange for a bank loan from which he and Mom personally delivered individual catch up checks totaling $4,745 to every faculty home on Christmas Eve, 1960. Talk about a great PR start with the faculty! It would take several more years to stabilize income and continuity of sustainable budgets – achieved through careful management, continual visiting in churches (he reported in that same January 29, 1962, Board meeting having travelled 13,000 driving miles during the first five months after he became president), and full disclosure to the Board about the realities of what was needed to maintain a viable college. It is important to realize that annual budgets did not pass the $100,000 mark until 1967. Enrollment usually hovered around 100 students, 82 his first year and 131 his last year. Tuition for the 1961-2 year was $125 a semester, or $10 per credit hour, far less than the $500-700 per unit charge charged at most Christian universities today. At the January 1961 Board meeting, $50 a month was authorized for library books and equipment, less than the cost of most single library books today. The college graduated an average of 10 students a year from 1960-68, from a low of 5 to a high of 18.

He inherited a terrific faculty, most of whom continued on throughout his time as President: George Alder, Emmett Butterworth (Academic Dean) and wife Katie (librarian), Ruben Ratzlaff and Ralph Holcomb (both hired in 1959), Harold Rea (retired in 1965 after 25 years at SBJC) and Wes Veach (who left in 1962). Added to the faculty were Jack Morrison, Dallas Meserve, Don Whitney, Hal Martin (as church liaison), followed by Loretta Carmickle as librarian (1966) and Bob Sargent as Dean (1967). Those closest to the college understood that George Alder was the *de facto* leader of the faculty during these years, and from whom other faculty and presidents sought counsel and advice.

Records indicate that in the fall of 1965 fulltime faculty were paid $130 per week, while the president was paid $140 per week. In June of 1966, the Board approved raising this weekly scale another $10 per year for the next three academic years. By 1968, faculty would receive $160 per week, those with doctorates $170 per week, the same pay as the president. That small differential between faculty and presidential pay would be unthinkable today. By this time a matching annuity program and health insurance benefits had been added to salaries.

Dad's physical stature and personality certainly was obvious, and sometimes overpowering. At 6'4", with an imposing stride and strong personality, he could be viewed initially as somewhat intimidating. That impression vanished quickly when his careful, considered, and concerned heart was experienced. I would not necessarily say he was presidential in demeanor or manner, but certainly was professional (save when playing golf, painting, or checking out landscaping on campus), organized, businesslike, as well as visionary, which are desirable presidential traits. In addition, he was a passionate builder. Ground was broken for a 50-bed men's dormitory on

February 2, 1962, just one year after he assumed Presidency. The following article appeared in the Broadcaster.

Gospel Broadcaster

SAN JOSE BIBLE COLLEGE   February, 1962   Vol. 21, No. 3

Ground-breaking Ceremonies

A large crowd gathered Friday afternoon, February 2, on the campus for ground breaking ceremonies to officially begin construction on Jessup Hall and the Cafetorium. Wayne Thomas presided over the ceremonies which featured the special address by Bryce Jessup, son of W. L. Jessup and now minister of the Lancaster church.

Very appropriately Bryce Jessup emphasized that he trusted the new Jessup Hall might serve to house young men training for the ministry and that they might capture there the same zeal which he gained from his father in years past.

Herm Link, speaking in behalf of the Board of Directors, reminded the audience that just a year ago the cornerstone plaque for this building had been presented to "Brother Bill" and that at that time we had not dreamed that we would have the building so soon. Mr. Link went on to say that God has most richly blessed our school in a way beyond our expectations, making possible not only the building of Jessup Hall but the Cafetorium as well.

Construction will soon begin. As was true of Beach Hall several years ago, we shall provide furnishings by special memorial gifts. Elsewhere in this paper details about this appear.

Pres. Tiffin, Board Chairman Herm Link, and former president, W. L. Jessup turn the soil for the new Jessup Hall.

101 ENROLL SECOND SEMESTER

The second semester began on February 8 with an enrollment of 101. Besides

NINTH ANNUAL CROSSBEARERS' CRUSADE

On Saturday night, March 31, the ninth annual Crossbearers' Crusade will begin with a youth banquet almost certain to exceed the 300 attendance of

Herm Link, Al Tiffin, Bryce Jessup and Bill Jessup

Then, the building of a cafetorium in 1963 provided a fully equipped cafeteria for students and faculty, a place for fellowship after Chapel, and released space in Beach Hall to house more students.

Cafeteria Under Construction and Completed

At the same time, a faculty lounge was established in a remodeled classroom adjacent to the new cafetorium. This not only served as an important get away room for faculty after 5 consecutive hours (7:30-12:30) of classes and chapel, but also provided an important venue for faculty interaction and fellowship. Spending an informal 45 minutes to an hour everyday with each other afforded more than just a time to eat and talk. There, from time to time, faculty would informally process important concerns, college challenges, and opportunities. The fellowship, the informal discussion, and the easy give and take in this faculty lounge environment was a key to faculty-administrative harmony and solidarity as president and faculty members daily shared this time together in which mutual respect and understanding was exercised and nourished. The fact is that faculty and administrators really liked each other.

This environment was the setting in which Dallas Meserve recalls the only time he ever saw Dad come close to making an arbitrary decision, prompting a very strong faculty response. Just after the opening of the faculty lounge, he walked in one day and pronounced there would be no coffee or food allowed in the new lounge. At first no one responded because they were so surprised. At that the last faculty member they would have expected to respond was Don Whitney, normally deferential, quiet, and very cooperative. He reacted swiftly, strongly, directly, and negatively. Surprised, Dad paused, thought about it, and on the spot acknowledged that his surprising and unilateral decision was inappropriate, and then rescinded his pronouncement on the spot. For Dallas, this incident demonstrated Dad's sensitivity and lack of ego.

Public Relations, today often referred to as "Advancement," was key to the ongoing viability of the college in these years. While Presidents Jessup and Tiffin spent significant time on the road, more was needed. Ralph Holcomb was assigned to this task in 1961 and served until 1963. Hal Martin carried out this task beginning in 1966 and early into Woody Phillips' presidency. Faculty spent several weekends a year in congregations, preaching and representing the college. Congregational support was the heart of the college because they not only sent students, but were the intended recipients of the work of the college in terms of preachers, staff, and educated workers.

This was closely allied with the need to raise funds to support the budget. Board minutes and Presidential reports throughout these years always included reports from the Board Finance Committee, Financial Reports and Presidential Reports – usually indicating deficits, some long-term, if not short-term, but always vexing. Short-term personal and bank loans bridged the gap sometimes, but there was always discussion about the impact of student recruitment, student retention, rates for tuition and room and board – as necessary components for a solution to remain solvent. As late as the June 1965 Board meeting, marking the end of the fifth year of his presidency, and after bringing very tight scrutiny to spending, Dad made a somber report to the Board: that by early spring the college was overdrawn by $3,077.00 (4% of the budget for that year). After offering analysis and explanation as to how the problem developed, and that faculty had once again each taken temporary payroll deductions for $10 to $50 a week (recall they were paid $130 per week), he then concluded: *I realize that the O.D. in the General Fund is an "unforgiveable sin." However, there was absolutely nothing I could do but allow it to come to pass. I am perfectly willing to accept any reprimand that may be offered by the Board. At the same time I would certainly appreciate your statement of an alternative.*

I read this as a friendly but subtle request for proactive help from the Board. The financial pressure was always present.

By this time, another building was very much needed. Early accreditation feasibility visits had clearly identified library holdings, organization, administration, and shelf space as necessary preludes to full accreditation. By late 1966, planning was underway to build the San Jose Bible College Memorial

Library which was accomplished in time for dedication in late spring 1968, at the transition point between presidencies. Built for about $75,000, it was a much needed stimulus to this essential part of academic life and progress. But buildings were not the only concern if accreditation was going to be achieved.

Before Dad became president, accreditation was viewed as an important step to long-term viability, academic respectability, and effective education for ministry. Dean Butterworth had been given the task of pursuing the groundwork for the achievement of this goal, which was progressing well by the fall of 1960. After a self-study was conducted and written, in compliance with the protocols of AABC (The Accrediting Association of Bible Colleges, now Association for Biblical Higher Education), an initial visit that could lead to associate membership occurred January 10 & 11, 1963. The two visiting accreditors (from Bethany and Multnomah Bible Colleges) produced a remarkable report summarized for the SJBC Board at their June Board meeting a few months later. The accreditors concluded that more needed to be accomplished before even a social membership could be granted.

Their report was a microanalysis of every aspect of campus life, governance, faculty procedures, and curriculum one might imagine. Likely meant to help, it was discouraging. Here are some of their suggestions, a few of which are surprising even to read today: obtain faculty transcripts, decrease drop-out rates, faculty should help recruit students, replace large library table with several small ones (I loved that big table – fun to slide down the middle on my "washboard stomach" when Mrs. Butterworth was out of the library!!), track student giving and mission efforts, build a gym, hold all classes on campus, restrict automobiles and the use of them for dating, study grading methods, rework faculty planning, and so it went. While each of these surely held merit, it would take four more years of diligent and persistent effort to move to full accreditation. Faculty, board members, students, and staff set to work to standardize procedures, leave audit trails of decision, expenditures, and activity, and become more like other Bible colleges. Federal aid to students (work study, grants, and loans) had now become dependent upon some form of accreditation, so when accomplished, this helped set the stage for the rapid growth that would follow after 1968.

SJBC was not accredited when I attended and graduated. While accreditation became and remains very important, the first 30 years of SJBC are testimony to the fact that effective education is based upon more than procedures, efficiency, standardization, and widely accepted protocols. These are important but no substitute for an ardently committed faculty, a caring and supportive environment, accountability for personal integrity and honor, and the power of mission and purpose to propel students to achieve beyond what any transcript can fully predict. The achievement of professional (AABC) and then later regional (WASC) accreditation confirmed what was actually occurring already.

Dad had always engaged in ministries which were in need of renewal which he accomplished and usually quite quickly. Mom and Dad left broken hearts in every congregation they served, but also left a foundation for future growth and effectiveness. This would also come to characterize Dad's presidency at SJBC, which provided a stable base for the rapid growth of the college in the early years of Woody Phillips' presidency. He was quite discerning as to timing, "when to hold and when to let go," which was true in 1968 when he concluded his work at San Jose.

Dad's accomplishments as President of San Jose were several:

1. He recognized the validity of the heritage of the Jessup presidency and never distanced himself from that foundation.

2. Given his extensive educational background, he provided a timely nudge the college needed to fully implement a collegiate structure, curriculum, and environment - this without trading the essence of the college for the sake of reputation, money, or status.

3. Like Bill Jessup, he was a builder – but since the foundation had been laid by Brother Bill, Dad expanded it to include initial accreditation by 1968 as well as three additional very much needed new buildings.

4. Dad understood financial management and blessed the college with careful accounting, forecasting, and management practices necessary to survive very lean times. There was never enough money, but faithful, prayerful, and visionary challenge moved the college to increased viability and stability.

5. He understood how to relate to people. He had always been very effective in challenging men to give their best, and likewise influenced women to do the same. His bark was much stronger than his gentle bite, which was usually withheld until no alternative was possible. He deeply loved students and faculty and they knew it and loved him back (eventually if not immediately – ask Bill Putnam!!).

6. He was involved. He practiced presence, even as he

taught in the classroom, travelled with students, kept an open office, perpetually traversed the campus throughout the day, and asked no one on staff or faculty to do what he had or would not do himself.

7. He was always a preacher first and an educator secondly, not that those are contradictory roles. This also characterized Jessup and Phillips in my view.

8. He kept mission as top priority, though sometimes camouflaged by his extensive efforts to build, manage, administer, and attend to needed details at the college. His passion for mission became focused and applied in the years following his presidency as he started 8 congregations in 10 years as director of the North Willamette Evangelistic Association, in the Portland area.

The Tiffin Presidency in Retrospect

In its origins, San Jose Bible College was built upon a vision shared by close associates, which then spread to like-minded congregations and willing supporters. Fueled by initial dogged commitment, special blessings of God, and an unflagging determination to succeed, it was World War II that ironically contributed to the permanent status of the college, with the influx of veterans returning from the war. As the 1950s played out, the college settled into the Northern California Christian support system it had actually created through church planting and home missions work. By 1954, the governance of the college had become more inclusive of representatives of that support system, which included Al Tiffin from Los Angeles and then later from Portland.

It is difficult to reconstruct expectations of Dad as he became president, but he surely was viewed as hard working, level headed, dependable, not likely to surprise, and predictably able to carry on the leadership of the college now barely 20 years old.

If the word consolidation applies to his presidency, it is not because repairs were needed, but that those 20 years of achievement could and should not be diminished or lost. Not as charismatic as Bill Jessup, Dad was effective as he sought to consolidate what he had received.

This surely was a transitional presidency. The SJBC I knew as I left in 1972 was a far different college than in 1958 when I first enrolled, and actually from 1965 when I joined the faculty. The essence had not changed, but the form, shape, impact, and importance had morphed in ways that most applauded. Sandwiched in between Jessup and Phillips, the Tiffin presidency now appears to have been an appropriate component in both maintaining the best of the past and preparing for what would be possible in a few short years. Late in his life, I asked him one time which phase of his later ministry roles, President of SJBC or Director of the North Willamette Evangelistic Association had been the most important and satisfying. His answer was revealing: both, because one was preparing others for witness, and the latter was direct witness.

Woodrow Phillips' First Four Years

Upon completion of my doctorate at Stanford in 1968, I moved from half-time to full-time faculty status that fall – which meant I would fully experience first hand the impact of the first four years of Woodrow (Woody) Phillips' presidency.

The news that he had been named the third president of SJBC created a stir among students, faculty and board members. After all, Woody, as he was known and called, had served as a missionary in Jamaica, ministered on the West Coast, and now headed an enviable missions department at Ozark Bible College. Along with Woody came a number of students who transferred from Ozark to SJBC. That number rose to about 30 by the fall of 1971. Some former students and supporters who had been reserved in their support for SJBC now became enthusiastic in anticipation of his coming. Faculty and staff were curious to see what the new president would do, change, and implement.

It did not take long! In those four years the student body *tripled*, Wednesday evening prayer meetings quickly filled the chapel as Woody led, preached, provoked, and generally spoke into our lives in ways most of us had rarely experienced. He was a charismatic personality, expressed with verve, zeal, and obvious commitment to educating a needed generation of witnesses for Jesus.

These early years of Woody's presidency were unique,

remarkable, and sometimes just wild and crazy. Up to this time, the SJBC student body overwhelmingly came from supporting and neighboring congregations. SJBC students (most but not all) traditionally had been raised in Christian homes, bringing with them a significant level of Bible knowledge, expected character, and somewhat conventional demeanor. While there was no collision of cultures, these were also the years of the Jesus People movement, open and aggressive street evangelism, open rejection of traditional values and a roaring youth counterculture. So the student body was soon peppered with newly converted youth, some wearing the Jesus People badge, and many straight from lives of rebellion, drugs, and non-conventional habits. Shorts, tee-shirts, sandals, and very casual wear on campus, including in the library, became increasingly and commonly accepted by many if not most on campus.

The number of freshman tripled within one year: 96 enrolled in the fall of 1969, 100 in 1970, and 123 in the fall of 1971. By fall of 1971, nearly one-fourth of the student body was from Oregon, and significant numbers were enrolling from Southern California. The 1971-72 academic year included the 1972 presidential campaign, the first when 18 year olds could vote. As I left the college that spring, those who supported a McGovern (Democrat) presidency were quite open and comfortable about that support. As I began at Pacific Christian College that fall, unlike at SJBC, the campus was overtly, overwhelmingly, and unabashedly for Nixon, which was likely true of many Christian colleges that year – but not at SBJC – which spoke to the tenor of campus culture. Teaching American Government in such an environment was a lively and sometimes raucous experience!!

The rapid growth of the student body was fueled by a number of factors. From the beginning, Woody Phillips openly gave Dad credit for having left behind a strong and compatible faculty, a sound and stable academic program under the leadership of Bob Sargent and expanded and up-to-date facilities, altogether forming a solid foundation which allowed for very quick growth. That strong faculty was now joined by Warren Bell, Willard Black, Al Hammond, Jim Crain and Bryce Jessup (1970) as Dean of Students, which gave students five more reasons to enroll. Woody Phillips was the right leader to relate to newly converted Christian students as well as those from more traditional backgrounds. Youth ministries in a number of congregations, such as led by Jim Crain at Central Christian in Portland, OR, were very effective in evangelizing youth, who immediately enrolled at SJBC. So by the 1971-72 academic year, the college had grown from 134 total students in 1968 to close to 350. Classes were larger, course offerings expanded (especially in general education now required by AABC accreditation), and the student body was increasingly populated by Christian youth for whom SJBC was first choice for college, even though some had been admitted to much larger and more prestigious colleges and universities.

SJBC had become a "happening" place, drawing 1500 youth from all over the west coast, to the 1971 and 1972 Crossbearer's Crusades, the annual spring youth weekend on campus. This event had drawn 450 youth 10 years earlier. During these years, notables such as Andre Crouch and Larry Norman were featured at major events on campus.

Crossbearer's Crusade with Andre Crouch

Woody supplemented his unique Wednesday night (not required, but always filled the chapel) prayer meetings with annual all-school retreats. Two of the most memorable were held in 1970 at Ponderosa Pines Christian Camp at Mt. Hermon in the coastal redwoods and in 1971 near Santa Cruz. This new camp was more luxurious than most homes students had left behind. While discussion groups, sports, a fabulous swimming pool, food, and activities were on the menu, most memorable and often life changing were Woody's long (usually 3-5 hours) confessional, prayer, and group counseling times attended by 150-200 students and faculty. These appeared to lack structure, but predictably drew out unprecedented moments of reality, honesty, forgiveness, and some of the most unpredictable group dynamics we had ever witnessed.

This was a time when so many students, new and long time Christians alike, were dealing with their own checkered backgrounds, broken family relationships, and facing their own missteps including abortion, promiscuity, and addictions of various types. In my naiveté, I was shocked that Woody would presume these past sins had been and likely still were common for many in the student body. But these sessions of raw testimony and confession confirmed that he understood youth culture better than me and most of the faculty.

Woody was often away from campus, in high demand as a speaker, conference leader, and consultant. That he could do so was testimony to the leadership of Academic Dean Bob Sargent, a conscientious faculty, and a faithful staff. We all knew he was the president in the formal sense of that title. But as part of that title and beyond it, he could surprise, but always supported us. He could be unpredictable, but predictably and passionately committed to the proclamation of the gospel. He could be very funny, but could turn serious very quickly. As if by stealth, he could make you feel bad about your shortcomings, sins of omission and commission, but at the same time, leave you begging for more reprimand, because he was absolutely correct in his presumptions and remedies, as painful as it was to admit.

Choirs, multiple music groups, expanded student interest groups, and lots of fun with faculty were commonplace. Faculty continued and expanded a tradition of providing an evening of just plain nutty, crazy, frolicking fun for students, which not only humanized the faculty in the eyes of students, but displayed some rather amazing faculty talent. For two years the event was named "Faculty Follies" a title unlikely to have been employed by faculty in the 1940's.

Basketball, volleyball, softball, and golf were available to students interested in intercollegiate sports. For years, players had purchased their own uniforms and wore miscellaneous sweatshirts for warm-ups. Now the college provided uniform uniforms. In a twist of history, we often quietly noted that basketball players from one rival team (holiness tradition) wore pants that came to the knee – how odd! Of course the University of Michigan Fab Five of the early 1990's led the way to that length as standard to this day. SJBC finally defeated archrival Bethany Bible College in basketball in 1971 to which the campus responded with great jubilation, even as some worried that sports would come to dominate the college budget! The faculty played the men's basketball team every year for a guaranteed win (students) and an even more predictable display of fading and waning faculty athletic prowess. The student body really enjoyed watching those old white skinny legs displayed by faculty.

Beach and Jessup Halls could hardly house this expanded student body, so arrangements were made to rent close-by housing in apartment complexes, vacant homes, and even at San Jose State U. This meant that students experienced both more freedom and responsibility and that the traditional "in loco parentis" function of the college no longer applied to upper division students. Few could remember it had always been this way before the building of dormitories in the 1960's. Home properties adjacent to campus were purchased when available in these years, both for housing as well as classroom and office space.

The college decided to build an activity center during the 1971-72 academic year. If you ever attended an event there, it was a simple open beamed structure, but with an athletic floor built by the same company that had laid the basketball floor at the newly built Pauley Pavilion at UCLA, the home of many John Wooden coached national champions in those years. So we were proud, but I was very frustrated! I was leaving the college just as the gymnasium was being completed, missing my chance to enjoy it. I was jealous of then Puget Sound Bible College where on their Edmonds, Washington campus they actually enjoyed two gyms. Ironically, in my many years in Christian higher education, I continued to be "early" for gymnasiums. PCC built theirs the year after I moved to Northwest Christian and then they built theirs the year after I left there. My only solace in 1972 was that the new SJBC Activities center was named the Tiffin Center in honor of Dad and Mom. As years went by, I usually could con Pacific Christian College students who knew the building that it was named "for" me – but only for a few moments! I now possess the brass plaque which adorned the Tiffin Center at the San Jose campus, a reminder of missed gymnasiums.

It would be hard to imagine a more energetic, dynamic, surprising, challenging, fun and sometimes scary four years in any institutional history. The class of 1972 shared those four years, a blessing to them, but also to the future of SJBC.

In the 1960s I viewed those who attended SJBC in the 1940s as part of the ancient history of the college. At this point, I look back and realize that the history recounted in this chapter constituted less than the first third of our history and the Tiffin era really is the ancient history.

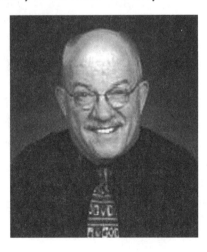

Brief Biography of Gary Tiffin

Gary Tiffin entered San Jose State U. in fall of 1958 and, additionally, lived with SJBC students and enrolled in one course a semester during his first two years at San Jose State, which were the last two years Bill Jessup was president of SJBC. He transferred to SJBC in the fall of 1960 (before he knew his father Al would become President on Nov. 1, 1960). Transferring from San Jose State, Gary graduated two years later (1962) from SJBC, as one of 10 graduates. After completing two degrees in history from California State University at Los Angeles, he returned to join the faculty (half-time) in the fall of 1965, teaching two courses per semester (history, science, and youth ministry) for the next three academic years, while completing his Ph.D. at Stanford. Coinciding with the coming of Woodrow Phillips as president of SJBC in 1968, Gary became a full time professor and served during the first four years of President Philips' tenure. He joined the faculty of Pacific Christian College in the fall of 1972, where he served the next 26 years as a professor of history and social science, and Dean of the College (his last 16 years). He then served as Provost of Northwest Christian University and now directs the doctoral program in education at George Fox University (since 2006), also teaching courses in the history of education.

Gary holds a unique position as having been a student at SJBC under the first two presidents, and then a faculty member under the second (Tiffin) and third (Philips) presidents. Interestingly, he succeeded Bryce Jessup as youth minister at Park Ave. Christian Church in Montebello, CA, in 1962, where he met his wife Pat, and then was in turn succeeded by Bryce as Dean of Students at SJBC in 1970, since a growing student body required a full time Dean of Students. The successions ended there!

CHAPTER FIVE

The Baby Boomer Surge and Decline! *(1969-1983)*

San Jose was home for me for most of my life. The college has been home for me for all but twelve years of its history. During those twelve years I was in youth ministry in Milwaukie, Oregon, graduate school at Pepperdine University, and a pastor of a church in Lancaster, California. While at Pepperdine I was contacted by the Central Christian Church in Lancaster during January 1962 about becoming their Pastor. Since I was going to graduate school, serving as youth minister at Montebello Christian Church under Don Meyer's leadership, and working twenty hours a week selling cameras at Sears & Roebuck in Compton to support the family, the preaching opportunity caught my attention. I was rather weary at this point but I still had six more months of graduate school. The Lancaster church made a generous offer. "How about becoming our preacher on week-ends, with the promise of moving to Lancaster in June and becoming our fulltime minister? We will pay you a full time salary so you can quit Sears and the youth ministry." Wow...that seemed an offer I couldn't refuse!

However, I remember going to one of my teachers for counsel and talking to him about the opportunity. One of the things that still pulled at me from time to time was my interest in playing baseball. At times I was conflicted about the issue. The baseball coach at Pepperdine had made me an offer via telephone while I was in Milwaukie to play at Pepperdine while in graduate school. However, when I got to Pepperdine the NCAA had changed its policy that summer and anyone who had a college degree was ineligible for collegiate sports. Being now at the age of 27, I shared my continuing love for baseball with one of my teachers, Logan Fox. I told him that the offer to try out for the Cleveland Browns was still good as it lasted for ten years. I shared with him that I was at times conflicted by this possibility. His response startled me! He said, "Well…go play baseball." What startled me was that for the first time I fully realized I had a choice. Having grown up in a Christian home where the ministry was our DNA, I just assumed that was where I would end up for the rest of my life. Mom and Dad did not shove it down my throat, but it was just a natural assumption on my part given my journey growing up. As I pondered his response, I realized that my deeper passion was people and their need to know and grow in Jesus, and I loved working with them and leading them to higher usefulness in life and God's Kingdom. Youth ministry had been fulfilling and fruitful and I enjoyed it! Plus, I now had a family to support. So I said yes to Central Christian Church in Lancaster and started preaching there on weekends.

The church was a loving and warm congregation as they welcomed a rather insecure pastor and his wife. I will always be grateful for the way in which they accepted us, encouraged us, and went to work to make the church a place where God was lifted up and drew people unto Himself. During our eight year ministry there, 1962-1970, we were strongly connected to SJBC personally and as a congregation. I had the privilege of serving on the Board of the college during the second half of my ministry in Lancaster, and chairman the last two years. It was a joy to keep connected to the college, to have singing groups down, and representatives from the college to speak at the worship services.

San Jose Bible College Board 1969

I was delighted with the way in which Al Tiffin had followed my Dad. He brought to the college a plan to move the college forward by achieving ABHE accreditation, building numerous facilities, enlarging student enrollment, and increasing the quality of the educational programs. He was always very complimentary toward Dad, and he was grateful for his legacy of training young people for ministry and church planting.

When Woodrow Phillips became President, there was an almost instant upswing in enrollment. As Gary Tiffin reported in the previous chapter, Woody was a very charismatic person who was willing and brilliantly equipped to speak to the issues of a confused generation. He was honest, confronting, forgiving, and able to communicate hope for the future regardless of one's past. The students responded to him because he spoke with courage, clarity, and conviction. This was the baby boomer and hippie generations. They loved Jesus, but they couldn't stand the church. Woody knew how to speak to these. He was a colorful communicator, great wit and much drama. Having been a missionary in Jamaica, he ignited one of the strongest missionary movements in our student history on campus. Many are still serving on the mission field today because of his impact. Woody and Marge quickly became very special to the students and staff at SJBC. Both he and Marge graduated from SJBC in the middle 1940s and so he not only understood the culture internally, but he was well connected to our constituency and churches.

President Woodrow and Marjorie Phillips outside his office door

As growth on campus approached 300 students in just a couple years of his presidency, he was scrambling to find additional staff to cover all the bases. On one visit to Lancaster to preach for us, he explored with me his interest in my coming to serve at the college. He wanted me to be the Dean of Students, coach the athletic teams, and teach two classes or six units each quarter. People wore many hats in those days! Though the church in Lancaster had grown rapidly and God had led us through an extensive building program, I was weary and near burnout. Being at my first church and very young as a senior minister, I at times overextended myself because of my immature need to prove that I could do it. So all things considered, Jo and I felt it was God's call to give us the needed change and to respond to increased usefulness in helping to equip the next generation to become world changers. So we said "yes" to Woody and accepted the opportunity to join the staff of SJBC. In a letter to the elders of the church in Lancaster dated January 30, 1970, I wrote:

> *It has been my privilege to serve as chairman of the twenty-one member Board of San Jose Bible College for the past two years. My father was the first president of this excellent preacher training institution. I am intensely excited about the tremendous progress of the school and the high quality of thoroughly committed Christian leaders that it is producing. The school is presently preparing to move into a massive expansion program to provide for the rapidly increasing student body.*
>
> *The school has often casually made contact with me in the past to see if I would be interested in serving on the faculty of San Jose Bible College. Last October, at their initiation, the board and faculty of San Jose Bible College extended to me a unanimous call to join them in the capacity of Dean of Students and teacher. After much prayer and seeking God's Will, I accepted this call in a letter to the school dated November 1, 1969, and herewith announce it publicly. We would like to begin our work with the school in approximately sixty days or around April 1st.*

It was tough leaving such a great church family, but we were convinced that saying "yes" to SJBC was what God wanted us to do.

The Return Move to San Jose

I started my ministry with SJBC in April as planned. My first assignment was to raise $200,000 by July 1 so that the college could build a gymnasium on campus. These were the days of the "Faith Promise" approach to giving. I spoke in chapel and the students committed around $20,000 in Faith Promises, which was amazing as I look back on it. Not sure how much was received from them, but I loved their hearts and generous faith commitment. However, God helped us reach the goal and soon construction was started. Our family moved to San Jose in June of 1970, purchasing a 1,600 square foot home on Lean Avenue in South San Jose for $24,500. This became our home for 34 years until our move to Rocklin in 2004. Coincidentally, I was 35 years of age when our family moved to San Jose to minister at SJBC which was the same age Dad was when he started SJBC.

Working at the college Dad had started when I was just four years old was both challenging and rewarding. My gifts were in the areas of relationship building and encouragement, a doer rather than a deep thinker, and so preparing for classes and teaching did not come easy, but it was rewarding as I had the joy of interacting with students and challenging them to become leaders in God's Kingdom. It was a delight to work under and learn from President Woodrow Phillips. In many ways he was my most significant mentor on how to lead as a college President. In fact, he told me early on that he felt I would one day be sitting in his chair. My private skeptical thoughts were "right...that will be the day!" Little did I know what God had planned down the road.

Attending the Wednesday night prayer meetings that he led for the students were so powerful and life changing for our college community. I loved to listen to him for he knew how to teach the Bible through his own personality in ways that disarmed the rebellious, challenged the indifferent, and shaped the willing hearts to obey God's call upon their lives to transform the world. It was an honor to fill in for him many times when he had to be gone, but it was also very humbling and difficult for none of us could lead the time together as well as Woody. Hundreds of lives were changed during his presidency at the Wednesday night services and beyond.

It was a delight to work in the early 1970s with a number of very special and gifted leaders at SJBC. I will always be indebted to them for what they taught me about how Christ-centered higher education can effectively be done to make a maximum impact upon students. Here are some of the workers at the college during those days.

Left to right: Woodrow Phillips, Jim North, Dean Cormany, Bryce Jessup, Mike Bowman, Don Whitney, Jim Crain (look at those pants!), Ruben Ratzlaff, Dallas Meserve, Dean Cary, George Alder, Al Hammond, Warren Bell, Loretta Carmichael

One of our professors, Jim Crain, has taught and led at SJBC/SJCC/WJU longer than any other worker and just one year less than myself. He continues his teaching responsibilities today with high energy and he continues to be a very popular teacher. I had the privilege of serving as his youth minister in Healdsburg, California, from 1954-55, during my Freshman and Sophomore years at SJBC. What a joy to see the way in which God has worked in and through his life. He has helped mold the lives of thousands of students through his teaching and mentoring. Below are some thoughts from Jim concerning his memories of the early 1970s.

SJBC: The Jesus Movement Years
By Jim Crain

In the fall of 1971 I came to SJBC as the youngest full-time professor ever hired at the then thirty-two year old institution. At 27, I was pretty much indistinguishable from the students themselves. It had been just five short years since I graduated myself, with twelve other young men from San Jose Bible College. Those years were spent in Portland, Oregon where I went to Western Conservative Baptist Seminary and worked as Youth Pastor at Central Christian Church. It was there that I gained the somewhat dubious title of "missionary to the hippies". The truth is that along with everyone else on the West Coast we were all riding a wave God generated in those days in what has now come to be known as "The Jesus Movement". They were exciting days. Yes, we looked like hippies. And, proud of it. In those early years I taught the Youth Ministry courses, Bible and Basic Faith.

In the early 70s SJBC was like a magnet for the youth revival that certainly wasn't limited to California. But to California they came. From Arizona, New Mexico,

Nebraska, Indiana, Missouri and even as far away as New York state. Everyone's hair grew long. Even the professors sprouted side-burns. Bell bottom pants and paisley shirts and tops were standard procedure on our little campus. Shoes were optional. And, of course, there was music, music, music. For the first time, young Christians had their own songs to sing and their own rhythms to clap and sway to. Every other student, it seemed, had a guitar and was writing and singing their own songs. New bands and singing groups popped up every day practically. It was a time of exuberant celebration. God was on the move. Soon, our students had their own Sunday night worship service in Tiffin Center that I was privileged to lead. Borrowing the title from the hip Peninsula Bible Church up the road in Palo Alto, we called it "Body Life". We sat on the floor, sang our hearts out, prayed and did our best to meet each others' needs. The offering basket was a boot. When it came past, you could put something in or take it out. If you could use some money, a light bulb or a ride to the airport, you didn't leave Body Life without it.

The early 70s will be forever known as the Woody Phillips years. Woody and his wife, Marge, came to us from Missouri, but they were Californians at heart. Come one, come all was the policy that they personified. If some school in the Midwest wouldn't let you enroll because you didn't have a Christian haircut, come on out; boys, we don't care how long your hair is. I even teamed up with some bushy students, Gary Dunn and Mark Neal to form a band. "Crain, Dunn and Neal" went everywhere singing our own brand of folk-rock and recruiting students. We raised a few eyebrows when we performed in some churches; but no one could challenge our sincerity.

For my wife, Cheryle and I, the students were more than students; they were friends. Living adjacent to campus on Orvis Street, our five little kids became campus mascots. Four years after we arrived and those first freshmen of ours graduated, we found ourselves grieving the loss of students that had become like family to us. But, of course, they were soon replaced by others, just as dear. Many of them are part of the internet fellowship these days known as "Former SJBC Folk". The truth is, for those of us who fondly recall those life-impacting days, San Jose Bible College is in our blood stream. Hold a reunion, we'll be back.

Student life on campus was a high-energy experience in the early 1970s. Many of our students served in churches, preached for SJBC Days in churches, played on our growing athletic teams, sang in our music groups, and filled up our dorms. The overflow of our dorms went into two apartment complexes at 780 and 781 South 10th Street, just around the corner from our campus. The library was frequented by students as Minnie Mick served as our librarian during those days.

And who can ever forget the delicious cinnamon rolls created by our own Doris Arneson? Students couldn't wait to get out of chapel to consume one or more of these in the cafeteria!

With the growing student body, there were increased needs in areas of counseling, mentoring, food services, health care, etc. Our college students have always worked to help support themselves while in college, but most students had little resources to draw upon for health care. Therefore, when one of our graduates from the early years of the college heard about it, he decided he and his wife would help. Dr. Wayne Bigelow, and his wife Rolly, decided they would drive over from Turlock each week to provide health care, medicine, and counsel to our whole college community. What an amazing gift this was. Rolly became the receptionist, keeping the books, and arranging for the visits with Dr. Bigelow. Thursday was his day off from his office in Turlock, and so for 10 years he and Rolly would drive over 100 miles to San Jose to provide free health care for the students, staff, and their families. Those of us who were on campus during the decade of the 70s cannot forget seeing a long line standing outside his door on Thursdays in the main administration building waiting their turn to see Dr. Bigelow. He not only provided health services, but he would use every opportunity to encourage and mentor our students. Dr. Rick Stedman, Sr. Pastor of Adventure Christian Church in Roseville tells the story of how as a student he saw Wayne for a medical appointment and shared with Wayne about his desire to become a medical doctor. Wayne used that as an opportunity to share with Rick that serving as a doctor gives you the privilege of helping people to live a little longer, but going into preaching ministry gives you the privilege of helping people to live forever with God. He asked Rick, "Why would you want to become a medical doctor if you have the gifts to become a preacher?" Rick has stated publicly that he took this as God's call upon his life for ministry. And with my wife and I now being members of the church he started from scratch and continues to pastor near our home in Rocklin, we have rejoiced in watching Rick grow a dynamic church of over 4,000 people during the past 20 years...Wayne had it right!

So Dr. Bigelow impacted the future of many of our students with his wise and seasoned counsel. Wayne, now in his early 80s, has been a great personal friend, counselor, and encourager to me through the years as he continues to minister through Adventure Christian Church as its Seniors Minister. Rolly went on to glory and Wayne remarried a few years ago to

Carolyn Hart, a wonderful lady who used to work at SJBC in the 60s and 70s. They are making a huge impact in the lives of our seniors at ACC. Here is a picture of a reluctant daughter of one of our students being treated at the Dr. Wayne Bigelow Health Clinic at our San Jose campus in the middle 1970s.

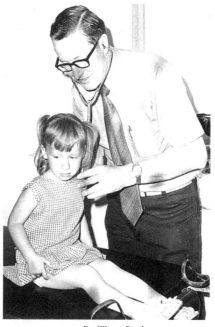

Dr. Wayne Bigelow

The campus at 12th and Virginia Streets was only able to accommodate about 300 students, even with the purchase of a number of the houses adjacent to the campus. During Woody's Presidency the student body peaked at 350 students in his third year as President. In total, we owned only about eight acres of land, and that was all that was available. Therefore, Woody started the search for another campus, looking even over in the Sacramento region at a large church site which was available, but unfortunately it was out of reach financially.

While serving for about three years as the Dean of Students, coach, and teacher at the college, I also went out most weekends to preach in churches to represent the college, taking with me many student groups to share in music and testimony. In 1973, I did some preaching for Central Christian Church in San Jose, as they were in transition and looking for a pastor. This was the church that Dad started in early 1939 which had given birth to SJBC, and thus my home church while growing up. I knew many of them as they had been my Sunday School teachers, youth workers, and partners with us at the college. They had continued to meet on the SJBC campus until around 1967 when they purchased land and built some facilities on Meridian Avenue in San Jose. As I preached there, they asked if I would consider becoming their part-time pastor on weekends as I continued on with the ministry at the college. The church was running around 150 people at the time. I was kind of itching to get back into preaching ministry again, and I felt I had learned some things during the past three years which would help me to balance my schedule. Therefore, I said yes and began my weekend ministry at Central Christian Church. As the church grew, it needed more and more of my time and I found myself working at two fulltime jobs. So I had to make a decision to cut back on one or the other. I decided to go fulltime with the church and to part-time teaching at the college in 1976.

As the college student body numbers peaked in the early and middle 1970s, Woody became aware that unless the college could relocate, it would not be able to grow beyond the 350 students attending on campus. However, he kept his hand to the plow, looking for relocation opportunities, all the while continuing to build a strong college community which was passionate about serving the Lord.

Added to this was the continued change which was taking place in our culture. The baby boomer population peaked in the early 1970s, and so the student pool was diminishing. There were many colleges and universities which overbuilt during the decade of the 70s to accommodate the large influx of students, only to then suffer significant decline in the late 70s and 80s and thus found themselves in financial jeopardy.

Woody began to feel discouraged when the college was no longer growing. He was doing all the same things he did when it was at its peak, but the rapid growth and momentum of the earlier years had slowed due to both the smaller student pool and the space limitations. The financial condition of the college was not good, due to the decline in student enrollment. I remember as a part-time teacher, Woody calling me into his office around 1977 and saying that he could no longer pay salaries for the part-time teachers, and so they were all being laid off. I remember asking him if he would accept volunteers. He seemed rather surprised by my question but indicated he would be happy to accept volunteers. Thus I volunteered to teach for a number of classes until I became President in 1984. Since he preached in churches most weekends, he was frequently presented with ministries opportunities in churches. There was one opportunity which caught his eye. The Overlake Christian Church, located in Kirkland, Washington, was the largest church in the state. At its peak it ministered to more than 6,000 people on any given weekend. Woody was invited to become its Executive Pastor to oversee the large staff and preach from time to time when the Senior Pastor, Bob Moorehead was out of town. After considerable prayer and conversation, he accepted the call to become the Executive Pastor of the Overlake Christian Church in December of 1978, and he started his ministry there in July of 1979. In the meantime, a search began for a new President for San Jose Bible College.

During the search process for a new President in early 1979, one name kept surfacing. Dr. Charles Boatman was a highly respected teacher at St. Louis Christian College, and he came from a family that had been engaged in Christian higher education for years. Chuck, as he was called by those who knew him, grew up in a strong Christian family and his father had been a very successful college president for many years. Thus Presidential DNA was in his blood. Having founded Liberia Christian College in Liberia, West Africa, he not only had classroom experience, but he had global experience in Christian higher education as a President of a Christian College.

After the interview process was completed, Dr. Charles Boatman was invited to be the fourth President of San Jose Bible College. Chuck accepted the invitation, and he and his wife Pat moved to San Jose early in the summer of 1979 to begin his Presidency at the college. He had a large challenge facing him with a declining student body, a campus that needed renovation, and many financial needs.

Chuck's first year the total number of students enrolled the first quarter was 195. This was the lowest student enrollment since 1969, which was ten years earlier, so he knew that he had his work cut out for him. He had some quality workers, but the school was suffering from fatigue both internally and externally due to the decline in student population over the past five years before his inauguration. Here is a picture of some of his workers and students with Chuck being seated in the far right of the picture.

As he put on his presidential shoes that first year, he developed a Long-Range Plan for San Jose Bible College (1980-1990) and presented it to the Board of Directors in May of 1980. Listed below are the seven goals that he presented. With each goal he had developed objectives and a detailed action plan to implement the goals. It was ambitious and well-stated.

Long-Range Plan for San Jose Bible College
(1980-1990)

1. Recapture the spirit and image of evangelism, i.e. the process of making and developing lifetime followers of Christ.
2. Increase enrollment for better stewardship of our resources.
3. Strengthen academic program by increasing library holdings and usage, encourage faculty upgrading, and improve vocational placement counseling of students.
4. Increase compensation for faculty.
5. Increase fund-raising.
6. Develop a campus setting conducive to a proper atmosphere for spiritual, mental, and physical growth.
7. Personnel should adequately reflect the needs of a growing student body and the requirements of good educational philosophy.

As he dove into connecting with the campus community, the region, and our constituency, he worked hard to implement the goals stated above. The first year of transition to his presidency went well, and he was able to launch a number of new initiatives which resulted in an increase in the student population to 235 students. That was encouraging, but the trend did not continue. In the three years which followed, the enrollment declined each of the next three years. This was true of many colleges during this time as was previously stated.

As Woody, his predecessor realized, a big part of the problem was that the campus was too small and was in a condition that would not attract students, so he set out to try and find a new location for the college where it could change its image and have room for growth.

The college began to again explore options for relocation. Guadalupe College in Los Gatos was discovered in 1982. A Catholic College that had gone out of existence, it was situated on 30 acres of land in a beautiful location. It seemed like a great possibility. The price tag did not seem out of reach, the facilities were in good shape, and it had marvelous potential for future development. Many of us had the privilege of taking the tour of the facility and I remember it well. It was on the side of a hill overlooking the Santa Clara Valley off of Blossom Hill Road with a marvelous view of the whole region. It had a beautiful auditorium that would seat around 800 people and the cafeteria and dorm facilities were well kept, but a number of classrooms would need to be built and athletic facilities would need to be constructed. However, the big challenge was going to be zoning as the town of Los Gatos did not want additional traffic going through the adjacent residential neighborhood. As the college representatives negotiated with the town of Los Gatos, they required building a new entrance road to divert the traffic around the residential neighborhood. The cost of the road would be around two million dollars and it would have to go over Lexington Dam to intersect with Highway 17 West of Los Gatos. This made moving forward with the purchase of Guadalupe College financially impossible. In retrospect,

God protected the college, for a few years later the earth quake that rocked the whole Bay Area destroyed a large portion of the college and it probably would have put the college out of existence.

The news that Guadalupe College would not become the home of SJBC was a devastating blow. The word had gotten out to our constituency through some of the college's mailings and people were getting excited about the possibilities, but it was back to the drawing board.

Due to the financial needs of the college, loans were taken out on a number of the college-owned houses adjacent to the campus in order to help cover the cash flow needs. This was during the time when interest rates were well over 12% thus adding to the increased financial burden the college had to shoulder. The college debt continued to deepen and was soon to put the future of the college in jeopardy.

Enrollment continued to decline, reaching a new low of 158 total students, with a fulltime equivalency (FTE) of 112. The actually number of full-time students was only 83. As a result of these issues and the uncertainty concerning the future, Dr. Chuck Boatman resigned his post as president of San Jose Bible College, effective at the end of the 1983-84 school year in June, 1984.

In spite of the challenging times in which Chuck served at SJBC, God used him to help set the course for deepening the relationships with the evangelical community and for a broadening of the curriculum. In one of his last Broadcaster articles in the March-April 1984 Presidents Corner he stated:

> *A good place to start our evaluation process would be*
> *to humbly admit we are not the Restoration Movement,*
> *but rather only one of many movements in the church's*
> *history which have articulated the need for the Lord's*

body to be simply Christian, guided solely by the word of God. Many of these movements made their theological point and later lost their vision, either to disappear or to become just one more denomination...The proliferation of "Bible churches" and "community churches" in our time has the potential of being a powerful, positive force for the restoration of Biblical Christianity...If we are really committed to the restoration of New Testament Christianity as a matter of principle (and not just as a code-word to describe our historical tradition), we may now have a golden opportunity. It may be the best opportunity for a movement toward restoration since the early 1800s. It is an opportunity to encourage others in the search for truth, to share with others in God's ministry of reconciling the world to Himself, and to accomplish the unity of His followers for which Christ prayed...Let us positively respond to our Christian friends, whatever their fellowship, as they show their desire to be Bible Christians unhindered by tradition, denomination, or any other impediment to the unity of Christians and the evangelization of the lost.

In another article in the same Broadcaster entitled "SJBC MAINTAINS ITS NON-DENOMINATIONAL HERITAGE" he records how all of this would relate to the composition of the Board of Trustees:

More important than the name of the congregation where a person worships is what that person believes. For the reasons stated here, the Board will be voting to change the By-laws of the college at its May, 1984 meeting. The change will replace the current Christian Church or Church of Christ membership requirement for Board members with a stipulation that all Board members agree with the basic purposes of the school as stated in the Articles of Incorporation and Statement of Faith…It is our belief that such a move is in keeping with the earliest spirit of our movement. It corresponds to the best and noblest ideals of our spiritual ancestors, who desired to be "Christians only."

In his final President's Corner in the June 1984 *Broadcaster*, Boatman wrote:

We look back in memory, with smiles on our faces (and occasionally with misty eyes) and gratitude in our hearts for what God has done through His people, both us and you. We look joyfully forward in hope, to new and exciting challenges in ministry for ourselves. And we confidently anticipate the good days that lie ahead for SJBC under Bryce Jessup's capable leadership. We commend him to you. We believe he is God's man for this time.

One of many times the ball field and basketball courts flooded on this campus!

"Sons of God" - 1970's Ron Rasmussen, Terry Thomas, Mark Neal, Jon Stedman, Dan Mackey, Kevin Levellie

"Touch of Joy" – 1970's Jerri Jessup, pianist, Penny West, Steve Mackey, Mollie Beasley

Crossbearer's Crusade Committee

Women's Volleyball with Coach Jeff Phillips

CHAPTER SIX

Recovery and Survival
(1984)

A New President is Installed

I am grateful that I kept most of the documents from the early part of 1984 when I was contacted concerning the presidency of SJBC. I received a mimeographed letter from the presidential search team of SJBC addressed to "whom it may concern". It asked if I was interested in applying for the presidency, or if I knew of anyone I could recommend for them to contact. I read the letter and remember thinking: "Good luck guys…I am happy with the growing ministry here at Central Christian Church and I don't have any desire to take on a new assignment, especially since the school is in decline and facing the possibility of closure. I am feeling quite secure with my present assignment as pastor here at the church." College records showed that there were only 83 full time students enrolled in the spring of 1984.

Having ignored the letter, I continued on with ministry and a couple weeks later I received a phone call from someone on the search committee asking if I would consider putting my name in the hat. I gave a spiritually correct, "I am honored to be considered, but I am happy in my ministry here at Central Christian Church. But I will pray about it." Little did I know what was going to take place. Shortly after this I received a phone call from Lee Shafer, minister of the Shasta Way Christian Church in Klamath Falls, Oregon, who was serving on the college Board and had been appointed chair of the search committee. We talked at some length about the opportunity, the need, potential candidates, etc., and then he asked me if I would be willing to have an informal conversation with the search team with no strings attached. Well, how could I say no? So I met with the search team made up of: Lee Shafer, chair and alumnus, Wayne Bigelow, medical doctor and alumnus, Mike Cook, minister, Al Hammond, professor at SJBC, Eldon Ewing, businessman and elder at Central Christian Church where I ministered, and Charlie Farrell, businessman. It was a cordial meeting as I knew all of the team members, appreciated their desire to see me apply, and I let them know that I would continue to think and pray about it.

Wouldn't you know, the word leaked out to my son Jim that I was being considered for the presidency. He was in a car with some of his basketball buddies on his way, as a Freshman at SJBC, to play a basketball game. Someone in the car brought the issue up and wondered how he felt about it. His compassionate but direct response I was told was: "Dad? What's he know about money?" (He knew his mother kept the check book in our family as I was lousy with financial details, and she grew up in the home of a banker!)

Shortly thereafter, I received another phone call to discuss the possibility of putting my name in the hat for the presidency. After a lengthy conversation, I stated I would put together some thoughts on paper about what I felt was needed at SJBC for the next steps of the journey. I deliberately presented some pretty strong new directions that I thought SJBC needed to take if it was going to survive, and hopefully one day to thrive. The college was not doing well and the future looked pretty bleak. A number of small Bible Colleges within our accrediting agency, the American Association of Bible Colleges (AABC), were in the process of folding due to the downturn in enrollment. A shrinking student recruitment pool, a declining number of high school graduates, and other cultural factors were thought to be responsible for the difficulties many colleges were facing at the time. After considering the multiplicity of challenges the school was facing I put together a rather bold four page document stating the things which I thought would need to be done if the college were to experience a turn around and have a future. (I found out six months into my presidency that papers had been drawn up, but not submitted, for bankruptcy for SJBC.)

In "Perspectives and Suggested Plans for San Jose Bible College," I addressed concerns such as low morale, the need to recapture the family spirit (as families are growth centers), low finances, low student spiritual climate, the need for additional pastoral role models on campus, and, the need for evaluating our doctrinal position. I stated, "We will need to hold to a non-denominational stance as outlined in the Articles of Incorporation, recapture the hearts of restoration churches, and make our program more visible to the local Christian communities with a non-defensive attitude. 70% of our students come from restoration churches, along with 95% of the finances. We need to invite and welcome everyone who wants to study the Bible and prepare for ministry. Our classrooms need repair and our dorms are in very poor condition." I went on to state, "We need to recapture a passion for the lost, plant cross-cultural churches, particularly Asian, Black and Hispanic, start a Christian Video College on Channel 65, strengthen the preaching focus on campus, add more mission and youth internships, move from a traditional to a contemporary music focus, and hire Woody Phillips and Bill Jessup as part time teachers." Additional suggestions included: change teaching philosophy from not do they have a Master's degree but can they teach for the Master, establish a Seniors Center on campus, cut the president's salary by 5% and raise fulltime teacher's salaries by 10%, have a weekly student Bible study which the President will lead and a Body Life service on Sunday evenings which Jim Crain will lead, increase recruitment in camps, develop a strong athletic program with a multiplicity of sports, establish President's area "Listen-In Meetings" for ministers and churches with follow up "Renewal Meetings" for vision casting in Northern California, and the Board needs to give more freedom for the administration to lead."

As for my personal role: "I am to establish and transfer an ambitious vision for the school, generate enthusiasm and a family spirit. An unwillingness to believe that a declining student recruitment pool determines the size of the college (300 students in three years seems reasonable). Preach in fifty churches a year. Speak in four summer camps each year. Direct involvement in mandatory chapel services. Continue teaching Counseling, Marriage and Family, and Pastoral Leadership. Be involved in student activities and have an open door policy for all students and staff. Maintain balance by continuing personal ministry through Central Christian Church, church planting facilitator, and Rotary International." I closed with: "It will take energy, prayer, unwillingness to get discouraged, and sacrifice... but SJBC is in a strategic location to significantly change our part of the world for Christ. The need is for Christian leaders, (Matthew 9:36), and for a vision to see afresh the fields that are white unto harvest (Matthew 9:37-38)." As I prepared this I thought this would probably set the search committee back on their heels and it would be the end of our discussion.

I met with the search committee and presented the document in March, 1984 at Eldon Ewing's real estate office in Campbell, California, expecting a negative response because I was suggesting so many changes. I was surprised; they liked what was shared and asked again if I would become a candidate for the presidency of SJBC. I had been thinking and praying for direction and this time I said yes. What they didn't know was that my wife and I had put out a fleece before the Lord. If He wanted me to take the presidency, then His sign to me would be that the vote of the search committee, the faculty, administration, and the board would have to be unanimous. I was very uncertain about whether I should take the job if it was offered. It would be a difficult assignment with a multiplicity of challenges, weeks and perhaps years of struggle and uncertainly about the future viability of the college. However, the one nagging issue that kept resurfacing was the legacy issue. Dad had started the college and I hated to see it possibly die. He encouraged me to explore conversations about the opportunity, but he was careful not to push me into something that he wanted. I needed to follow the Lord's leading. In addition, I personally felt a strong passion for the college: that it was needed and could have a future. The church where I ministered was doing well and I felt another could come in and keep it moving forward. So I felt a peace about the possibility of leaving Central Christian Church.

Soon after the meeting Lee Shafer phoned me and said, "The Search Committee is unanimous in wanting to recommend you as the next president of SJBC." So I met with the administrators and faculty and shared my planning document also. They interacted with me for a couple of hours and then voted anonymously on small pieces of paper which I still have in my file. They were to say "yes" or "no". I was taken back as they left the meeting and I sat alone to count the votes.

They voted unanimously "yes". Faculty and administrators are rarely unanimously united on anything, let alone an important issue like this one. However, there was still one more hurdle to clear – the Board. Eldon Ewing, Board chair, sent out a letter to the Board on April 16, 1984, which stated: "The Search Committee has completed their selection process and are recommending that the Board approve Bryce Jessup for the Presidency of San Jose Bible College. Bryce has agreed to serve should the Board of Directors extend a call." A telephone poll of the Board was taken on Monday, April 23, and Eldon made a call to me stating that it was a unanimous vote by the board for me to be the next president of SJBC. I was stunned! God had made it clear that I should become the president, even though I had some reservations and fears about what all of this was going to mean. I shared the decision with Central Christian Church where I ministered, gave the closing prayer at SJBC graduation in May as my formal installation service, and officially began as the fifth President of SJBC on June 4, 1984. I suggested that we not have an inauguration service, as the one for my predecessor was so poorly planned and attended that it was embarrassing. I just wanted to get to the work that needed to be done. The public announcement was made in the Summer 1984 Broadcaster and the San Jose Mercury News.

I was grateful for the legacy handed to me from my Dad, Al Tiffin, Woodrow Phillips, and Chuck Boatman, but now it was my turn to put on the walking shoes, and start running! The first few weeks in the new role were filled with meetings both inside the college community and outside in the church community, just trying to get my arms around things. It wasn't as though the situation was new to me. I grew up with the school, graduated from it, and served on the Board during the middle 1960s. Plus, I had worked both fulltime and part-time at the college continuously since 1970, so I knew something of what I was stepping into, but it always looks and feels different when you actually sit in the president's chair. The task was a daunting one. It was hard to know where to begin, and so I just jumped in, hitting the road running as there was little time for careful planning. I ran around like a crazy man trying to find out how to repair the ship, keep it from sinking, and ultimately to find ways to head it in the right direction.

As we met for the first Board Meeting of my presidency, I was encouraged by the board members who stood with me in wanting to see the school move forward. Don Whitney, Senior Minister of Napa First Christian Church was now the board chair. Others who served with him were: John Bigham, minister; Franklin Bixler, minister; J.E. Blanton, business; Mike Cook, minister; Ed Craig, business; Eldon Ewing, business; Darrell Foote, minister; Pat Fuller, business; Donna Hahn, business; John Henry, minister; Bob Hicks, business; Jay Hoffman, minister; Marty Neese, minister; Steve Rundle, minister; Tom Salter, minister; Jim Sinclair, minister; Steve Tolliver, minister; Harold Uhlig, business; and Ted Williams, business. These were committed men and women who encouraged me greatly during my first year and they were a good fit for a Bible college. There were many changes that needed to be made internally at the college: difficult staff changes, program and policy changes, renovation and financial needs, etc.

It was difficult making the needed changes in personnel, and just as hard in trying to find replacements who would come at the meager salaries we were offering. In fact, in the first year not only was I working at the college, but Jeff and Jerri Bigelow, my oldest daughter and son-in-law, Frank and Jan Schattner, my younger daughter and her husband, and my wife were all working at the college, and our son Jim was a student. I had hired all of them, with the exception of Jeff who was already teaching at the school when I became the president. I remember overhearing one of our staff members say about a future hiring need, "Yes, we need to hire someone as long as it is not another Jessup." Then they went on a long dissertation about "nepotism" in my hiring practices. They were right, but the truth was I could not find others who would work for the low wages my family was willing to accept, or perhaps pressured to accept. Hiring family came in handy on a number of occasions, but one specifically stands out in my mind. The students were about to arrive for the Fall quarter in 1984 and the lawns were in need of mowing along with a lot of tall weeds around the parking area. I phoned up my family on a Saturday morning and "invited" them to join with me in mowing the grass and cutting down the weeds. The maintenance crews were unavailable or unwilling to join with us, so I pushed my mower along with my family members for several hours until the job was completed. I recall one of my sons-in-law getting so ticked that he took it upon himself to phone up one of the maintenance guys and said to get down here and help, that even the president was mowing grass. His appeal went on deaf ears, but somehow we all survived the ordeal and welcomed the new students with cut grass and warm, grass-stained hands!

Records show that there was an increase in total full-time student enrollment (F.T.E.) in the fall of 1984, from 112 F.T.E. to 152 F.T.E. We were delighted at the significant bump up in F.T.E., but there was a very small increase in total student populations counting all full-time and part-time students. The chart below shows the total student population growing slowly up through 1990.

Had it not been for the Multi-Cultural Bible Institute, (MCBI) our total student population would have hit new lows in the second half of the 1980s.

SJCC Students
1980–89

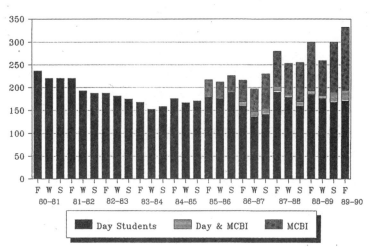

Multi-Cultural Bible Institute

Thousands of refugees from Asia were pouring into the San Jose region in the early 1980s. One day in 1982 as I drove into the parking lot at Central Christian Church where I was ministering, my son-in-law Frank left the church lawn he was mowing and came running across the parking lot to speak to me before I got out of the car. God was obviously stirring in his heart and he said, "There are thousands of South East

Asian refugees coming to Santa Clara Valley…if we don't do something about it…I believe that God will hold the Church responsible." Though I didn't fully agree with everything he said, I deeply appreciated his heart and his desire to minister to the refugee community. The initial seeds for the MCBI program had been planted in his life by God, and they would soon take root and bear fruit.

Frank came to the region in the early 80s from the University of Massachusetts where he had graduated with a BA in Sports Medicine and Human Performance. He came west to train for the Olympics in the decathlon at San Jose City College hoping to make the Olympic trials. However, after having trained for four years, his ham-string was injured and he was unable to participate in the trials. When he first moved to the region he found San Jose Bible College while reading a road map of the San Jose area and came to the campus. One of the students recommended Central Christian Church, where he soon met my daughter. They both had a love for missions and soon for each other, and the rest is history. Frank completed his BA in Bible and Theology in 1984, and they have been serving as missionaries to Thailand and beyond for the past 25 years.

Al Hammond was the chair of our Missions Department and he also encouraged Frank and Jan to do something about the need to reach the various ethnic communities surrounding SJBC. Though there were many Asian immigrants surrounding the college, very few ethnic students were attending the school. In the meantime, Frank and I had been in contact with Moses Samol Seth, a Cambodian pastor in Southern California through Laverne Morris who brought him up to speak to some of our area churches and leaders. Moses had been a governor of a Cambodian province and then served as a major in the Cambodian army. He was driven out of Cambodia by Pol Pot and the Khmer Rouge and some of his family members were killed. He found refuge in the Khao I Dang refugee camp on the Thai/Cambodian border. While there, he became the refugee camp pastor and evangelist, led more than 25,000 to the Lord and baptized them. Frank and I flew to Southern California on September 21, 1984, to visit with him and to challenge him to consider coming to San Jose to start both a Cambodian Church, and a minister training center for his people on campus. Many in the Cambodian community already knew him from the refugee camp. He said he would send us a pastor to get it started. Praise God he ended up coming himself, along with his wife, Samantha. The church grew rapidly on campus and for special occasions such as New Years and Christmas celebrations, they would have more than 1,000 Cambodians attending the celebrations. It was a sobering thing to preach to these people. I marveled at their great faith and was amazed at their confidence in God's love and goodness in the aftermath of the senseless slaughter of so many of their friends and family in Cambodia.

Moses taught in Cambodian at the San Jose campus in our MCBI program. He later moved to Stockton to establish a Cambodian Institute along with Don Byers. The refugees settled there since it was a farming community more like what they had been used to in Cambodia. In fact, MCBI extensions were scattered throughout the Central Valley. Moses trained and graduated more than 70 Cambodians for the ministry, and helped plant a number of Cambodian churches in Northern California through his students. When it was safe to return to Cambodia in the late 1990s, he rejoined some of the pastors he had trained and sent back to Cambodia. Together they have planted over 1200 churches in Cambodia and almost 100 churches in Viet Nam. This is being done under the umbrella of Agape International Missions (AIM), a ministry to

Cambodians which he started with Frank's help when he was in San Jose. The ministry has expanded in recent years under the leadership of Don Brewster, one of our graduates, to rescue hundreds of girls out of the sex trafficking industry through Agape Restoration Center and to give them hope in Jesus. I have the privilege of continuing to serve on the AIM Board.

Frank and Jan worked with the Cambodian refugees while still working full-time in their regular jobs, helping them with social issues, language, cultural adjustments, spiritual and psychological issues, church planting, etc. The standing joke around campus was that you could always tell which Cambodians were ministered to by Frank, for they would have a Bostonian accent in their English.

One day Al Hammond asked Frank to consider starting an institute on campus to train not only Cambodians, but other ethnic communities as well, and to do it in their native languages. So Al appointed Frank the Director of the Multi-Cultural Department at SJBC. Frank jumped on it and established the Multi-Cultural Bible Institute (MCBI). The classes were taught in the evenings by ministers of the various local ethnic communities. These relationships were built by Frank through extended time visiting ethnic pastors within their communities. He encouraged those that had a specific vision and burden to train their own people for evangelism and church planting. SJBC simply provided the venue so that they could fulfill their vision to reach their own people. Though no budget was set aside for this ministry, God sustained the ministry through prayer and from the discounted tuitions collected from the students. Below is a chart of the ethnic diversity which existed in the 1990 school year.

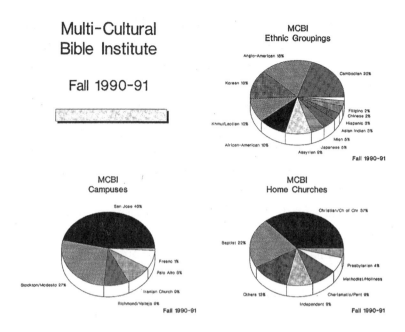

Multi-Cultural Bible Institute

Fall 1990-91

MCBI Ethnic Groupings

MCBI Campuses

MCBI Home Churches

It wasn't long until the Bible was being taught in seven different languages: Farsi, Tamale, Korean, Cambodian, Vietnamese, Spanish, and Amharic. There were also integrated classes where simple English was used along with other language helps to encourage learning and added proficiency in English. MCBI also built strong relationships across various and diverse ethnic communities, breaking down walls of bigotry and suspicion. It was an exciting time as over 150 students at the peak were being trained for ministry for their people and in their native tongue. Al Hammond reported that out of this group of students many ethnic churches were planted in Northern California during the later 1980s and 1990s. In a 1996 report he counts: Cambodian 14, Korean 6, Khmu 3, Iranian 4, East Indian 3, Hispanic 3, Filipino 1. Many of the Korean churches were planted under the leadership of Yoon Kwon Chae, a SJBC grad and President of Seoul Christian College, and Nam Soo

Woo, professor at SJBC. Iranian churches were started under the direction of Hormoz Shariot, a SJBC grad, and Pastor Feredoun; Spanish churches were planted under the leadership of Cesar Buitrago also a SJBC grad. Multi-cultural rallies were held frequently to express our unity in Christ with several hundred attending from various ethnic communities with their choirs and flags. These were great times of celebration and worship. Many churches were started on the campus of SJBC and then grew to acquire their own facilities. It was not unusual to have 5 different ethnic congregations meeting at various times on Sundays.

The Santa Clara valley was becoming more and more diverse with people flooding into the region from scores of different countries. This provided us the opportunity to reach people who came to us and were eager for ministry training. Thus the entire student body of SJBC during these days was approaching 60% non-European American from more than 30 different birth countries. From 1990 to 1996 there were 322 graduates; 177 of these were non-European-American which is 54% of the total. Of the non-European American graduates, Koreans made up 43%; Cambodians 26% and 20 other nationalities made up the remaining 31%. Ethnic students made up 59% of the total 1996 graduating class. This was the most diverse of any Bible College within the American Association of Bible Colleges in the United States. Later, as we sought regional accreditation, the integration of the MCBI program into our traditional program became necessary and thus many of the required subjects were only available in English. Thus our MCBI program had to become eliminated. MCBI was a freewheeling enterprise in those days, numbering as many as fourteen sites in the Bay Area and Central Valley, with classes taught in as many as nine different languages. Although we attempted to monitor the quality of instruction, the need to require course documents in English, per accreditation standards, presented a challenge. Some of the students were unable to meet the English requirement, but some were able to do so and they continued on and eventually graduated. However, the impact of the MCBI program lives on today through the hundreds of ethnic communities which are continuing to have a witness for our Lord through the Christian ministers and leaders that were trained and sent forth through the MCBI program, and the churches which have been planted globally.

During the 1990s, we gave many full scholarships to students who applied from their home countries and then came to us for an education in ministry. Since we wanted them to return to their countries for church planting and Kingdom growth, the only stipulation to receive the 100% scholarship was that they need to return to their birth country. We felt this was an additional tool for reaching the countries of the world for Christ. Though it produced Kingdom growth, I'm sure many stayed in the U.S. and we rarely received any tuition payments from them! This costly generosity forced us to re-think our strategy for reaching the world. We began to focus on equipping those that God had already brought to the U.S. This was a strategy far different from most other schools. By 1996, thirty-three birth countries were represented on campus: Argentina, Australia, Bahamas, Bolivia, Brazil, Cambodia, Canada, China, Columbia, England, Ethiopia, Germany, Haiti, Hong Kong, India, Indonesia, Japan, Kenya, Korea, Laos, Liberia, Mexico, Nepal, Philippines, Russia, Sierra Leone, Taiwan, Thailand, Tonga Island, United States, Venezuela, Vietnam, and Western Somoa. These were exciting days of multi-culturalism on campus.

On-Going Challenges

Not only was the ethnic composition of the local community changing, but the church communities were undergoing changes also as they attempted to build the Kingdom of God. SJBC needed to change also and be open to God's direction concerning our place in Kingdom work and the next steps that we should take. Our facilities were old, run down, small and inadequate to provide for growth opportunities. Around 350 students were all that we could accommodate on our eight acre campus. The curriculum needed to be broadened to include ministry opportunities beyond the pulpit and missions. We needed to become more inclusive of Bible believing Christians, regardless of the name over the church building. These changes were not motivated by the desire to simply survive, but rather by the growing conviction that God wanted us to change. Some were worried we were heading down a slippery slope and said goodbye to us, for they saw us as having abandoned our roots. Others encouraged us to "stay the course, if God is in it then He will prevail and the college will move forward."

There were so many buildings which needed immediate attention. I recall standing in the parking lot outside Jessup Hall with Professor Bev Wiens looking at the buildings with her. It grew silent and then she looked at me with tears rolling down her cheeks and said something I have never forgotten, "I wasn't called to work in a rescue mission." Well, out of that conversation I challenged her to do something about it, and she did. She raised funds, organized work crews of students and staff, informed churches and individuals who gave and brought work crews, etc., and did a remarkable job of fixing up large portions of our campus as our Director of Campus Renovation.

A number of Christian business men and women were key supporters of the work: Bennie and Hope Ingraham, Lyle and Mary Ottinger, Glen and Jay Comstock, Karen Toft, and Dr. Dean and Bonnie Smith. Additionally, I was blessed by Dean as he was a treasured source of counsel to me personally on many personnel and policy issues, in addition to his generous financial support of the school. The school was in bad shape before Bev and all of these supporters made it their mission to renovate the campus facilities. Almost all maintenance had been deferred for years due to lack of funds. One time a toilet fell from upstairs through the floor to the downstairs of Beach Hall, the men's dorm. We were so glad no one was in the lower bathroom! Earl Doise, a former board member and friend of the family and the college since the middle 1940s, stepped up and said, "The parking lot is in horrible shape, I will hire a company to repave the parking lot and supply the cement bumpers for each parking space." It was the classiest thing on campus. When people came on campus and wanted to see our facilities, I would say, "Let me show you our parking lot!" The following article appeared in our Broadcaster in the Summer 1990 edition.

PHON-A-THON A GREAT SUCCESS

You people were great!! We couldn't believe your generosity! What we thought would be scary turned out to be a lot of fun!

For those of you who don't know what I am referring to, recently we had a phon-a-thon to solicit funds for the renovation of Beach Hall--our men's residence hall. It is in pretty sad shape and we knew it was time to address this problem and prepare the building to receive our new residents this fall.

So, we tried something we've never done before. We mailed out a letter to all of the alumni, telling them about the problem. Then we got a team of students and faculty together who were willing to commit to calling the alumni who had received the letter to see if they could help with the project. On the nights of May 2, 3, 7, and 8, this team made a total of 533 phone calls!

A total of $20,425 was raised during the phon-a-thon--commitments to be given toward the Beach Hall project in the months of May, June and July. With these commitments we will be able to recarpet and repaint the entire interior and furnish both lounges and the kitchen. Additionally, we will be able to install closet doors in each room and put bathroom sinks with vanities in each bathroom. That building will be so much better when the men arrive on campus in August!

It was important for us to remember as we called that we were calling friends--people who really do care about the school and its students. It was so gratifying to find that you are indeed friends and you are willing to help. It was great to visit with you and hear of your ministries. It was so nice to pray with some of you over the phone.

And your generosity has overwhelmed us! Thank you so much! Please be assured that we will make every effort to be wise stewards with what you have given. And please--come visit us soon so that you can see the fruits of your investment!

WHAT I LEARNED LAST NIGHT

Bev Wiens
Director of Campus Renovation

Thought you might be interested to learn what I learned last night! I attended a "college review" lecture for parents whose children will be high school seniors next year. It was an excellent program informing the parents about the "ins and outs" of colleges/admissions/financial aid. At one point in the program the presenter discussed the importance of *campus tours* and noted for the parents the various things to "check out" in evaluating a college.

At the end of this section of the presentation he flipped the overhead off and said, "Now, you'll need a quick way to rule out some colleges. Here's the quickest way: walk on the campus and check out how well they are caring for their facilities and grounds. If things are poorly cared for, don't bother to check any further!"

The audience looked startled. He continued, "'Why?', you ask. It's because facilities are usually the last priority for any institution so you can be fairly sure that if they are caring for their facilities, they are caring for all other parts of the program."

I left with a renewed sense of the importance of facilities in the recruitment of new students and I'm grateful that SJCC has made real progress in this area.

Bev Wiens, Director of Campus Renovation

CAFETERIA RENOVATION

Have you been wondering how our cafeteria renovation is coming? We surpassed our goal for phase one by raising a total of $51,019 for the renovation of the cafeteria! Now we can get started!

A fine Christian businessman has agreed to manage the project. Pray with us that we will quickly pass through any red tape involving the various permits/inspections required by the city of San Jose. At this point, it feels like it will take a miracle akin to "parting the Red Sea" to see that happen.

We must complete the first phase of the project before mid-August so that the cafeteria is ready to operate when school starts. The first phase of the renovation will involve remodeling the dishwashing area and serving area of the kitchen. We also hope to expand the dining area and develop an outdoor patio.

A portion of the money raised has already been spent to cover architectural fees, permit fees, and the purchase of some new kitchen equipment. So, as you pray, also ask the Lord to stretch the remaining dollars to accomplish the necessary remodeling.

Thanks for your giving! Thanks in advance for your prayer support for this project!

Broadcaster in the Summer 1990 edition

We owe a great debt of gratitude to Bev for helping us improve student recruitment and retention by renovating our campus during the 1990s, thus making it a more attractive destination for students.

Finances continued to be a challenge. No one would lend us any more money and interest rates were more than 12% in the early 1980s. Money had been borrowed on the houses we owned adjacent to the campus to pay the bills. So many times it seemed we were about to go under, salaries not paid, trade debt rising, and creditors literally banging on our doors. Would we have a future? Though unknown to the college community or board, soon after I became president I was made aware that preliminary papers had been drawn up for bankruptcy. I recall on one occasion a creditor to whom we owed back payments came to the campus and blocked the door with one of his body guards and refused to let us out of the room until we wrote him a check. It was a scary time. However, it seems God always came through at just the right time to help us get our noses above water again and again. Not more than a year into my presidency we were on the edge of financial collapse when we received our portion of the Art Rickard Will distribution. Art and Dad were friends from the early days at Ceres Christian Church. Art wanted to become a preacher like Dad, but his father died when he was in high school and so it became necessary for him to go to work to support the family. He became a successful realtor and since he could not go to college to become a preacher, he decided to support those who could. He supported the college throughout his lifetime, but his largest gift came at the end of his life. I will never forget the euphoria and spiritual rush I felt when I received word that we would be receiving a check of around $400,000 from his will. What a grand day of celebration we had, now able to get caught up on our bills, back salaries, etc., and it gave us another glimmer of hope for the future and an increased confidence that God was up to something in His plans for SJBC.

In 1988 something similar happened. We were again very low on finances, back salaries needing to be paid, and the trade debt was rising. I remember meeting on a Thursday morning with the Executive Administrators and deciding that we were going to have to tell the faculty at our Faculty Meeting that afternoon that we all were going to have to take a 5% cut in salary. Then I headed off to a noon Pastors prayer meeting at a local church. On the way I was opening my mail as I was driving, throwing the junk on the floor and keeping the good stuff on the passenger's seat. I was about to open an envelope when I noticed it was from a lawyer. I thought, "Oh boy, we are in deep financial water and now here comes a lawsuit from a lawyer." As I slowly opened the envelope, there was a check and a letter from a lawyer. The letter explained that the check was from a lady in Morgan Hill who died five years earlier and her estate had finally been settled. She had heard one of the SJBC students preach at her Presbyterian Church in Morgan Hill a number of years earlier and was so impressed that she wanted to leave something to the college. The check was for $42,500. So when I returned to campus and met with the Faculty I told them the story. Therefore, instead of cutting salaries and having a prayer time for our needs, we had a praise service together. Again, I was assured, especially because of the timing that God had his eye on us and was going to provide to keep us going!

Around that time, I knew that only God had the capacity to move the college forward, so I formed a prayer committee to seek His presence, leadership, resources, and future. I felt that if 120 people were needed to pray before the outpouring of God's Spirit on Pentecost, Acts 1, then I needed that number on our prayer team for God to show up in a dramatic way to lead us. So for a number of years I sent out a monthly email to 120 of our friends and partners who committed themselves to be our "prayer warriors". In the email I listed the "praises and prayer requests" and kept the team informed about almost every aspect of the college journey. I am convinced that the school is where it is today because of the prayers of God's people, from Mom and Dad forward to the present hour. It is the foundation upon which the college is built.

One of the most intriguing demonstrations of God's hand upon us took place on a Friday morning about 7:30 a.m., in the late 1980s just before the Board of Trustees was to meet. They had spent the day on Thursday in various committee meetings. The property committee was overwhelmed with the need to repair large portions of our facilities. One of the areas they examined was the shower area in the men's locker room in the gym. The tile was falling off the walls, but we had no funds to repair it. As the Board was beginning to assemble for their meeting, the sister of one of our students who had just gotten her driver's license came speeding around our class room building and into the parking lot, out of control. The accelerator was stuck in her Volkswagen. The car jumped over the curb by the gym, past the huge oak tree, and landed right in the men's shower. Many rushed over to help and discovered she was only slightly injured with a knot on her head. She was pulled out of the car and shortly after brought into our chapel service where we prayed for her and then thanked her for her insurance policy. It paid for the rebuilding of the whole shower area including beautiful new tile. It was our showpiece room on campus for a couple of years. We didn't need for the car to ram into the building twenty feet East from where it hit, for that part of the building was fine, but we needed it to hit exactly where it did. All of us, including the Board, had a renewed confidence that day that God had His eye on us and we could trust Him to give us a future. It seemed He was saying, "See that Volkswagen? Watch this and you will be blessed." Amazing how He speaks to us if we are open to listen to His voice!

The 50th anniversary celebration of SJBC was held January 25-27, 1989. The celebration began after our Board Meeting on Wednesday evening and continued throughout the day on Thursday on our San Jose campus. College singing groups, both past and present performed. The preaching was done by graduates, teachers, and administrators of SJBC/SJCC. Friday evening was a sit down dinner and program at the Fairmount Hotel in downtown San Jose. We had a great celebration with more than 1100 people in attendance. The speaker for the evening was Wayne Smith, a well-known preacher from Louisville, Kentucky, frequently referred to as the Bob Hope of the Restoration Movement. His humor and heart for the Lord and people made him a great fit for the evening. The following article was in the San Jose Mercury News, January 21, 1989.

Brother Bill remembers
the years of struggle and salvation

San Jose Bible College turns 50

By Joan Connell
Mercury News Religion & Ethics Editor

MUCH of the brimstone is gone, but the fire still burns bright when 83-year-old Bill Jessup talks about San Jose Bible College, which he established here five decades ago.

Jessup — Brother Bill to those who know him best — had been the pastor of an independent country church in Visalia in 1939 when he established the San Jose Bible College on the fringe of what was then the San Jose State College campus.

Though his vision of a Bible college never wavered, Bill Jessup admits to one major change in his thinking over 58 years. He has mellowed.

"I started out a legalistic, cocksure conservative," says Jessup, recalling the early days of fire-and-brimstone preaching. "But I've softened, and so have many of my peers. There's a broader, more generous spirit here than there was in the early years."

This week, the non-denominational school celebrates its 50th anniversary and the achievements of its 1,100 graduates with a Bible conference at its downtown campus and a banquet at the Fairmont Hotel.

Filling the need of this world

"It was my burning conviction that the need of this world is Christ, the hope of this world is Christ," says Jessup, looking back on his career as an evangelist and educator. "It was my burning conviction to train young people to take that love and that hope out into the world. That need was great, and the need was fulfilled." That is a bit of an understatement.

Graduates of the school have gone on to establish 75 churches in Northern California. In addition to the Central Christian Church of San Jose (now numbering 700 members), which Bill Jessup established, his Bible college has sent out ministers who founded the Christian Church of Redwood City, Green Valley Christian Church in San Jose, Santa Clara Christian Church, and churches in Martinez, Morgan Hill, Turlock and Merced, to name a few. Nearly 300 have become missionaries, serving in 62 foreign countries.

In recent years, San Jose Bible College has turned its attention to mission fields closer to home. Reaching out to the immigrant populations in Santa Clara County, the school offers Bible classes in Vietnamese, Cambodian, Farsi, Spanish and Korean, and has trained ministers who have established a dozen local ethnic churches.

Many things have changed for Bill Jessup since 1939, when he, his wife, Carrie, and three students transformed two tiny houses on South Fifth Street into a non-denominational training ground for independent ministers. Now a 12-acre campus at 790 S. 12th St., it has a 14-member faculty, a 32,000-volume library and 342 full-time students. And its current president is Bryce Jessup, Bill's 53-year-old son.

Accredited now only by the American Association of Bible Colleges, the school is in the process of applying for regional accreditation through Western Association of Schools and Colleges as a liberal arts college, to attract a more diverse student body. On July 1, Bryce Jessup says, the school will change its name to San Jose Christian College and will add more science, arts and social science courses to its curriculum.

Begun with three students

Though Bill Jessup was the one who made the dream of a Bible college a reality, the idea of a Bible college originated with one Eugene Sanderson, whom Bill first met when he was attending Northwest Christian College in Oregon. Sanderson, by then ill and in his 80s, convinced the young pastor that he was the man for the job.

"I guess I inherited a dead horse," Bill Jessup chuckles. "There were no students. The mortgage payments on the two houses hadn't been made and they were about to be sold for back taxes. But the owners gave me free rent for six months and the opportunity to pay off the taxes."

He built a small chapel and began preaching and teaching. Tuition was $25 a semester and scholarships were always available.

"We never asked anybody for support," he says. "We never passed a collection basket, but we had a box at the door. If anybody wanted to put anything in it, they did. And a number of local churches helped us."

One of Bryce Jessup's clearest memories of those lean years was that a friend of the family who worked for Clapp's baby food company would bring dented cans of baby food to the college.

See BIBLE, Page 14D

Michael Rondou – Mercury News
William Jessup, right, and son Bryce have seen their school's graduates begin 75 churches

The highlight for the evening was the awarding of the first honorary doctorate from SJBC/SJCC. It was appropriate that it should be awarded to my Dad as the founder and first President of the college. He received a standing ovation for his dedication and service to our Lord. Dad thanked the Lord for the privilege of serving at the college through the years and his desire to continue his partnership until he would be called home. He thanked Mom, his family, friends, and churches for their support and friendship through the years. It was indeed an inspiring time of gratitude. He also commented that he appreciated the award of the Doctor's degree, but don't you dare call me Doctor! It produced a good round of laughter.

In attendance for the 50th anniversary celebration were all five Presidents of the college who served on the San Jose campus, perhaps the only time all five were together at a college event. It was an historic event which gave us renewed hope in the midst of all the challenges we faced. Below is the picture of the five presidents and the years they served in the presidential role.

William Jessup	Al Tiffin	Woodrow Phillips	Chuck Boatman	Bryce Jessup
1939-1960	*1960-1968*	*1969-1978*	*1978-1984*	*1984-2010*

STUDENT LIFE COMMITTEE

The purpose of the Student Life Committee was to plan certain events for the school such as the Halloween party, an "ON CAM-PUS" program for high school Juniors and Seniors to check out the school as a possibilty for future education, and the week of Spiritual Renewal for the students and staff at SJBC. (They also told us which movies were O.K. to watch!) They also were involved with any disciplinary actions, and finding Resident Hall Directors and Resident Assistants for the dorms at SJBC. Members of SLC were Dennis Nichols, Bev Weins, Steve Meyer, Frank Schattner, Tina Miranda, John Coleman, and Jocela Bigham.

Dennis Nichols enjoys another funfilled student life committee meeting. (top)
Bev Weins takes notes in a meeting. (above)
Decisions, Decisions, Desicions!!! (left)
Frank diligently reads the rule book.(fr lt)

181

Kim Alderson

Jennifer Olegeriil

Julie Johnson

Alicia (Lisa) Spiker

Love In Any Language

Karen Spray

Mimi Stoker

Gary Taylor

Carl Thorsted

Andi Bacon

Brett Titsworth

Lorni Wright

DORM PARENTS

Frank and Jan Schattner have served SJBC as Beach Boy Dorm Parents since 1981. During these four years, they have been there for the guys, giving them encouragement, building their character, disciplining their habits, and making all the gaps feel at home. They have freely given their time above and beyond any call from any Beach Boy.

Of course, all the Beach Boys have had a wonderful time being big brothers to the joy in Frank and Jan's life, Ryan. Ryan adds joy to all the Beach Boys life, just by being himself — playing ball in the hallways, wandering up the stairs, parking in everyone's rooms.

Frank and Jan are appreciated and loved very much.

(above)—Frank asks, "What's going on up-(left)—Jan Schattner flashes a smile.
(bottom left)—Ryan Schattner just flashes.

CHEERLEADING

"WARRIORS" Clap, Clap, "WARRIORS." That was one of the che that could be heard at any of the home basketball games, or at a p rally. The culprits of such noise was (you guessed it) SJBC's cheerlead Filled with excitement and energy, the cheerleaders sold M & M'S (ph and peanuts, mind you), homemade cookies, and other goodies order to earn money to outfit themselves in proper cheerleading ge

Executed jumps and precision movements performed by these sho looking cheerleaders showed their two nights a week of hard work. Tl along with their laughing faces and occasional bewildered looks mo the cheerleaders fun to watch at a game. Always encouraging the tec and keeping the spirits of the crowd high, the word that comes to m for this group is SUCCESSFUL.

FRANK & JAN SCHATTNER
Residence Hall Directors

CHAPTER SEVEN

New Beginnings *(1990)*

There were many new beginnings in the history of the college: changes in programs, boards, teachers, presidents, etc. In the 90s it became obvious that another change was needed. Our eight acre campus, with deteriorating facilities, was not going to accommodate the needed growth for the college to have a viable future in our rapidly changing world. In addition, we were accredited by the American Association of Bible Colleges (AABC), but on the West Coast, the Christian colleges that were surviving were also regionally accredited through the Western Association of Schools and Colleges (WASC). This would lead to changing our name, broadening of our program and curriculum, hiring additional personnel, demonstrating financial sustainability, and creating a strategic plan to guide us.

The college chose to begin the process of seeking regional accreditation with WASC in 1989, and the first on-campus visit by their team was in November of that year. The name of the college was changed from San Jose Bible College to San Jose Christian College in 1989 as we applied for regional accreditation. We were already in the process of expanding our curriculum beyond the traditional Bible College model. However, we continue with program accreditation with the AABC, now called the Association of Biblical Higher Education (ABHE) in all of our vocational ministry programs to this day. We applied to WASC to begin the process of becoming regionally accredited and the WASC commission voted to grant eligibility to the college in January of 1991, which allowed us to proceed with the writing of documents to prepare for the initial candidacy visit. There were 13 criteria for eligibility for initial candidacy which included such things as governing board, administration, educational programs, faculty, learning resources, planning, finances, etc. After the visit, there were a multiplicity of recommendations which were given to us. It was important that we would roll up our sleeves and go to work in order to come into compliance with the criteria. Below is the history of our journey to initial accreditation.

It proved to be a lengthy process before we would receive candidacy for accreditation in 1996. It took another six years before we would receive initial accreditation in February 2002. This gave us the specified authority to develop new majors in the Liberal Arts at the Bachelor's level and individual authority for Associate degrees. In addition, credits from the college could now be transferred to virtually any college or university as we had received the highest accreditation that is available. Dr. Kay Llovio led us remarkably well as our Accreditation Liaison Officer (ALO) through the whole process from application to initial accreditation. She continues to this day as our ALO to WASC in addition to serving on numerous accrediting teams for WASC to evaluate other colleges and universities in their accreditation process. We had a grand celebration in Chapel on February 12, 2002 with confetti, sirens, balloons, refreshments, and we gave out tee shirts to everyone in attendance.

Initial WASC Accreditation Celebration

February 2002

Dr. Joe Womack   Dr. Roger Edrington   Dr. Kay Llovio   Dr. Bryce Jessup
VP for Advancement   Executive VP   VP for Academic Affairs   President
(& ALO)

One of the non-negotiables was that we keep our roots as a Christ-centered, Bible-based institution which is committed to its mission of transforming world cultures to the glory of God. I was thrilled that WASC did not tamper with our mission, but rather they pushed us to clarify and unify the institution in its resolve to fulfill its mission.

I had the privilege of attending San Jose Bible College and graduated in 1958. Following a two year youth ministry in Milwaukie, Oregon, I attended a Christian liberal arts school, Pepperdine University, where I experienced firsthand the value of a Christian liberal arts education, in addition to the Bible College education I had received. I remember saying to my Dad shortly after attending Pepperdine, "Dad, you started a Bible College. How would you feel if someday I started a Christian liberal arts college?" He replied with "Go do it!"

Well, after accreditation, it dawned on me that it had occurred almost without my realizing it. We were still a Bible College in that we still offered all of our church vocational degrees with the required Bible courses, but we now also were a Christian Liberal Arts college. The two were now joined together in one institution and continues on in that arrangement today. Kay Llovio, serving as our VP for Academic Affairs and our ALO during the accreditation process, has written a brief overview of our accreditation and program development from the early 1990s up through 2012.

Dr. Kay Llovio
Accreditation and Program Development

The mission of San Jose Christian College remained closely tied to its roots: to provide Christians with an education that would prepare them for Christian ministries. With little substantial revision, this has been the purpose of the institution since its origin.

The original articles of incorporation of San Jose Bible College, written October 12, 1945, stated that the purpose for the founding of the College was to "operate a school for the one purpose of training young people to preach the Gospel in all nations and to establish churches of Christ after the New Testament order." Through the decades the staff and board of the College continuously tested the validity of that purpose, resulting in modifications in 1954, in 1963, in 1982, and most recently in 1991-93. The testing had to do with the fundamental nature of the College. Should SJCC continue as a single-purpose institution, training men and women for ministry, or should it broaden its purpose to become what might be referred to as a Christian liberal arts college?

Consistently, SJCC reaffirmed its original purpose, maintaining itself as a Bible college. The decision to remain a single-purpose institution was based on a number of sound reasons. SJCC existed in a setting that contained liberal arts colleges with far greater resources to present a liberal arts education than did SJCC. On the other hand, San Jose and its surrounding communities had a number of churches, some of which were growing and some of which needed renewal. All of these needed trained and well-educated Christian workers. Only two other Bible colleges existed in the San Francisco Bay area: Bethany College in Scotts Valley and Patten College in Oakland. Consequently, SJCC had an almost exclusive access to the broad evangelical Christian community in Santa Clara County.

Therefore, given its limited resources and relatively restricted traditional constituency, SJCC focused on one particular form of training. This particular emphasis of training for ministry is consistent with the change in the institution's name. Although the name Bible College historically had denoted an institution whose main focus of study is the Bible--as is San Jose Christian College-- that name in contemporary use was beginning to be associated only with smaller, non-accredited schools attached to local churches. A Christian college is one that studies all subjects in higher education from a Christian worldview and was not limited to those that offer a liberal arts program. The focus becomes not only the content but also the approach to education.

This revised Statement of Purpose appears in the 1992-93 College Catalog as:

> *In partnership with the Church, the purpose of San Jose Christian College is to educate, train, and prepare Christians for service and leadership in Christian ministries.*

Five general principles follow the Statement of Purpose, elaborating the type of education offered at SJCC.

1. It is Christ-centered education.

2. It is biblical education.

3. It is general education.
4. It is practical education.
5. It is multi-cultural education.

Three components by which the College accomplishes its mission were specified in a 1993 revision: Christian higher education, spiritual formation, and directed experiences. Specific emphasis on the latter two recognized that Christian higher education itself is both lifestyle learning and lifelong learning. A variety of learning experiences are required in order to reach the whole person and effect significant life change.

The 1993 version of the mission statement was sufficiently broad to direct the institution in its growth from Bible college to Christian college to Christian university. With only change in the name, the mission remains:

> In partnership with the Church, the purpose of William Jessup University is to prepare Christians for leadership and service in church and society through Christian higher education, spiritual formation, and directed experiences.

Each degree-seeking student at SJCC earned a major in Bible and Theology and a major or minor in one of eight ministry areas. Historically, these second majors were church-related vocations, e.g., Pastoral Ministry, Music, Missions, Christian Education, and Youth Ministry. As the church itself adapted to society's needs, the College added majors in Counseling Psychology, Christian Leadership, and Management and Ethics. Proposals for new educational programs were required to meet the dual requirements of serving the church and society in tangible ways. One-year certificate programs continued to equip Christians to serve the Church in specific areas of ministry.

SAN JOSE BIBLE COLLEGE   SAN JOSE CHRISTIAN COLLEGE   WILLIAM JESSUP UNIVERSITY

After the move to Rocklin, however, an enlarged vision was emerging, from preparing students for ministry, whether that ministry would be in the church or in society, to a Vision "that our graduates will be transformed and will help redeem world culture by providing notable servant leadership; by enriching family, church and community life; and by service with distinction in their chosen career." The broader understanding of the mission statement allowed the University to include the more traditional liberal arts outcomes of preparing students for graduate school and offering a broader variety of majors in the liberal arts and sciences. In the first three years as WJU, majors were added in Liberal Studies, Business, Public Policy, and English, and the Psychology and Music majors were revised to reflect a liberal arts rather than a ministry focus. We added our first post-baccalaureate program, a California State Multiple Subject teaching credential.

These academic program changes signify a much larger change in self-perception. Our sense of ourselves as a small Christian college focused on Bible, theology, and ministry has broadened, until we now see ourselves as a Christian university, committed to educating students in a liberal arts tradition. To facilitate the process of establishing a widely understood institutional identity, the first goal of the strategic plan was to "Strengthen WJU identity as a quality Christ-centered university." In many unforeseen ways, WJU tackled this objective, by identifying a set of core values and curriculum design assumptions to guide new program development.

General education requirements were modified in the traditional program to expose students to a wide spectrum of knowledge that offered more opportunities to sample areas of interest as they explore fields that could be considered as a major. The transfer-friendly requirements retained distinctive courses in both traditional and degree completion programs that were designed to assist the student in formation of a Christian worldview, in addition to biblical studies requirements.

A more sensitive area of progress was to refashion the biblical studies component of the curriculum, long considered the heart and soul of a Bible college. Recent changes in the standards of the Association for Biblical Higher Education (ABHE) allowed the University to move from institutional to program accreditation of the biblical and ministry programs only, designing two sets of foundational studies for different majors while providing a biblical education for all students.

Students entering the church-related ministry majors continue to take 30 units of biblical studies. The 18 units of Bible and theology that had formed the core of the universal Bible major were retained to provide a Christian worldview for students entering liberal arts and degree completion programs.

Currently, the academic mission of the University is fulfilled through the offering of nineteen majors in the undergraduate program, a Master of Arts in Teaching degree, two associate degrees, and two certificates. As we have added majors in subjects like History, Mathematics, Biology, and Creative Arts, we are multiplying the impact of the core principles of San Jose Bible College – in Fall 2012 almost half of the students in our traditional program were enrolled in the majors developed in Rocklin!

During the accreditation process, we continued to realize that the major obstacle for growth was the lack of resources to expand or relocate. God provided in some amazing ways to show us that His hand was not only on us, but it was on some friends of the college through whom He would work to accomplish His dream for us "far beyond all that we could ask or think". Little did we know how He was going to do this, we just kept praying and believing that He would, and so we continued to simply keep putting one foot in front of the other, with the confidence that one day we would look back and see how He had guided our footsteps to where He wanted us to be.

One of our first friends to step up in 1991 was Ed Harris, who was led to the Lord by one of our graduates, Marvin Rickard, pastor for many years at Los Gatos Christian Church. Ed went onto glory in January of 2012. I was the interim pastor at Los Gatos Christian Church in 1988-89 where he and his lovely wife Sandy were attending. His financial advisor, Carl Mel who also attended LGCC, had shared with Ed that he might want to check out SJBC as he was looking for some ministries to partner with as his business was flourishing in the Silicon Valley computer industry. He stopped by the college one day to get better acquainted and to inquire if there were some things he could do to help. Of course I said, "No...we were doing just fine!" Actually, I almost went into shock as I was so excited I felt like jumping up and down for this was the first person of high resource during my presidency who had ever initiated this kind of an offer. How did he know to show up when he did? The timing was perfect and the journey to connect was absolutely amazing indeed. My decision to preach at LGCC was for Kingdom purposes far beyond this large congregation of more than 4,000 people who were worshipping there at the time. How God connects the dots is frequently unknown to us at the time until we look back over our shoulder and see what He has done; then we stand in awe of Him and overflow with gratitude.

When Ed approached us, we had been in the red for the last 2 years! If we were to have a third year in the red our accreditation with AABC would be in jeopardy. Making any overture to WASC to begin the regional accreditation process would have been out of the question. It was in May 1991, just one month before the close of the third fiscal year in the red, that Ed showed up. When he asked how he could help, I openly explained our situation and without hesitation he asked how much we would need to balance the budget. He immediately took out his check book and wrote a huge check to San Jose Christian College. One month later we found out that we would need an additional $12,000 to actually finish in the black, and so he wrote another check for that amount on June 28, 1991, and we finished the fiscal year with a slight surplus in the general fund! Ed repeated that same scenario the next year and by the time of his homegoing Ed and Sandy had invested hundreds of thousands of dollars in the ministry of SJCC. Therefore, on August 16, 2012, we dedicated a memorial plaque in his honor in our new gym as he was an outstanding basketball player who was a star at Sonora High School and went on to play for Baylor University. The words on the plaque will remind players for generations to come to be "Constantly In Training For Christ," as this was his life's goal. I Cor. 9:25. I doubt that WJU would exist today were it not for the generosity and encouragement of Ed and Sandy Harris.

As for basketball itself, during the 1990s it was under the capable leadership of coach Glen Miller. Glen was our basketball coach, campus pastor, popular teacher, and one of my closest friends and partners in ministry from the 1970s forward. He led the team to four national championships, in 1991, 1993, 1994, and 1995. We were members of the National Bible

College Athletic Association, Division 1. Melvin Adams, in the red hat below, went on to play professional basketball for the Harlem Globetrotters for five years.

Dad's Homegoing...

It was always an honor to speak in churches throughout the region on various themes. One speaking date in the early 90s will forever be etched in my mind for there has never been and never will be one quite like it. My Dad, my son Jim, and I were invited to speak at the South Valley Christian Church in Morgan Hill on Palm Sunday evening, April 12, 1992. The theme for the evening was Growing Multi-generational

Christian Families. We were to share some Biblical principles and then some stories from our family of six generations of Christ-followers. We had done this on a number of occasions, with the first being a workshop presentation at the North American Christian Convention in July of 1985 in Anaheim, California.

The evening in Morgan Hill started like many others we had done before. I welcomed the more than 150 people in attendance and explained to them the purpose and program for the evening. I then introduced and welcomed my 86 year old Dad to the platform for his 10 minute message. I still have his Bible and the message that he gave tucked within it...what a treasure! He started by saying:

> *75 years ago I was united with Christ. I moved out...Christ moved in. 70 years ago...Carrie did the same. We promised to be faithful, to love and serve Him. There were times when our promise was not kept. Like the prodigal son, there were times when we disobeyed. But we saw the error and returned to the father. Carrie and I met at Eugene Bible University, we were both in college, committed to Christ, and 63 years ago we promised to love, serve, submit, be faithful to each other until death. We were both in Christ, Christ in us, and we became one in Christ.*

He brought an excellent message as he spoke on love, joy, and peace. He emphasized that these virtues are needed in all relationships but needed most in marriage. From the tape that we have of the evening, I have copied below word for word his closing comments which became his final words on planet earth.

After 63 years of marriage, yes there have been problems, but we have forgiven each other, prayed for each other, loved each other, and I frequently sing that song "sweeter as the years go by" for the love is stronger than ever before.... I believe Christian friend that there isn't any problem that two Christian people can have who possess the mind of Christ and the spirit of Christ, there isn't any problem but what those two people can solve at the feet of Jesus Christ.

The people clapped enthusiastically as Dad sat down in the audience next to Jim's wife Liz, my wife Jo, and our granddaughter Meredith Bigelow. Meredith was in the eighth grade and was scheduled to play a special number on the piano later that evening. Mom was not in attendance as she was not feeling well. I got up and thanked Dad and told the story of how just three weeks earlier Dad called my brother Velt and his wife Eilene, and my wife Jo and me to come to his mobile home for a family gathering. I shared that Dad talked about the fact that he wasn't getting any younger and he wanted to share with us some of his thoughts about how we should do things upon his passing. We were somewhat uncomfortable with the conversation, but he wasn't for he could talk about death as easily as he could talk about life. He joked with us that he had an insurance policy that would pay us double if he were killed in an auto accident rather than natural causes...so he suggested that if he should get to looking peeked we should put him behind the steering wheel of his car and point it down Monterey Highway. Everyone had a good laugh. As I shared these comments with the audience, Dad sat there listening and laughing at my reflections, not aware of what was to follow or maybe he was aware!

However, I didn't share that he also told us that he did not want an open mike at the memorial service for he said there is always a preacher who has a sermon that no one has asked him to preach and this becomes his "call" to deliver it! Also, he wrote down on his instructions which he then gave us that he wanted no guitars at the service, and underlined it for emphasis. Following the giving of all his instructions about what we should do when his "time of departure" should arrive, he fixed ice cream sundaes for all of us...which were very strange mixes of different ice creams and syrups.

Well...following my comments about Dad at the service in Morgan Hill, I introduced Jim and nine minutes into Jim's presentation as he was about to wrap it up, Dad slumped over into Liz's lap and Liz called out to Jim. Jim said, "Grandpa," and he went leaping over the chairs to get to Dad as the people scattered. There was a doctor in the audience, and he and Jim did compressions and mouth-to-mouth resuscitations, for which Jim had been trained as a volunteer fireman, but Dad was gone. People gathered in groups around the auditorium and prayed. I stood there in shock as I watched Dad being worked on. Something I will never forget is Dad's face after the first "mouth to mouth" by Jim. It may have been just a physical muscle reaction to what was happening, but I will simply share what I saw. Dad had a recognizable smile on his face. I wonder if it was because he saw things he had never seen before, the wonder of heaven, seeing Jesus and hearing "well done, good and faithful servant," the reunion with his mom and Dad and thousands of friends, the glory of God and the discovery of his marvelous new eternal home. I would like to think that these were some of the things he saw which brought the smile to his face!

Soon the paramedics arrived and took him to the St. Louise Hospital in Morgan Hill, the very hospital that one day we would attempt to purchase for the relocation of the college. It was the first time Dad had ever been a patient in a hospital, but he didn't stay long as his body was willed to Stanford University for medical research. He believed that since God had worked through his body to touch others with God's love while he was alive, why not have the same thing happen at his death…plus Dad being financially conservative thought it the best way to preserve his assets for Kingdom purposes and family so money would not need to be spent for burial of the body. He was such a responsible steward of his resources that one time our family noticed it took him a long time to eat because he only had about a dozen teeth left, and we suggested he might go to the dentist and let him add a few more teeth. At dinner time we would ask him what more he wanted and he would respond by saying, "just a little more time." He told us frequently that it was his desire for his last tooth and his last day of life to occur at the same time…didn't quite make it!

Well, Dad graduated with honors, without a moment of pain. He never wanted to graduate while he was preaching, he thought that would be too traumatic for people, but he sure did cut it close. In the Summer 1992 Broadcaster I wrote concerning his home going. Here is a portion of what I said:

To Me, He was Dad

Some called him Mr. Jessup, many Brother Bill, but to me he was Dad. He was a church   planter, teacher, Bible College President, encourager, pastor, writer, unity worker and scholar, and to me he was my friend, counselor, and mentor. No one taught me more about life, about graduation, too – his graduation.

Dad was good at doing a lot of things. But what I treasure most was his desire to spend time with me. He really cared how things were going in my life and I knew he was praying for me. I will miss the moments when he looked into my office, said hello, greeted me with a big smile and firm handshake, then slipped out because he didn't want to take too much of my time. He taught me how to fish, preach, play baseball, pray, golf, love the Lord, encourage, and how to love people and be a husband and father. He invested time with me so that his values, loves, and commitments could rub off on my life. He gave me a treasure more valuable than all the wealth of the world.

My wish is that of Elisha to Elijah, "let me inherit a double portion of your spirit" (II Kings 2:9). For what radiated from Dad was not just competence in service, but the spirit in which he served. I would love to inherit a double portion of his spirit of optimism, sacrifice, gratitude, joy and humility.

A service of celebration was held at Central Christian Church the day after Easter. This is the church that he established in 1939 and that gave birth to San Jose Bible College. It was a time of joyous praise which reflected his life in Christ to the more than 600 people who attended. An endowed scholarship fund was established in Mom and Dad's honor. Dad left $50,000 in his will to start the scholarship, and today it totals around $80,000. All the profits from this book will be given to this fund which is now called "The William and Carrie Jessup Endowed Memorial Scholarship Fund." Many students entering ministry have received help from this fund, and will continue to do so for as long as WJU exists.

What a wonderful legacy of vision, faith, hope, love, joy, dedication and sacrifice Dad and Mom have given to us! It will continue to change the landscape of eternity.

Shortly after this, I had the privilege of preaching at Cathedral of Faith in San Jose. Kenny Foreman had been a pastor and friend for a number of years, and he had led the congregation dynamically into becoming one of the largest and most impacting fellowships of believers in the Santa Clara valley through its TV and many outreach ministries. Following the last worship service on Sunday morning, a man came up to me and said, "Swish." I said, "Swish…guess I'll need an explanation." He went on to say, "We played basketball together at Roosevelt Junior High School in the seventh grade. Every time you shot you said, 'Swish!' The ball never went in, just kidding, but I never forgot you and our basketball games." Amazing indeed, we had not seen each other for more than forty years. That renewed a friendship that continues to this day. He introduced me to his lovely bride Nancy. Jack and Nancy Horton, more than any other couple, have been the most responsible for helping SJCC/WJU in its long relocation journey.

Jack, who recently retired, was the most successful dry wall contractor in Silicon Valley. Jack and Nan live in a beautiful home on a multi-acre site in Los Altos, overlooking the San Francisco Bay area. He invited me to do lunch with him to reminisce, to get caught up on our journeys, and to learn more about our ministry. The next time we got together he wanted to come see our campus at 12th and Virginia Streets in San Jose. I will always remember his initial response; it was something like this, though I don't recall his actual words: "Bryce, this is a dump! We have got to do something about it." My response was "You got that right! What do you have in mind?" His reply, "We need to build some quality buildings to upgrade your facilities and provide room for growth." I stated, "Great idea, but Jack, I can't even pay our teachers let alone think about building some new buildings." He then let me know that he wanted to pray and think about it; soon after he came to see me and said he would personally hire an architect to draw plans that we could take to the city so we could build some new buildings out front along 12th street. I was ecstatic to say the least. It wasn't long until the plans were drawn for a signature building to be built at the entrance of our campus. The pictures below shows some of the houses that married students and staff occupied which were to be torn down and the new buildings would be built in their place. We were deeply appreciative of the work that the Hortons and our architect had done, and we were anxious to take the plans to the city of San Jose for approval.

The architect's renderings of the proposed facilities to be built on the corner of 12th and Virginia.

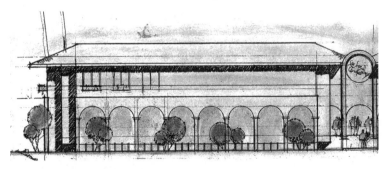

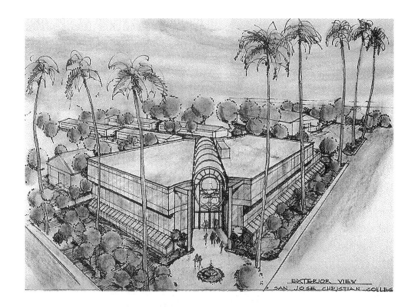

SAN JOSE
CHRISTIAN
COLLEGE

When we took the plans to the city, they informed us that they had serious reservations about granting us a building permit. One of the first things they required of us was to hold a neighborhood meeting to let the people see the pictures of the proposed buildings and hear from us concerning our plans. Around 200 people from the immediate and surrounding neighborhood showed up and it was not a pleasant meeting. They complained about everything from increased traffic, congestion, and noise, to contributing to increased crime in the neighborhood. We left the meeting very discouraged.

We then approached some of the San Jose City Council members and explained to them our desired plans. We discovered that only one of the twelve city council members was in our corner and was willing to speak on our behalf, the others were not. Therefore, with much consternation and disappointment we abandoned our plans to build any new buildings on our 12th Street campus. "Lord...what's next? We cannot survive on our current campus." The only alternative to going out of existence was to start looking again for a new location which would allow us to grow. As stated earlier in the book, the college had looked at property in the Sacramento region under Woody's presidency and Guadalupe College in Los Gatos in 1982 under Chuck's presidency, but neither of them became viable options...so it was time to roll up our sleeves and keep looking.

We explored fourteen sites for relocation during the 1990s and the early 2000s under the outstanding leadership of our Executive VP, Dr. Roger Edrington, and our VP for Advancement, Joe Womack. These two men exercised great initiative in finding properties and negotiating on our behalf. In May 1994 we began conversation concerning land named the Kring Property adjacent to Los Gatos Christian Church. Since I had been doing interim preaching there, LGCC was open to a merger of some kind which would allow us to use their facilities during the week, and they could use ours on the weekends. Ed Kellar was a wonderful Christian man, developer and President of Cornerstone Church Development company and a leader at LGCC. We commissioned him to lead us in this project. It seemed like a win/win situation. The Kring property adjacent to the LGCC property was 34.41 acres of land which would provide the needed space to build dormitories, athletic facilities, cafeteria, additional classrooms, etc. However, there were a couple of big hurdles that we would have had to overcome in order to make it work. The 34 acres was in the county and would need to be annexed into the town of Los Gatos. In addition to this, we knew the road and utilities for the campus were going to be a major challenge as well as the resistance from the neighborhood. When we took it to the Los Gatos city council it was obvious that the requirements to build and occupy the land were going to be beyond our capacity and time table. Plus, LGCC was going through some tough financial challenges themselves and so they needed to pull out of the discussions to concentrate on remodeling their facilities and funding the existing ministries. So we prayed again, "God…what's next?" And we resumed our search again because we could not bring ourselves to believe that we were supposed to wait for something to be dropped in our laps.

Another site that we found, and became serious about, was the Dade Behring Building on the East Side of San Jose. It was a beautiful building in the foothills which belonged to a technology company which had been unable to make it in Silicon Valley. The buildings were only about 10 years old and they were in immaculate shape. It had a beautiful cafeteria which would seat 600 people, many smaller rooms which would serve as classrooms, and an attractive appearance. It was three stories high, had a large open area in the middle of the facilities for gatherings such as Chapel, etc. The sticker price was $60 million dollars. Our Board of Directors, in walking through the facilities, was excited about the location and the charming quality of the buildings, but not the price tag! So after much prayer and discussion, the board decided we should keep on looking, and I reluctantly agreed with them.

Soon after that we discovered a convent in Saratoga. We took our Board and development team to view this campus to get their impressions. I personally thought it had some real potential. It was on about twenty acres of land, and though the facilities were a bit old, they were very well kept. It had lots of dorm space, meeting rooms, and it was situated in a quiet, upscale residential neighborhood. There were about five acres of bare land where additional buildings could be built. It would raise the image of the college considerably and be an attractive recruitment tool as it was located in the most affluent region of Silicon Valley. However, the city of Saratoga made it clear early on in our dialogue with them that we would need to build a large new road to the facility which would circle the neighborhood rather than going through it. It would require the purchase of a number of plots of land in a very expensive neighborhood, so that alone put a stop to any further negotiations with the city of Saratoga. So...we kept praying and believing that God would ultimately get us to the Promised Land, though we had no idea where it would be.

Continuing our search, we looked seriously at a couple of empty electronic facilities in South San Jose, one large piece of property on a hill overlooking the valley in East San Jose called Evergreen, open land in Coyote which is south of San Jose, and a shopping center at Union and Camden in San Jose. In one update from June 2, 1996, I was reminded that we also looked at the property across Coyote Creek at the back of our property. We would have built a bridge across Coyote Creek for easy access. The update to our constituency stated:

The City of San Jose has given us preliminary approval to develop the 13 acres of Parks and Recreation land immediately to the east of our campus. Hopefully, we will provide a ball diamond, soccer field, and tennis courts in exchange for a 55 year lease on the rest of the land for college development. This will allow us to grow from the current student body of 312 to around 900 students. The drawings are now at the City Planning Department.

That would have been a convenient plan and it might have served us well, but the planning department turned us down because the city was not interested in working with us to make it doable. In addition, the city of San Jose in the late

1990s developed a policy that the twenty large open parcels of land that were left in San Jose would be reserved for industrial development and not available for churches and non-profit organizations. Only one was set aside for a church or a non-profit organization, but it was in a very undesirable and hard to get to location in South San Jose.

One day as I was praying and thinking about the next steps of the journey, I recalled all the churches that I had been speaking in throughout Santa Clara Valley for a number of years. It seemed that almost every weekend I was in another church sharing a message, bringing an update on the college, and challenging the congregations to continue to "fight the good fight" in the middle of a fast changing, rapidly emerging global technology culture, in Silicon Valley. It dawned on me that there were a number of Ed Harrises and Jack Hortons in these congregations who might have a personal interest in partnering with the college in some way if asked. I wondered what might happen if I pulled them together for a breakfast meeting and had them dream with me about the future of SJCC as they see it. I couldn't escape the thought of *"Dream A Dream And Build A Team"* and it seems God burned those words into my mind, and reminded me of them frequently until they drove me to action. I have reflected on that concept on a regular basis ever since. Dr. Clark Dickerson, our fund raising consultant, strongly encouraged me to move forward with this idea. So I made a list of successful Christian businessmen I had gotten to know and I invited them to a breakfast meeting at the Hayes Mansion in San Jose on September 15, 1998. When I invited them I told them it was going to be just the one meeting where I wanted to have them help me dream about the future of SJCC. Here is the list of the guys who served with me on the Dream Team. That one meeting turned into a partnership for more than a dozen years and launched the college into a spectacular future.

Dream Team

John Crawford, top chip architect at Intel and Fellow. He was the co-designer of the 386, 486, and Pentium chips. He retired in February 2013. I had performed his wedding to Norma almost 30 years ago.

John Davis, President of Air Systems, Inc., a heating and air conditioning company in Santa Clara County.

Jack Horton, owner of Jack Horton Drywall, Inc., the largest drywall company in Santa Clara County, recently retired. I played basketball with him in the seventh grade.

Greg Sivaslian, Principal of Sivaslian & Associates, a financial planning company.

Mark Lauback, President of Royal Roofing Co., Inc.

David Davenport, Former President of Pepperdine University, a fellow at Hoover Institute at Stanford University in Palo Alto.

Ed Kellar, President, Cornerstone Church Development Inc., a private contractor.

Greg Jamison, President and CEO of the San Jose Sharks and the Compaq Center...in negotiations to become the owner of Phoenix Coyotes, Arizona hockey team.

Norman Nason, President of Saratoga Investment Company, a large real estate company in Santa Clara County. He led us in many of our real estate explorations including Rocklin campus.

Frank Bergandi, President of a software company, now a business consultant.

Pat Gelsinger, Corporate VP and Chief Technology Officer for the primary business of Intel, now CEO of VMware. I performed his wedding to Linda almost 30 years ago.

Mike West, President of VinaTech and former CEO of Octel, the largest automated voice mail manufacturer in the world, now a private corporate consultant.

Walt Wilson, President of Palo Alto Research Group and author of the *Internet Church,* now the Founder and Chairman of Global Media Outreach.

Ken Kerley, owner and manager of Joe Kerley Mercury/Jeep dealership in San Jose, now retired.

David Seeba, owner and manager of Hanish & Seeba, a large accounting firm in Santa Clara County.

Mike Ainsley, financial planner, executive business coach in Silicon Valley.

Ed Harris, Chief Development Officer of a large Software company in Silicon Valley, went to be with our Lord in January 2012.

Grover Sinsley, Retired Contractor, passed on to glory in December 2009.

Gary Radonich, President of Silicon Valley Roofing Company.

Clark Dickerson, President of Dickerson and Associates, a resource development company.

Joe Womack, VP for Advancement, SJCC/WJU.

Roger Edrington, Executive VP of SJCC/WJU.

Here are a couple pictures of two of our later Dream Team Meetings at the Shark's Tank in San Jose. Greg Jamison graciously hosted us in his suite for the dinner meetings and then the hockey games. Lots of special memories of our times together…what a great Dream Team!

At the urging of our consultant Clark Dickerson, we had our first breakfast meeting in September of 1998. I shared with the Dream Team some of my dreams using the slides copied below. We had an architect draw a second drawing seen below to hopefully renovate the old campus and this time impress the city of San Jose. The fourteen men in the room were engaged in the presentation and they responded with numerous interesting comments.

San Jose Christian College

Vision Goal
To be a regionally accredited college
of 1000 students from 40 birth countries
preparing to serve the Lord
through the local church
around the world
by the year 2010.

San Jose Christian College
60 Years of Ministry

★ Over 2000 graduates serving in 50 countries
★ 60% enter ministry
★ 34 ethnic churches planted
★ 54% growth in last three years

San Jose Christian College
60 Years of Ministry

★ 383 Students
★ 50% non-European American from 33 countries
★ Only non-denominational college in N. Calif.
★ 80% of student body in ministry

Santa Clara Valley in 2040
Mercury News, December 20, 1998

■ 44% Asians
■ 38% Latinos
■ 15% Whites
■ 3% Blacks

California population will double to 60 Million

Strategy

1. Christ Centered and empowered
2. Committed to Biblical Truth
3. Communicating A Global Vision
4. Continue Single Purpose Focus of Ministry
5. Create Trans-Denominational unity
6. Church Planting among ethnic communities
7. Cooperation With Harvest Seminary
8. College Excel Degree Completion Program
9. Challenging Young People to Ministry
10. Church and Individual Partnerships

Project Goal

■ Build New Learning Center
■ Build New Classrooms
■ Build New Administration Offices
■ Build New Chapel
■ Purchase Property for Expansion
■ Phase Projects

Financial Goal

■ $6M Campaign over 3 years
  ▸ $3M to building program
  ▸ $3M to operations
■ Long term financial stability
  ▸ Endowments
  ▸ Foundations

Draft Concept Drawing

Draft Concept Drawing

Where Do We Go From Here?
Five Questions

1. Is this a reasonable dream?
2. Do you think the Christian Community has a desire to see this happen?
3. Are there resources within the valley to bring it to pass?
4. How can these resources be found?
5. What are the next steps?

Here are some of their words from various guys following my presentation as copied from the minutes of the meeting.

> *If God has given you the vision, stay with it and He will provide the resources. God may have a location for you that has not yet been discovered. Don't say it is just this location, but maybe somewhere in Santa Clara Valley. Do you have a Foundation? Foundations could help you with fundraising. You are the only one with the vision and you need to keep at it. I'm a firm believer in walking down the track until the Lord closes the door. I'm real excited to see how, with prayer, that Rag Factory is yours. Maybe if you put us in a room once a quarter, out of that would come a working relationship with us and more encouragement for you. Funding is not a problem with God...maybe we could help you with that. Abraham as the father of the nations of the world got in a hurry and didn't wait for God's timing. How to reach the goal is important. Patience is a real good thing. Everything you do is bathed in prayer. I assume your dream and God's dream are connected. If you have to stay the course and be a significant Bible College, you need to stay doing that. There is a lot of fruit being reaped. You are in the center of a big mission field. What is the plan, the strategy? Put four or five sheets down and let us stare at this with you. Those of us who have run businesses have had to have strategy to get to the end of the game. I don't want to walk away without accomplishing something.*

The outcome of the meeting was the underlining message that my dreams were way too small. To put it bluntly, they kicked the doors off of my dreams and wanted them to become much bigger. On one occasion, I remember being invited by

Pat Gelsinger to share my dreams after breakfast in our home and he tactfully replied with one word, "Wimpy"! I got the message, but what impressed me most about this, and the first meeting at the Hayes Mansion with the Dream Team, was that they were willing to step up and join with us in exploring the future together. So they invited me to not simply have this one meeting, but to meet together on an ongoing basis to dream and explore the future of SJCC. Needless to say, I was thrilled at their response and it was huge in depositing to my heart a confidence that something important was going to unfold down the road under God's direction. That first meeting was a landmark meeting in setting a whole new direction and certainty about the future. These leaders would not let me step down from the Presidency during the times when I would get discouraged and want to turn in my letter of resignation. These guys were just what I needed, unafraid to speak truth into my life, encouragement to my soul, and hope concerning the future. I was not alone, I had a team who believed in us at SJCC and stood with us as partners.

Greg Jamison invited us to be his guests for our second meeting on January 11, 1999. He hosted us for dinner at 5:30 p.m. at the Shark's Tank, we had our "dreaming meeting", and then enjoyed the hockey game at 7:30 p.m. in his suite. This became an annual gathering there in addition to the other meetings we would have during the year. Not only did we meet as a team, but I followed up with most of the guys frequently for lunch to connect and draw insights from them about the future of SJCC as they saw it. What was a special and unanticipated blessing was that a number of them began to take the initiative to phone me to schedule time to get together to see how I was doing, and to connect on recent developments and plans. These guys knew that I might bail from the whole process, as it was filled with much more disappointment and discouragement than blessings and hope. These were busy guys, but they carved out time to listen, laugh, and at times shed a tear with me over the journey. I will be forever indebted to them for their heartfelt friendship, direction, and the hope that they constantly restored to my heart. They are some of God's special treasures! Were it not for the Dream Team, I would not have survived as President of SJCC and we would not be in Rocklin today with a magnificent campus, a flourishing student body, and a certain hope for a marvelous future. To God be the Glory!!

CHAPTER EIGHT

The Morgan Hill Fiasco
(2000)

In the late 1990s, we continued to explore properties for the relocation of the college. Norm Nason, President of Saratoga Investment Company, a large real estate company in Santa Clara County, was our real estate partner to help us find a new place for SJCC. He was an aggressive and knowledgeable developer with a Kingdom heart. He had led us to investigate and negotiate several of the properties we had explored. I will always remember a phone call I received from him during the week of Thanksgiving 1999. He wanted me to take a look at a former hospital in Morgan Hill which was soon to cease its operations. He wanted me to look at it on the day before Thanksgiving, but I was scheduled to leave town to join with some of our family for the holidays. In his own insistent way he reeled me in so that I had to delay my leaving town for a few hours to go take a look at the hospital, along with Joe Womack, our VP for Advancement, and Kay Llovio, our VP for Academics. With reluctance and a bit of frustration, because I felt it was too far from where we wanted to be in Silicon Valley, I went with him and the team to look it over.

Former Saint Louise Hospital of Morgan Hill

On November 25, 1999, there was a front page article in the Morgan Hill Times which read "Saint Louise ready to shut down operations." It went on to state, "In less than a week Saint Louise Hospital will close its doors. Through the Thanksgiving holiday weekend, the emergency room will continue to be open and functioning as it has since the hospital opened in 1989. Catholic Healthcare West (CHW) purchased Columbia South Valley Hospital in Gilroy in August and announced that it would move all hospital functions from Morgan Hill to Gilroy and rename the hospital the Saint Louise Regional Hospital. Both hospitals, in competition with each other, had suffered losses of $65 million during the last 10 years." There was just too much hospital for the limited population of the region.

As I thought about the hospital over the Thanksgiving holidays, I kept thinking it was too far from our current campus, being 19 miles to the south. But then as I kept looking for some positive indicators, I was reminded that Joshua led the children of Israel across the Jordan River and into the Promised land as God backed up the water 19 miles upstream to Adam. As a result, they walked on dry land to inhabit the land He had prepared. Just maybe God was working 19 miles upstream again on our behalf. Coyote Creek which was at the back of our 12th Street property had its source near the hospital at Anderson Dam. In one of my lighter moments I thought, "Well, at least students under stress would have oxygen in every room, and for the problem students we would have urgent care." Then on a more serious note, the memory of Dad's passing in Morgan Hill and then being taken to the Saint Louise Hospital was almost overwhelming. To think that the college might be growing a global ministry on the very campus where its founder went on to glory was indeed intriguing.

In an email to our Board and Dream Team members dated December 13, 1999, I stated:

Please Join us in Prayer

I need your prayers and input. Today, I toured for the second time St. Louise Hospital in Morgan Hill with Clark Dickerson and Joe Womack. It is just 17 minutes from our current campus at HWY 101 and Cochrane Avenue. The hospital is for sale with a minimum asking price of $23,000,000. At the current time there are 20 offers on the property and the bidding will close on Wednesday at midnight. It eventually got down to three offers and so we had to up ours to $23,500,000. There are approximately 100,000 square feet of buildings, almost double our current situation at SJCC. It is a two story building with beautiful architecture that is more collegiate than hospital in feel. The buildings are just 10 years old and are in great shape.

There are more parking spaces than we need. The buildings are located on 25 acres of land with an additional 12 acres right along the freeway...wonderful visibility and accessibility. The 12 acres could be sold to help finance the main hospital property, though it would be good to hold onto it.

We have had estimates on the value of our property from 8-12 million...One of the major hurdles will be the zoning of the property by the city of Morgan Hill... There has never been an opportunity for relocation or the building of buildings for the college that has so excited me, and the rest of the administration, as this one. It has so many positive aspects to it, but it is also a huge undertaking. Personally, I believe it is doable if we are given a chance...what do you think? Obviously, I am not looking for a formal vote as there are way too many questions that we all have, but is the dream something we should pursue?...I will keep you updated on the progress.

Wouldn't it be something if God started moving on this? It is such a long shot at this point, but I'm praying for a wonderful surprise as He is in the business of giving to us the desires of our hearts. This is a Kingdom desire and I'd love to see Him agree and respond!...With Anticipation, Bryce

As we soon took faculty, board members, students, Dream Team, architects, builders, and others to look at the 25 acre campus, there was a unanimous consensus that this would be a wonderful place where the college could relocate. There was additional land nearby that we could purchase someday for expansion, but after some renovation, we could accommodate around 1200 students on the current campus. It was located right off of the well known and traveled freeway, Highway #101. Thomas Kinkade, the Painter of Light, had his international studios and warehouses within walking distance on the other side of the freeway. He later even gave us 2,500 paintings of the

"Mountains Declare the Glory of God," a beautiful painting of Bridalveil Falls with the Merced River in the foreground. This painting represented Dad's favorite place on earth, Yosemite National Park. We began to sell these as a fund raiser for the purchase of the hospital. We discussed with him having a Thomas Kinkade Art Academy on campus. He agreed and he was willing to be one of our featured artists. Little did we know at that time that he was to have a very challenging future and soon pass from this life.

The big unknown was how we could possibly fund it? The asking price was $23 million, add to that the multi-million dollar renovation it would take to make it usable for a college and it looked out of reach, but we felt led to explore purchasing it anyway. The more we explored it, the more the possibilities began to loom. Jack Horton, my long time basketball friend from the 7th grade and the largest dry wall contractor in Silicon Valley, said he and his wife Nancy would buy the 12 acres between the hospital and the freeway for $5 million. That brought the purchase price down to $18 Million. He had helped us with providing for the architectural drawings for the 12th street campus when we tried to expand there, and now he would be helping us to explore purchasing the hospital. A local Chinese Church now wanted our 12th Street property and were willing to pay us $10 million...it began to look like it might work. In reading some of my thoughts during that time it is obvious that I was riding rather high as reflected in this Broadcaster statement in Winter 2000:

> *To put it metaphorically, over the Christmas season I saw the Bethlehem star and it settled over St. Louise Hospital and I have gone there to worship Jesus. Now, I'm waiting for the Wisemen to show up, bringing gold, frankincense, and myrrh. On second thought, forget the frankincense and myrrh.*

Hospital is Purchased!

In a meeting the first week of January 2000 in Santa Clara with the Catholic Healthcare West sales team, we were able to reach an agreement. Larry Winger, President of Provision ministries and Doug Crozier, then President of Church Development Fund, were our invited partners at the meeting. When the meeting reached an impasse, Larry asked for a recess and they discussed with us what it might look like if CDF provided the funding for the purchase of the facilities. We were elated and CHW readily accepted their offer. Therefore, our Board of Trustees voted on January 14, 2000, to purchase the hospital and to proceed with the application process for zoning from the City of Morgan Hill. There were many tears of gratitude and joy that were flowing, including mine! In the Winter 2000 Broadcaster I wrote:

> *In my wildest dreams I could not have envisioned what has just taken place! I am still in a state of shock, excitement, and overwhelming gratitude for God's amazing provision... Who could have predicted when we started our planning for our 60th anniversary celebration over a year ago, that on the same day of the dinner meeting our board would receive word and vote unanimously to enter into negotiations to purchase the hospital? If all goes well, it is our plan to open SJCC at the new facility by January 2001.*

That Friday evening, around 500 people gathered with us at the San Jose campus to celebrate the 60th anniversary of SJBC/SJCC. As I showed pictures of the hospital and told them of our moving forward in the purchase of the property, there was a standing ovation and I can still clearly see in my minds eye our students running around shouting for joy and high fiving one another all over the old 12ᵗʰ Street gymnasium. It was a great time of joy, celebration, and spontaneous euphoria. On January 26, 2000, a press release read: "CATHOLIC HEALTHCARE WEST ANNOUNCES SALE OF MORGAN HILL PROPERTY." Little did we know the challenges just around the corner as owners of the former Saint Louise Hospital.

In the midst of all that was happening, Mom was not doing well in the convalescent hospital where she had been for the past six years. She ate breakfast, went to sleep and graduated into the presence of our Lord on January 19, 2000. She no doubt found Dad soon and I'm sure she began singing one of her favorite songs, "We're together again, just praising the Lord." A memorial praise service was held at Central Christian Church in San Jose on January 27 to celebrate her life and to express gratitude for God's grace in her life through the years. Mom never got a chance to see the former St. Louise Hospital. She was a wonderful mother, a great teacher of song leading and music at SJBC, and a very special first lady to my Dad through 63 years of marriage. She was Dad's biggest fan! Dad left part of his assets to establish a William Jessup Endowed Memorial Scholarship Fund when he died. Mom wanted people to contribute to that fund on her passing, also. So with what Dad gave to start the fund along with what others gave at his homegoing and Mom's, the fund is now more than $80,000. Worthy and needy students each year receive scholarships out of this fund from WJU to assist them as they prepare for the ministry. All the proceeds from this book will go to their scholarship fund.

Mom had a big heart, a soft spirit, and I never heard her complain except for the one time when Dad was fly fishing along a brush filled stream in Mount Lassen National Park. She always wanted to hike along with us, but in this instance there was no trail, just brush everywhere. So Dad took the easy path and walked straight up the center of the river, catching fish as he sang with great delight. Mom, getting more deeply entangled in the brush with each forward step felt her frustration level rising and finally yelled out at Dad, "You, you, beast!" I still crack up every time I think about it because I can still hear Dad's insensitive response of loud laughter when he heard her. I owe so much of who I am to my loving and sacrificing mother. She always put others ahead of herself. She believed in people and especially her family. Mom was a lady who had affluence growing up and great need as the wife of a founding President, but she always made us feel rich because our family had those things which money can't buy; love, joy, peace.

Well, we continued to celebrate big time the purchase of the hospital and our future in many ways. We held one of our chapel services there and surrounded the buildings in prayer. The students were excited. I hosted the Dream Team on site for breakfast, gave them a tour, and sought their help in our newly launched Capital Campaign, "The Future Is Now." Our Board of Directors had some of their meetings there, some of us even slept overnight in the hospital rooms to bask in God's goodness in what He was providing. I enjoyed that, though I have to admit it was a bit spooky as I considered the many sick and dying who probably slept in my bed. I would take people on tours of the hospital, show them the room where Dad went on to glory and say to them that I looked forward to the time when this room would become the prayer room on campus. Our architects were busy designing the renovation project and we were accelerating the fundraising. It was an exciting time, but also a time when we realized it was not yet a done deal!

However, as June, 2000, approached, we began to feel confident that the deal was going to come together and we were going to move to Morgan Hill! Therefore, since this was going to be the last graduating class from the 12th Street property, I was asked to give the Commencement address on June 2nd . From my sermon notes, here is what I said as I started:

> *Distinguished graduates and friends. What an honor to be asked to address you…you who are heading out into ministry…you who are the last graduating class on this campus and the first graduating class of the new millennium.*

I shared with them that our prayer for them is that they would choose to build "An Extraordinary Ministry For Extraordinary Times." For that to happen I stated we would be giving to our graduates three things as they come across the platform. 1) Something for their Head…a diploma. 2) Something for their Heart…a Bible. 3) Something for their Hands…a towel. It was an exciting time of celebration and a time of challenging our graduates to go forth as the last graduating class in San Jose to become extraordinary world changers by giving God full access to their head, heart, and hands! We sent them forth with prayer, joy, and overwhelming gratitude.

Two weeks later, on June 16, 2000, we officially became the owners of the hospital after many weeks of negotiations with Catholic Healthcare West to work out the details of the purchase with Church Development Fund and ourselves. We closed Escrow and gave thanks again to God for His making our dream come true.

We continued our dialogue with the City of Morgan Hill concerning the Use Permit. Early on in our conversations with individual city council members they indicated openness to our occupancy which encouraged us to move forward, but that soon shifted. Many people from the community, especially the older people, wanted their hospital back, though there was no one interested in buying it. Therefore, there began a long and often intense series of meetings with the City Council, sometimes going past midnight where we listened to the complaints about taking away their hospital, adding noise, traffic congestion, and some even complained that there would no doubt be late night parties with lots of drinking and reckless driving.

However, we continued to move forward with confidence that God was going to see us through these meetings and deliver us to our new campus, the Promised Land. I wrote in the Fall 2000 Broadcaster a word of concern about the zoning issues but then I hastened to again express my excitement in what God had provided.

> *We had hoped to be started with our renovation project at our new campus by now, but the zoning issues with the city of Morgan Hill are taking longer than we had planned…*
>
> *However…what an exciting time this has been, and the excitement is building toward that day when we will have a new home to which we will be inviting you to visit*

and celebrate God's goodness and future with us. What this will mean to the growth of the Kingdom cannot be measured, but it will be 'far beyond all that we could have asked or even imagined.' In my 45 years of journey in the ministry, these are the most exciting yet!

Well, the meetings became more frequent and heated as we tried to move forward. The City Council reported that having done a phone survey of the city, approximately 75% of the residents wanted to take back the hospital by eminent domain. Many of us from the college spoke from time to time at the Council meetings. At one of the meetings in April there were some 350-400 people who attended the City Council meeting, with only about 40 people to vote for taking the hospital back. This is in light of the fact that a flyer was sent to over 30,000 people who live in Morgan Hill encouraging them to attend in support of getting the hospital back. Over 300 people were there in support of SJCC coming to Morgan Hill and to make it a WIN/WIN situation. We had a large prayer meeting on the lawn behind the Council chamber before the meeting. We then presented to the City Council over 2,400 signed statements from Morgan Hill residences who wanted us in Morgan Hill. After about 200 hours of late night meetings, thousands of letters sent to the community, newspaper articles, phone calls, TV interviews, scores of high level business and church communities endorsing us, the launching of an $18 million dollar capital campaign The Future is Now, and our spending around a million dollars in fees, taxes, consultants, etc., the City Council of Morgan Hill voted 4-1 against zoning our new property for education. We were stunned...crushed!

Pacific Justice Institute and Brad Dacus, their President, got wind of our situation. He is a wonderful brother in the Lord who later served on our WJU Board of Trustees. We discussed our predicament with him and he volunteered his organization to partner with us to seek to reverse the decision. A recent federal law had been passed called the Religious Land Use and Institutionalized Acts which gave broad protection for religious institutions against governments imposing substantial burdens on properties. Though the law had yet to be tested, Brad and his team felt we had a good chance of winning and setting a precedent for the future for America on these kinds of issues for religious institutions. Therefore, the Summer 2001 Broadcaster stated:

> *In order to protect the new campus that we own, we filed a law suit last month. The City of Morgan Hill denied our zoning earlier this year. After we had exhausted all other possible negotiated settlements, we were advised by our negotiating team and the Board to file suit. Hopefully, we will have resolution to the issue within the next couple of months. Where do we go from here? I believe we keep putting one foot in front of the other and keep moving in the direction that God is leading. He led us to purchase the new campus and I am confident that He will get us where He wants us to be on His time-line and in His own special way so that Christ can be increasingly exalted among the nations. He has not led us this far to take us down a dead-end street. He will provide the resources to do this.*

So off to court we went. We eventually ended up in the Ninth District Federal Court in San Francisco. As I sat there and listened to the arguments in February 2002, it seemed so simple, and as I prayed and listened and listened and prayed during the session. I felt we had a good chance of winning. But I was wrong; they failed to overturn the decision of the

Morgan Hill City Council. The only option left to us was to appeal the decision to the Supreme Court. PJI and their staff felt we had a good chance to win. The problem was that it would be costly and it would take us around five years to have our case tried in the Supreme Court and we would probably go into bankruptcy in the process. So I looked at Joe Womack and Roger Edrington and said something like, "Guys, go look for another site…this one is history!" Though we were greatly disappointed with the outcome, we still held confidently to the conviction that God was not yet finished with SJCC. We believed that if we kept banging on doors, (we were done with gentle knocking), one of them God would open in His timing.

My life has been blessed since 1990 going backpacking every year with usually about eight guys to some 10,000 ft. elevation lakes on the Eastern side of Yosemite National Park. We begin our hike at Tuolumne Meadows and hike about 13 miles to the lakes. It is always a very inspirational time of being out in God's great out-of-doors. My Dad taught me a love for the Sierras and fishing which I continue to enjoy to this day. As I reflect on our journey to Rocklin, I stand in awe of how God connects the dots, usually not seen at the time, but clearly seen in retrospect, to accomplish what He wants done. I sent out a development or fund raising letter on March 9, 2001, right after the city of Morgan Hill denied our use permit for the hospital. The caption at the top read **"ZONING DENIED"**. We had lost around a million dollars, $275,000 in taxes alone. Non-profits only pay taxes on the properties and land that they are not using, so since we were not using the hospital and of course we couldn't, we still had to pay taxes anyway. In the letter I was focusing on the devastating impact of Morgan Hill on our finances and at the same time trying to give hope to our partners concerning the future. Given all the failed attempts to relocate, it is surprising that most of our constituency hung with us during that time rather than choosing to find a seemingly more fruitful ministry to support. I concluded my appeal for donations with this interesting metaphor which I have used many times since in presentations and sermons and always think about it as I backpack each summer. Here is part of what I wrote in March of 2001.

> *In a recent quiet time, I was reminded of an alpine lake at 9,000 ft. in the back country of Yosemite, where I have gone backpacking for more than 10 years. About 5 years ago a storm came through as I was fishing this lake. I sought shelter under a huge boulder and decided to wait out the storm. While there I studied the landscape and realized that there was an underground stream that fed the lake from above. After the storm passed, I climbed another 1,000 ft. and there I discovered an alpine lake twice the size of the lower one, much deeper, magnificent in beauty with snow capped mountains surrounding it, and teaming with larger trout just for me. I have been going there ever since.*

> *God has brought us to the first lake (the former St. Louise hospital in Morgan Hill)...it may be there that he wants us to fish when the storm is over! However, He may well be showing us through the storm that there is something magnificent, beyond our view, but prepared for us that is far beyond the previous fishing hole. I stand, squinting my eyes to try and see it...and I believe when the storm is over, it will be good beyond our imaginations!*

Lower Lake

Lower Lake from Upper Lake

Upper Lake

The Catch of the Day...Upper Lake

In the middle of the Lower Lake picture is the stream that led us to the upper lake. In the second picture I'm looking down on the Lower Lake from the Upper Lake with Half Dome in the distance. The beautiful Upper Lake is well over 10,000 ft in elevation with no trail to get there! Frank, my missionary son-in-law, caught the biggest catch of the day on one of our first trips into the Upper Lake. Little did I know how powerful and prophetic these words would one day become. After the storm of Morgan Hill was over and we were led to Rocklin, my wife became inspired and penned the following poem in the fall of 2004.

THE UPPER LAKE

After the storm at the "lower lake"
A stream of water revealed

The presence of an "upper lake"
Was above the ridge concealed.

The beauty of that upper lake
Was awesome beyond compare
But without the storm at the lower lake
I wouldn't have known it was there!

Climbing to the upper lake
Was the fulfillment of a dream
But the glory goes to God Himself
For His leading was in that stream.

So when the storms of doubt appear
And threaten to overtake
I remember the stream from the ridge above
And the view of that upper lake!
Jo Jessup 2004

The poem tells the whole story. God knew that after the storm of Morgan Hill there would be an "upper lake" available that He would lead us to after the storm if we would but follow the stream, and it would make the "lower lake" look pretty anemic by comparison. Our call was to be faithful to His leading! I am so glad our team persevered through the storm...for the fishing is tremendous at the "upper lake". It was stories like this and metaphors of the children of Israel and their journey through the wilderness to get to the promised land that inspired us and gave us hope concerning the future.

Well, after a hard fought battle in Morgan Hill, in the Summer 2002 Broadcaster I concluded my article with this statement of hope:

This has been a tough year, but God has shown Himself strong and continues to unfold a powerful future for SJCC. Thank you for your prayers, encouragement, and support. We still don't know where He will guide us to relocate the campus so that growth can continue, but we are holding on to the vision with confidence that He will open the door to the place He wants us to enter. It is that vision and eternal hope which drives us. Its fulfillment will be good!

Thankfully, we were able to negotiate a settlement with Catholic Healthcare West and hand the hospital back to them. The buildings still sit there today, relatively empty, but no hospital. What a waste, but it was now time for us to move on. We would have gone out of existence had it not been for our Dream Team and a number of friends who stepped up to do more than verbally encourage us and pray for us, they gave of their resources so that we could have a future. For these and others who have partnered with us through the years, I will be eternally grateful. By the way, I carry with me on my key ring a key to the hospital as a daily reminder of God's faithfulness in not answering every prayer the way that we pray them for He sometimes has something better in mind for us, though unknown at the time.

Goodbye Morgan Hill!

CHAPTER NINE

The Promised Land
Rocklin *(2003)*

The week of February 18, 2002, will always be one of the most significant weeks ever in the history of SJBC/SJCC/ WJU. What took place during that week changed the future of the college forever. Three things took place which changed our thinking, reshaped our vision and plans, and would eventually multiply the impact and broaden the college's global ministry in a powerful way. And it all happened within one week!

First we received the decision from the 9th District Federal Court in San Francisco telling us they would not overturn the ruling of the Morgan Hill city council. The decision from the Federal Court brought an abrupt halt to our proposed journey to Morgan Hill. Amazingly, and to their credit, Catholic Health Care West was willing to buy back the hospital from us, which was not required in the original agreement.

The second thing took place at the Annual WASC meeting which just happened to be held at the Fairmont Hotel in San Jose. We had been working on our regional accreditation with WASC for more than ten years, and now was the time to make our final defense concerning our progress and materials and await the decision of the commission. We made the presentations on Thursday the 21st, and on Friday we were notified verbally that we had received initial regional accreditation. The formal letter of being granted Initial Accreditation was dated March 1, 2002. You can imagine the rush of joy, gratitude, and celebration that occurred among those of us who were at the conference. Shortly after that we had a grand celebration in chapel and then an evening banquet at Los Gatos Christian Church with many from our constituency attending.

The third thing was an email I had received which was sent to hundreds of private colleges and universities in America. I remember showing the email to our Executive Team who were attending the WASC Conference. The email told of an offer of 1,000 acres of land to be given by Angelo Tsakopoulos, a prominent real estate developer in Sacramento, to a private, regionally accredited, four year college who would establish a college in the Sacramento Region, for there was none in the region. The land was located about 10 miles North West of Roseville near Sacramento. The email stated that half of the land could be sold in order to generate resources to build the college or university on the other half. It sounded interesting now that we had just received regional accreditation... though there was a lot of skepticism among us about why Mr. Tsakopoulos would do that, what was in it for him, what would be the obstacles, etc.

We felt it was worth exploring with at least a phone call or an email response to see where it might lead. Perhaps what was different for us from other colleges who received the email is that we were desperate to relocate, and this property was located in a region that had been on the SJBC radar screen back in the 1970s. President Woody Phillips realized that the school needed to relocate to be able to grow and had looked at the facilities of the former Bethel Temple, (now Capital

Christian Center in Sacramento) which was relocating in order to expand. The buildings were originally built for a small Technical College near Cal State, Sacramento, and thus had lots of classrooms, 100 dorm rooms, gymnasium, etc. The facilities were on 13 acres of land in the heart of Sacramento along the American River. There was interest on the part of SJBC, but the price tag of $4 million put it out of reach for the college at that time.

In addition to the interest in the Sacramento region back in the 70s, we had started SJCC's only extension site for a Degree Completion Program and it just happened to be in the city of Rocklin. It was started back in 1997 through Adventure Christian Church. Dr. Rick Stedman, one of our graduates from SJBC in 1980, is the senior pastor and founded the church in 1992, a church that now is impacting around 4000 people each week. Rick has served on our college Board of Trustees at various times during our journey; he kept challenging us to have an extension site in Rocklin because of the growth of the community and church, and the potential for a great fit for the region. Therefore, when he offered his rented church offices at Sunset and Whitney for our use at no charge, we could not refuse. I remember well coming over and teaching classes myself in the evenings for one of the first modules of the program. I soon saw the potential of the region, its fresh look, the growing churches of the area, the safe and family feel of the community, and the conservative perspective on many of life's issues. It was obvious that the region would be a good fit for the college if anything should become available.

Well, we contacted Angelo Tsakopoulos and set up a time to meet with him to hear about the land offer. When we arrived, I was shocked, as one of the first people we met in his office was the lawyer who had fought against our zoning proposal in Morgan Hill! I could hardly believe it! I paused to roll my eyes heavenward to our team as things got started on a less than exciting note, though he assured us this was a new and different deal. Amazingly, we had come all the way from San Jose to Sacramento only to discover that our meeting is with the lawyer that shot us down in Morgan Hill. He had been mayor of Folsom and was a friend of the mayor in Morgan Hill. He was also Angelo's lawyer who handled his legal land issues. We met two or three times with Angelo's team, but it was obvious that it was not going to work for us. The land offer was land that was set aside as protected game reserve land. Angelo was hoping that the county would change the zoning to accommodate a college or university thus giving him the opportunity to develop thousands of acres of his land that was adjacent to the proposed university. Our team realized that we would have law suits from the Sierra Club and other environmental organizations that would take years and hundreds of thousands of dollars to fight. Some estimated that even if we won, it would take 10-15 years to get the approval to use the land. Therefore, we pulled out and Drexel University started working with Angelo, but has recently pulled out of the process also and the land is still sitting there unable to be used.

It became another disappointing journey. We continued to wonder what God was up to in reference to the college. We refused to take these decisions as a sign that God was finished with us and thus we had no future. We chose to believe that He still had His eye on us and that in His own timing, He would yet guide us to the Upper Lake or to use the a biblical metaphor, the Promised Land. Both of these metaphors were discussed frequently to encourage us. Having made a number of trips over to the Sacramento region to speak with Angelo's team about his property, we became aware of other opportunities that we decided to explore in the region since Silicon Valley no longer had a place for us. So we decided to keep looking at the Sacramento region for available land. We looked at land in the El Dorado Hills area south and east of Sacramento, but it was way out in the country. We also looked at the former Ace Hardware warehouses on Sunset Blvd., in Rocklin. They were located on 25 acres of land, in good shape, but it would not allow us room for the expansion of the facilities that we would need to do.

So, it was time to head back to San Jose, but we made a wrong turn on Sunset Blvd., and headed north instead of south. As we drew near to Highway 65 there was a For Sale sign on the property near the freeway that was the west coast home for the Herman Miller Office Furniture Manufacturing Company. As I read the sign to our Real Estate Broker, Norm Nason, I said something like, "Look at that, 156 acres, 340,000 square feet of buildings…What about that property Norm?" He replied, "I don't know." By this time my frustration in not being able to find the right property surfaced and I said, "Isn't that what you do for a living? Go find out!"

On our way out of town I phoned Ted Gaines on my cell phone. At the time Ted served as the chair of the Placer

County Supervisor in the region. I had heard that he was a great Christian man who would be open to a conversation with me about the college if I ever wanted to do that. I was blown away by his response. We talked for about 45 minutes as I told him of our journey and the For Sale sign we had just seen. He went into great detail to tell me all that he would do if anything should come together for us in the region. Ted was highly respected in the region and he said he would go ahead of us to have conversations with all of the players who would have a part in making a decision about changing the zoning from business to non-profit education. It was an amazing conversation as he described the culture of Placer County and how it was so different from Silicon Valley. He convinced me that we would not only be welcomed to the area, but that Rocklin would be eager and proud to have the first regionally accredited, residential, private, four year university in the whole Sacramento region in their community. Needless to say, I was extremely excited as we drove back to San Jose, but I needed to try and keep a lid on the excitement as all we knew at this point was that the land was for sale, we knew nothing of the details.

During the next couple of days Norm and Bob Rispoli, a Christian developer and friend in the region, did their research and they found out that the land was already in escrow with Grupe Homes. When I was told, my response was, "Oh boy, here we go again...will anything ever come together for us?" This seemed like something that could be a fit, but it looked like we were going to be shot down again. It was the first time we felt we would have the strong support of the region if something were to come together. However, it looked like it was probably all over now with Grupe wanting to build homes on the property and they would probably have a greater chance with Placer County and Rocklin because of the tax revenue they would be generating. Placer County would be making the decision concerning the issuing of the use permit, but it was also in dialogue with Rocklin on the decision, for Rocklin was soon to annex the property into the city.

Bob Rispoli, Norm Nason, and now Mike Emmert from Church Development Fund, recommended to us that we would give a back-up offer of $18.5 Million in case things didn't come together with Grupe. When Grupe, who had completed their due diligence on the property, met the very next week to speak with the Herman Miller representative, an amazing thing happened. It seems that after Grupe did their due diligence it was determined that it was going to be too costly to tear down the existing buildings with all of the concrete, etc., so that they could build their new homes, and they also would have to pay for a huge sewer line to be built through their property. So they withdrew their offer. Wow...amazing! I was speechless!! The team was excited too but they encouraged me to calm down a bit as this was only the beginning point, that there were scores of things that would have to come together to make all of this work for the college. Well...they could calm down a bit, but not me! I was off the chart excited about the possibility. To add to my excitement, I was informed that during the negotiations with the Herman Miller representatives they informed us that they would leave behind about $1 Million worth of top of the line Herman Miller Aeron chairs, quality desks, and excellent office partitions.

Soon our team went back up to take a closer look. Three big warehouses, with some administrative offices and I thought to myself, those will be three really huge classrooms with over 100,000 square feet of space in each of them. Frankly, I had a bit of a hard time visualizing how the big warehouses could be utilized, but not our architect. Russ Taylor was salivating about what could be done. The buildings were originally designed by Frank Gehry, a world renowned architect who has received numerous awards plus 13 honorary doctorates from prestigious universities for his work. He also designed the popular Walt Disney Concert Hall. In 1991, this Rocklin facility was awarded the National Honor Award by the American Institute of Architects (AIA). On this visit we invited Rick Stedman and a number of other influential Christian leaders in the region to walk around with us to examine the buildings. They were all encouraging us to move forward with the negotiations.

At our Faculty Retreat at Roger Edrington's home on May 29-30, 2002, I shared with the Faculty and Administration this prayer: "Help us to understand our situation accurately so that we do not miss the opportunity for greatness." I shared with them that our mission must always reflect God's purposes, and then I defined it with four statements:

1. A corporate seeking of God's heart reflected in Jesus
2. A passion for the lost
3. The development of servant leaders, rooted in scripture, who will disciple others
4. A commitment to build the church globally

I shared with them the failed exploration of the Tsakopoulos property and other properties and then the current opportunity to explore the Herman Miller property. I stated that we may need to move aggressively, with confidence, expecting resistance both internally and externally, but with determined faith in God we may be asked to pack up and head to the upper lake in Rocklin! I closed with saying that one thing we must decide is that we will move forward, refusing discouragement for it is not an option! I kind of gulp as I look back to those written statements delivered to our team with some nervousness, but with a gut confidence that God would get us to a better place.

About six weeks later in an email to the Faculty dated 7/19/02, I gave them the following information:

Dear Faculty,

This email is a follow up on our discussion at the Faculty Retreat when we discussed the possibility of a move to Sacramento. I want to give you an update so we can all be on the same page and I wanted you to be among the first to know what is happening.

We have made an offer on the Herman Miller property at the corner of Highway #65 and Sunset Boulevard in Rocklin, about 3 miles north of Inter-State Highway #80 to Lake Tahoe. There are three large buildings on the property with a total of 340,000 square feet. The buildings are situated on 156 acres of land overlooking the city of Rocklin to the South and Lincoln to the North. Until two weeks ago, we were in second place in the running, but we have now moved into first place after a developer (Grupe Co.) deciding to step aside.

The contract is being worked on by Church Development Fund lawyers and Herman Miller lawyers and should be completed for signing within the next couple of weeks. We will then have 60 days of "due diligence" to determine if this is a move that should be made. During the "due diligence," the architects and builders will be determining what work will need to be done to convert the buildings to college use. A study of classroom needs, offices, dorms, cafeteria, athletic facilities, chapel, etc., will be done. A professional feasibility study will be done to determine the market for a college like ours in the Sacramento area. In addition, contact has already been made with the Placer County Board of Supervisors and the Rocklin City Council to determine their willingness to zone the property for college use. At the end of the 60 days we will decide whether to actually purchase the property, or to back out and receive our down payment back. !

If it should be determined by our Board of Directors that this is what God is leading us to do for the future growth and progress of the college, then work would begin immediately following the purchase of the new facility. The hope would be that the college could open at the new campus in Fall of 2004.

I am aware that should this be determined to be the best for the future of SJCC, that it will be a difficult thing for many of our SJCC team. Some will be delighted, others disappointed, a number will be frustrated over the move, some will feel unappreciated, upset that they were not heard or felt valued for all of their work at the current campus, some will go and others will choose to stay. All of us will feel different degrees of being overwhelmed. If we should move to Sacramento, my highest prayer is that we could retain our current campus, or at least a portion of it as a branch campus for both a traditional program and our Excel program. We may not have the luxury financially to be able to do this.

I have run the gamet of emotions from "thrilled to panic" concerning this opportunity. And I have those feelings almost daily for this would be a huge undertaking. I have put together a 25 member "Relocation Commitee" composed of Sacramento pastors, businessmen, builders, lawyers, former & current college presidents, finance people, venture capitalists, and developers. There is agreement from all of these and others who are working on our project that this is a terrific opportunity if it should all come together. Bob Rispoli, a developer said he sees this as a "once in a lifetime opportunity for the college." Of course, we felt that about Morgan Hill also.

I would be very interested in your thoughts about this opportunity. Please email them to me or speak with me personally if you would like. I have not been down this trail before and I want to make sure it is the right one before I recommend to the board that we go there. Please pray about this and for clarity of direction, especially for Roger Edrington who is again doing a great job in leading us in all of our negotiations concerning the property.

The staff does not have this same information yet.

Trust you are having a good summer!

Bryce

Early visits to the Rocklin facility

There were some who had strong feelings about the potential move and resisted the idea. One teacher said to me, "Why do you want to move to that cow town?" It would be a hardship for some to move and for others it was almost unthinkable early on. One said, "It is a slap in the face to those of us who have already sacrificed to be in San Jose." I appreciated one faculty member who sent me this Leaders Prayer by Bill Pile to encourage me to be strong in my resolve.

> *Like Moses, I accepted leadership with great reluctance,*
> *O Lord. And now, many years later and several cultural*
> *shifts later, I'm conflicted, Lord, from the voices out there*

243

and I'm wondering: Am I to find out where people want to go and take them there? Am I to find out what they want and give it to them wrapped in holy wrapping? Or, am I to find out what You want for them and help them find it? It has to be the latter, but it's so hard.

We did not get off to a good start in getting our faculty over to see the facility, 130 miles North East of our San Jose campus. We took a number of the faculty and staff over and our bus broke down around Concord, which is not quite half way to Rocklin. We phoned back to San Jose and three or four of our workers drove their cars up and picked us up after a two hour wait and drove us to Rocklin. At times it seemed like things were not going our way and I'm sure that Satan was very happy to help see that things would work against us. But in spite of all of that, after people saw the campus and all of the 156 acres of land which held such potential for future growth, understood a bit of the accepting culture of the region, and realized there was a chance we might be able to reel this one in, their reluctance soon shifted to support and anticipation.

Our development team did their due diligence work during the summer of 2002. Bob Rispoli and Mike Emmert were long time developers from the region. Bob, as a private developer and home builder, and Mike was the land developer for McDonalds and then with Church Development Fund. They were strong Christian men who wanted to see us move to the Rocklin site. They knew all of the issues to confront and the people who needed to be confronted. They saw the tremendous potential of the move for growth and for regional and global impact for the Kingdom. They not only knew the region well, but the region knew them. Bob knew many of the civic leaders and how they would view our owning the property. Bob led us in working out a strategy with the city of Rocklin that really sweetened the deal. We told the city of

Rocklin that we would be willing to sell the 30 acres on the corner of Sunset and Hwy 65 for commercial development. This would give the city tax income off of a portion of our property. The city quickly warmed up to us, plus it would give us around $10 million from the sale of the property and we would own the remaining 126 acres of property and buildings for $8 million instead of $18 million. The city of Rocklin was really in our corner after this offer, and it was a great deal for us also. A genuine win/win opportunity!

Joe Womack, our VP for Advancement, did feasibility studies concerning regional education needs, the local economy, spiritual and political climate, the current educational systems, church receptivity, personal and business partnerships, etc. Roger Edrington, our Executive VP and chair of our relocation team, led the team as it negotiated with both the county and the city concerning the zoning issues. Both Joe and Roger led us very effectively in these arenas.

After our due diligence period, the Board of Trustees had a special Board meeting on September 20, 2002 at the Rocklin facility and voted unanimously to move forward with the purchase of the property conditioned upon Placer County and the City of Rocklin giving us our use permit for education.

Front row left to right: Hormos Shariot, Phyllis Lanyon, Laura Gschwend, Barbara Jackowski, Dave Stram, Yong Garcia, Dan Converse, Bill Yee, Ann Gibson, Kay Llovio
Second row left to right: Marc Bigelow, Mike Stipe, Gerry Matsumoto, Randy Christian, Roger Edrington, Ron Carter, Bryce Jessup, Frank Bergandi, Joe Womack

Unanimous Vote September 20, 2002

A Time of Thanksgiving for God's Provision and Direction!

In the Fall 2002 issue of the Broadcaster, I wrote the following article to re-affirm my belief that God had us on His radar screen and that He would come through...we would yet have a future! The foundation that Dad had laid back in 1939 was being built upon in ways he could never have envisioned, but I can't help but feel he would wholeheartedly endorse it if he were alive today. The story lives on and the dream continues to unfold!

The two years that we worked to try and get into the hospital in Morgan Hill was all in God's timing for the Herman Miller facilities were not available at that time. God was working upstream for us during those days of frustration.

Page **2**

President's Corner

HIS GLORY. . . OUR GOAL

Be exalted, O God, above the heavens; let your glory be over all the earth. Psalm 57:5 The desire of my heart is that God and His glory would be seen over all of the earth, including San Jose Christian College.

As you know, we at SJCC have been trying to re-locate our campus for a number of years. We thought that it was going to be Morgan Hill, but that did not work out so we had to consider other options. In recent months we have been looking at a site in Rocklin, near Sacramento. The site is the former Herman Miller industrial facility located on 156 acres of land with 340,000 square feet of buildings. It is in a prime growth location and it would provide opportunity for significant growth for many years to come. Our Board has made the decision to continue exploring that site, while maintaining a branch campus in Silicon Valley, should this connect. We will not know until around the end of this calendar year whether or not a use permit will be granted for the College so that renovation work could begin. It looks promising at this point, but as we have learned in the past, there can be unforeseen obstacles.

In the meantime, we continue to dream of what God might have for San Jose Christian College, for no one can take away our dreams. Let me share a few of mine with you as it relates to the future of the college:

* I dream of a college that brings glory to God through the integrity of all of its students, staff, board, constituency and all its programs.

* I dream of a college that reflects the glory of God by its Christ-likeness.

* I dream of a college that is seen as a leader in preparing students who have a deep passion for the lost and desire nothing other than to touch God and others with His love.

* I dream of a college that is supported by the church for its excellence in producing world-changers for Jesus Christ.

* I dream of a college where all learning is integrated with God's truth.

* I dream of a college that gives scholarly information to reach the goal of student transformation.

* I dream of a college where all the students and staff are 100% sold out for Jesus.

* I dream of a college where the major recruitment is done spontaneously by the excitement and passion of the students.

* I dream of a college where its graduates seek God and His Kingdom first and are prepared to be innovative, confident, humble, servant/leaders for the church and society.

* I dream of a multi-cultural college that lives as one family, with the education being accessible to all who want to come and study, from the needy by providing scholarships, to the affluent by providing opportunity.

* I dream of a college that will be faithful to its roots while reaching out to welcome as equals all of God's family to prepare for ministry.

* I dream of a college that is debt free with an endowment of 50 million dollars to fund scholarships, student mission internships, and faculty chairs.

* I dream of a college that will bring glory to God in the community of which it is a part, seen by the local community as an institution of excellence, integrity, community involvement, and outstanding graduates.

* I dream of a college that will bring glory to God by having a powerful "end vision" of changing the landscape of eternity by filling up heaven with people from every nation.

* I dream of hundreds of students praising the Lord, preparing to serve by going deep in their walk with God, possessing self-awareness of all their potential, and clinging to a big dream of usefulness that has been ignited in their hearts.

HIS GLORY. . . OUR GOAL! That's my dream. Dad started the college in 1939 because he had a dream. . . that dream lives on! I remember Dad speaking at a high school camp at Mt. Toyon in the Santa Cruz mountains when I was a junior in high school. I went forward to give my life to "full time" Christian service. I remember saying to him on the way home in the car that I wanted my life to make a difference. I wanted to contribute to the lives of others. I wanted to do something more with my life than play baseball. Dad had taught me how to throw a knuckle ball, fast ball, drop ball and a curve. He taught me how to hit, stand and swing, but he also taught me how to preach – and I wanted to preach. I saw so many small, struggling churches and I felt God was capable of producing something larger – and I wanted to give it a try if God could use me.

There was no bright light, no vision of God on the throne, just a teenager believing that God had something He wanted him to do. In the midst of busy ministry I have been reaching for that "something" most of my life. Some opportunities to leave the college during the past 18 years have come my way. Some of them looked so attractive – but I couldn't. I had my resignation typed on more than one occasion, but I could not bring myself to turning it in, yet I was confused because it was so limiting to stay in a setting that had only minimal growth opportunities because of the facilities, even though lots of good things were happening.

However, I continue praying about that "something" special that God has planned for the College. When it occurs, and I believe it will, I will stand back in awe, rejoicing with tears, and say, "This is the 'something' that I was put on planet earth to accomplish for our Lord." It will be the fulfillment of a high school dream – and we will be playing in the world series for our Lord. I believe it will become a "sweep" against the forces of evil. We will give God all of the GLORY. . . for that is our GOAL!

It had been quite a ride but it looked like the future might just be gloriously bright. It seemed our dream was beginning to take shape. Our confidence and excitement were building as we sought in prayer the continued direction and provision of our Lord. Was He about to perform the greatest miracle in the history of the school, the moving of the college 130 miles from San Jose to Rocklin? Would the San Jose campus be able to be appropriately sold in a timely fashion? Would our students and staff be willing to come with us? How would God provide the resources for the renovation of the new campus? Would we be able to maintain unity among our administrators, faculty, staff and our constituency?

In reading through the Bible in 2002 I had written in my personal devotional journal these words on "July 15, 2002. Proverbs 13:12 - Hope deferred makes the heart sick, but a longing fulfilled is a tree of life. Yes Lord, please don't lead us down another rabbit trail!" Then on August 1, 2002, I wrote, "Romans 15:4 - For everything that was written in the past was written to teach us, so that through endurance and the encouragement of scripture we might have hope. May the God who gives endurance and encouragement give you a spirit of unity among yourselves as you follow Jesus Christ, so that with one heart and mouth you may Glorify the God and Father of our Lord Jesus Christ...Yes Lord...I feel it is unfolding in Sacramento...we have HOPE! Endurance is being rewarded."

The due diligence period would last for about 3-4 months, allowing us the time to submit preliminary drawings of the renovation to the county, do our research to see if we have the potential resources to move forward with the purchase and construction, find out if we can sell our San Jose campus at the needed price, and have a multiplicity of meetings with both Placer County and the City of Rocklin Planning Commissions to negotiate the arrangements. On December 19, 2002 I wrote in my Devotional Journal..."Haggai 2:79 - I will shake all nations, and the desired of all nations will come, and I will fill this house with glory,' says the Lord Almighty. The silver is mine and the gold is mine, declares the Lord Almighty. The glory of this present house will be greater than the glory of the former house, says the Lord Almighty. And in this place I will grant peace, declares the Lord Almighty. I longed to see this happen in Rocklin. All the nations come...the buildings filled with glory...the resources being adequate...the glory being more than the former house (SJ)...and peace will be ours!" I prayed that prayer fervently and frequently as we waited for the big decision day by the county.

The big day was finally on the calendar, the meeting with the Placer County Planning Commission in Auburn was scheduled and our prayers and planning was now focused on that day, January 19, 2003. This was the day when we would receive the decision of the Planning Commission concerning our use permit. I remember well driving there with Bob Rispoli and talking with him about the possible outcome of the meeting. He was to be the one to represent us before the County Planning Commission. In addition to our being there, we had a team of more than a dozen people who had been involved in our planning. We had engineers, builders, architects, and college representatives. The Planning Commission took a few minutes to present their findings and asked if there were any comments or questions. One man went to the microphone and talked about the added pollution our presence would bring to the region with the increased population, heating and cooling emissions, etc. After he made his presentation he sat down and no one else went to the microphone.

Therefore, the chair of the Planning Commission read his prepared comments and said something like "having done our research on your proposed usage of the former Herman Miller Office Furniture Manufacturing Plant we hereby grant you approval to use the facility from this day forward...

congratulations and welcome to the community. Do you want to make any response?" For the first time since I had known him, Bob Rispoli was speechless, but then we all were! We were not only speechless, but stunned. We were ready to fight the good fight if needed for we had done a lot of that over the past 15 years with city councils in San Jose, Los Gatos, and Morgan Hill. But not this time, in just 14 minutes we had received our approval. It was a miracle! We left the meeting hugging one another, our engineers, builders, and architects high fiving one another in the parking lot. What an amazing move of God. The man that spoke against us came up to me and said "just want you to know that I didn't want to be here, but my boss made me come." We couldn't believe it...we were unanimously accepted into the region by both the Placer County Planning Commission and the Planning Commission of Rocklin. God showed up big time...we had arrived at the Upper Lake and it took a number of days for it to fully sink in. We had been in the wilderness so long that we didn't know how to respond when we finally reached the promised land, but our "joy cup" was full and running over and we were drinking from our saucers.

We had received some encouraging information before the meeting that it looked promising that we might receive the use permit, but having gone down similar routes before, we were cautious going into the meeting. So I sent this article to our board a couple days before the meeting to express my thoughts as to how I felt about where we were headed.

It is Sink or Swim Time

As a child I remember bouncing up and down in a lake with water up to my ears, trying desperately to keep my feet touching the bottom for security. It was scary to go out any further...but I knew that was the only choice I had if I wanted to swim. It was worth it! I survived and thrived as I made it to the floating platform. We are at that stage of our college development. It is much safer and feels better to keep bouncing along...it is scary to push out any further for we have not been there before. However, it is time for us to boldly take the next step where we will either "sink" or "swim". I choose to believe that when we no longer can feel the bottom, we will swim. It will be a struggle at first...but later we will wonder why we hesitated. There will be a grand celebration, and an echo of the voice that we will hear clearly one day "well done!"

When you fail to do what you know to do, what you don't know will paralyze you. We know what to do...step out in faith...and more faith will be developed as we see God respond to build His college and Kingdom.

The time has arrived to take the bold step! We cannot any longer stay in the security of the shallows but we must now launch out into the deep. It is a huge step with many unknowns. I know of no other college our size that has undertaken such a huge step of faith. There will be many anxious moments...but I am determined to not let the resistance and unknowns keep us from doing what we know to do and ultimately touching the heart of God and His Dream for SJCC.

We signed the papers with Herman Miller to officially move forward with the purchase of the facilities, with Church Development Fund as our financial partner, and escrow closed over Easter vacation of 2003. We now owned the property. We had an All Personnel Meeting on April 24th to share the great news and to celebrate God's faithfulness and provision. My typed notes document the content and tone of that meeting:

We are now the owners of a wonderful new facility in Rocklin. We have the conditional use permit in hand!

It is a done deal...a slam dunk...give somebody a high five...this is a huge victory...can anybody whistle...the facilities 340,000 square feet of building and 156 acres of land were valued at $29 million in 1988...we purchase it last week for $18 million. We are moving to Rocklin to open classes there in Fall of 2004. It has been a team effort! Tell the person next to you...you are my hero! I love you...I would kiss every one of you but in this day of lawsuits it is to risky...so here are some candy kisses instead! (I threw handfuls of them to the staff)

This is a huge step of faith for us all...we are walking on water...we could sink...but not if we keep our eye on Jesus...not been here before...don't know how we will do it...what I do know is that Jesus said come! Here is what I can see...but a lot that I can't! We are selling this SJ campus for $11 million to a home developer who will build 61 homes on this property...we will continue here until June of 2004 and then close escrow and the money comes to us and it will be used to pay down our loan. We will have a capital campaign of $25 million... in just 3 months we have almost $5 million committed to the campaign. Here is a hand written check for $1 million...I tried to print copy it and cash the prints, but decided that would probably not be a good idea. Now the tough work begins...I have no way of seeing how we can raise $25 million...we just need to do it! We will be selling off 30 acres of our land in Rocklin for $10 million, so this will certainly help.

There is a huge gap from where we are to where we need to be...want all of you to come with us... high percentage are...some unable because of family or economic situation...wish it were different! Grateful that all of you are working here...you could be compensated better in the secular world...but you are here because you feel this is where God wants you to be…I am grateful… we will be helping you with your relocation expenses…did research on 15 other colleges to see how they compensate employees and we have decided on a plan that is on the high end compared with what other colleges do…see your supervisor for the details.

We hired a Construction Manager this week. He will oversee the whole building project and be our CFO. You will get to know Gene DeYoung…he is a wonderfully gifted Christian man…experienced in building projects… wants his life to count for our Lord.

What a memorable celebration we had on that day with our college community! A few days later the Herman Miller representative presented me with the keys to our new campus at 333 Sunset Blvd., Rocklin, California! New life is seen in the April trees and felt powerfully in my own heart. We were now ready to shift into high gear to get the campus renovated and ready for it to become a university.

There would be a lot of work to be done if we were going to be open for classes in Fall of 2004. It would take until summer of 2003 to finalize the architectural plans and get everything cleared through the county and city planning commissions. Once that was done constructions could begin.

Gene DeYoung, our VP for Administration and Finance continued to work with our architect, Russ Taylor, and Reeve-Knight, our building contractors. Bob Reeve and Joe Knight had built a number of churches in the region, and they, along with Russ Taylor, were great Christian guys with global Kingdom hearts. They were a joy to work with and they continue in those roles at WJU as we continue to expand and increase our impact.

We knew that we needed to begin connecting with the churches, businesses, education, government, etc., in the region. My son, Jim Jessup, just happened to be in transition in ministry in the Winter of 2003 and he talked to me about perhaps moving to Rocklin and connecting the churches in the region to the university if everything should come together for the move. I replied, "Great idea but we don't have funding for it." He replied, "How about if I raised most of my own support?" My reply, "You're hired!" Jim had been on staff as our recruiter shortly after college, and he also had been a youth pastor and a pastor and so he was a good fit for his new role, plus he was already well connected with many churches in Northern California. He began his work on February 1st and started to immediately connect with the churches in the region and their pastors to get acquainted and to let them know about the college coming to the region. In the October Board report of October 9, 2003, he reported that he had given 63 church tours of the new facilities and contacted over 100 churches, along with directing the alumni portion of PR and working with area schools and college fairs. The first pastors' gathering was on January 28, 2004. More than 250 pastors came to the campus to hear about the university and its plans, and to see the new facilities. This was astounding to us, for in San Jose if we had 75 pastors show up for a gathering on our campus we felt that was huge. It was another indicator of great things to come! Here is a picture of that 1st pastors gathering. It was a thrill for me to stand there before them, to get acquainted, and to share our vision for the future.

Pastors' Luncheon January 28, 2004

In addition, Jim formed a local pastors support team, made up of about a dozen influential pastors in the region. This team met a number of times to give feedback to us on what they would like to see the university become in the region and beyond. They were extremely helpful in connecting us to the churches; helping us to understand the region and how best to move forward to become a premier Christian university in Northern California.

Joe Womack, our VP for Advancement, also moved early into the Sacramento region to begin connecting the university to the community, working with the Chamber of Commerce of Rocklin, and getting acquainted with the business and educational community in the area. He placed over 35 significant articles in area newspapers, 6 television stories (one appearance on a local/network talk and news show), and two radio interviews. Rocklin Chamber of Commerce hosted the University's full-time employees for a "welcome lunch" at the Sunset-Whitney Country Club where several community, county, and state officials offered words of welcome. In addition, Joe led us in our search for a new name for the school. It was obvious that we could not use the name of San Jose Christian College. A firm was hired to help us in our research and they came up with about eight viable names. Their recommendation to the team was William Jessup University. Our research team was some SJCC administrators, faculty, and staff. They chewed on the recommended name for a few weeks and ended up recommending it to the Board of Trustees. At first I felt uncomfortable about the name as I felt it drew too much attention to our family and it took me a while to begin to relax about it. I will always remember the Board level discussion. After they had discussed it, they asked me, "Bryce, how do you think your Dad would feel about the college being named after him?" I said, "I don't think he would like that." The first comment was, "Well, what is the next item on the agenda? Let's move on." They voted unanimously to name it after the founder! I have thought a number of times about what I will say to Dad on that day when I meet him at the Pearly Gates of heaven. He will no doubt affirm me for the job that was done in leading the college to Rocklin, but then he will say, "But why did you let them name it after me?" My response will be, "Dad, you know these Boards, sometimes you just can't control them."

Our Board of Trustees Chair during the time of transition was Dave Stram. Dave was the senior Pastor of the Creswell Church of Christ for more than 30 years and is currently the mayor of Creswell, Oregon. Below are his reflections on the decision to move from San Jose to Rocklin. I am so appreciative of his steady, skillful, and God-directed leadership during that time.

Memories of San Jose Christian College and William Jessup University – *By Dave Stram*

At the May, 2002 Board meeting of SJCC I was elected Board Chair. We had just been through the painful experience of purchasing a hospital in Morgan Hill then losing it. One of the thoughts that passed through my head was, "Will I chair the Board that closes San Jose Christian College?" It was not a pleasant thought.

Sometime later that month (May) or early June I received a phone call from Bryce asking me to fly to Sacramento and look at some property as a possible site for a move. My response was, "Sacramento? Bryce, we're San Jose Christian College." But Bryce was insistent. He had found a new location and wanted me to see it. And so I flew down and took my first tour of the former Herman Miller facility in Rocklin. It was quite impressive: three large buildings, some office space, and lots of land. But I must confess, I couldn't see how it could be turned into a Christian College campus. In fact, I remember saying to myself, "I can't see it. I can't envision our college here." This was so totally different than the small, intimate setting we had in San Jose.

Looking back, it's a good thing that the future of the college didn't depend on my ability to see it! Others could see it, and God did a wonderful work in spite of my first impression and lack of vision.

Still later that summer Bryce called again, asking me to return once more to Sacramento. "We have been approached by Hope International University about a possible merger with them." Back to Sacramento I flew for a meeting at the Herman Miller site for a day of conversation with the President of Hope and members of the administration and executive Board. Bryce Jessup (SJCC) and LeRoy Lawson (HIU) were visionary leaders, looking into the future and considering what shape Christian higher education might need to take in the future in order to survive and be viable into the 21ˢᵗ century. These were exciting conversations to be a part of! At the end of this meeting it was agreed that both Boards would discuss the possibility of a merger at their fall 2002 Board meetings.

That October, our Board met at the Rocklin site. Traditionally the fall Board meeting had the flavor of a retreat; we met at the beach one year, at Tahoe another, and on the campus of the Morgan Hill hospital another year. This October saw us in Rocklin, touring the facility and discussing some rather large ideas: relocating from San Jose to Sacramento and merging with Hope International University. There was a new vibrancy to our board as we sat in the conference room in Rocklin overlooking the city below and dreaming about the future. At the conclusion of the meetings it was clear that the board was very interested both in relocating and merging with HIU.

Early in January of 2003, the Board Executive teams and key Administrators of both SJCC and HIU met on the Hope campus in Fullerton to continue the merger conversation. The proposal coming from Hope was that we would make the move first to Rocklin, selling our property in San Jose, raising the necessary funds to purchase the facility, then transitioning staff and students and holding classes for a year. The following year Hope would join us. It was going to take them a little longer to sell their facility, prepare their constituents for the move, and relocate their staff to Sacramento. The concept was that the two schools would cease to exist and would create a brand new University with a new name and a new Administration.

In addition, Hope President LeRoy Lawson and Bryce had been having some conversations about the possibility of both retiring from the Presidency, so that a younger man could be the President of the newly formed University. One possible scenario had us creating a new University with one campus in Rocklin and the other one in Fullerton; selecting a new President who would lead the University once it was formed; moving Hope's undergraduate school to Rocklin a year later, while maintaining their post-graduate school in Southern California. What became apparent to me was that our President, Bryce Jessup, was probably not going to be the President of the newly formed University.

The mood of the SJCC executive Board was very positive at the end of this January meeting. But it was evident that our Administrative team had concerns. The task ahead was daunting: relocate to Sacramento while planning for a merger. Could it all be done in the coming year? That was a question we had to consider.

It was clear to me that our Executive team was prepared to recommend that we move forward with the merger. Yet I was troubled by the change of direction in our Administration.

One week later both Boards were set to meet for their own January Board meetings. It was agreed that a final decision would be made at that time. The ball was in our court. Our meetings convened on a Thursday, with the Hope Board meeting on Friday. Since we were the ones set to purchase the facility and make the move first, it was understood that ours was the first decision to be made. Were we ready to merge with Hope? At the conclusion of our Thursday meetings, I was to call the Board Chair of Hope with our decision. If it was a "Yes," then he would take the news to the Hope Board and see if they were in agreement.

I will never forget the Thursday morning that I drove from Creswell, Oregon to Portland to catch my flight to San Jose. During my two hour drive to Portland I pondered the future of San Jose Christian College: we would move to Rocklin, raise millions of dollars to make it possible, relocate teachers and staff, bring as many students along as we could, recruit new students, rename the college and become a University - all in the next 18 months. Much of this would fall upon the shoulders of our President, Bryce Jessup, yet it was unclear who would be the President of this new University. It did not look like it would be Bryce.

This was the scenario I imagined: our Board would give Bryce the charge to raise a few million dollars, keep the staff unified and the morale high during the transition, represent the college to a questioning constituency, be the *"voice" of the school to potential donors and new partners in the Sacramento area, then successfully complete the move to Rocklin. But . . . when the moving vans came to San Jose, they would not be coming to his door. And I wondered: Can Bryce be the leader we need him to be in the coming months, full of energy and commitment to this process, all the while knowing that he will probably not be the President of this new University he has dreamed for, worked for, and helped to create? The answer in my mind was a resounding, "No."*

By the time the plane touched down at San Jose International Airport I had serious misgivings about the direction we were heading. Arriving at the college, I went to the Administration office and inquired whether Bryce was available. He was, so I went in to see him. I shared my morning's ruminations and conclusion. Bryce's response was, "Who have you been talking to today?" I said, "No one. I had breakfast with Jocelyn, got in the car and drove to the airport. I don't have a cell phone and have not talked with anyone today until I arrived here. It's just been me, my thoughts and God."

Bryce was a bit incredulous. He said that he had also been troubled and so, the previous day, he had talked to one of his advisors who had given him this counsel: "You cannot effectively lead in the transition to Rocklin and the merger at the same time. You will not function at your best if you know that you are creating something that you will not be a part of. You need to stay at the helm, be fully engaged as the leader, make the successful move to Rocklin, be the President of the new University and then, if you want to consider a merger, do it in a year or two."

The streams of thought were converging; it appeared God was leading Bryce and me to the same conclusion. We agreed on a new presentation to be made to the Board that afternoon. When the Board convened I made this presentation: We would table the merger talks, affirm Bryce as our President both now and in the creation of the new University, make a successful move to Rocklin in the next 18 months, and then once successfully established reconsider a possible merger with HIU. My commitment, expressed to the Board, was that we would need Bryce at-his-best in the coming 18 months. He had the dream and the ability to communicate it; he had our full confidence and that of our staff, students, and constituents; he was the leader we needed at this critical juncture in our school's history. We could afford no compromise of his passions and dedication at this hour. Talks of the merger would have to wait; for now, SJCC needed to go it alone.

Conversation followed and the Board concurred with this new direction. A strong decision was made by the Board of SJCC that day: Bryce was the leader we needed, talks of merger would be tabled, we would proceed to move the college to Rocklin and establish a new University. At the end of the meeting, there was elation in the room. Now I needed to make the call to the Hope Board chair. Bryce and I went to his office and I placed the call. The Hope chair was very gracious in receiving our decision. He wished us the very best in the months to come. We agreed that once we had successfully made the move, we would reconsider entering into talks of a possible merger.

From that moment on, so many exciting things

happened. As the vision spread through the Silicon Valley and into the Sacramento area and beyond, partners came on board. The religious and business community in Sacramento received us with open arms. In May, our Board met again at Rocklin and voted unanimously to purchase the former Herman Miller facility for the price of $18 million dollars. Next was the matter of renaming the school, since San Jose Christian College would not be appropriate once we were located in Rocklin. A finer name could not have been selected than that of our founder, William Jessup. And so William Jessup University came into existence! One of our Board members, Frank Bergandi, generously presented each Board member with a sweatshirt sporting the name, "William Jessup University". Our present campus, the beloved 9-acre postage stamp in the heart of San Jose, was put up for sale.

During the final months of my term as Board Chair, I had both the honor of signing the purchase documents for our new campus in Rocklin as well as the sad duty of signing the sale papers on our San Jose campus, where I had met my wife in 1977 and graduated in 1982. At commencement in May, graduates received diplomas that said, "San Jose Christian College" and "William Jessup University".

And then, as I walked off the stage at the conclusion of this historic graduation, my term of service came to an end. During the six years I had served on the Board we had gone from a six-million dollar campus renovation project that never got off the ground, to the purchase of a hospital where we would never hold classes, to a beautiful facility 100 miles north that would become the home to

William Jessup University. It was an amazing, God-filled six years in the life of this Christian college.

There were so many fine Board members who served during this time. We were blessed to have a dedicated team of Administrators, led by Bryce Jessup along with Roger Edrington, Kay Llovio, and Joe Womack. The end result, I believe, is to the glory of God and the furthering of the mission to "make disciples of all nations"!

CHAPTER TEN

Construction and Entry
The Promise Land! *(2004)*

Classes continued at the San Jose campus for the 2003-2004 school year. Enrollment dropped some to around 350 students during our last three years on the San Jose campus as students knew that we would be relocating.

Our construction team continued their negotiations with Placer County and the City of Rocklin building department concerning our renovation project and soon received the necessary building permits. The renovation work started on our new campus in July of 2003. Here are some of the early pictures of the construction that was occurring, building buildings inside of buildings!

The 2003-2004 school year was a time for preparation for the move with staff and teachers continuing their work in San Jose, but making frequent trips over to the Sacramento region to look for housing and to survey the new campus development. It was exciting to see the enthusiasm begin to build toward the Rocklin move. My wife and I purchased a four-year-old JMC Home in the Fall of 2003 in a housing community that was the closest one to our campus. I wanted it close so that I could ride my bike to the campus and later…my wheelchair.

In November, I drove to Rocklin from San Jose to attend the annual breakfast meeting presentation of the Placer County Economic Board. I arrived the night before to stay in our unfurnished home to sleep on a temporary bed. Around midnight I crawled into bed but soon remembered that I had left some things in my car in the garage that I intended to bring into the house. As I walked into the garage the door shut and locked behind me. The door had springs in the hinges and I was locked out of the house for my keys were by my bed. There I stood, in about 45 degree temperature in my shorts with a thin tee shirt and bare footed, wondering what to do. I couldn't knock on my neighbors doors for I didn't know them, plus everybody was in bed, plus it is risky knocking on a door at midnight! I looked around the garage and saw my chest high neoprene waders that I had brought over on a previous trip. I put them on for warmth, crawled around the garage floor looking up under my 1999 Tahoe for I was sure I had hidden a car key there in earlier years, but none was found. So I got in my SUV, tilted the seat back, put my arms down inside my waders for warmth, and decided to sleep there until morning.

About 6:00 a.m. I knew I had to do something soon, especially if I was going to make it to the breakfast meeting. I remembered that my son had a key to my new house and I had a key to our new college facility in my car. So I headed out walking in my waders, with my arms tucked in them as it was very cold, and I set out for the new facilities about a mile away. As I walked I prayed, "Dear Lord, please keep the policeman out of the area for if they see me I will be in deep trouble and locked up before I can get them to understand what has happened." As I walked past the open field behind the Oracle Plant toward the college I was sure their surveillance cameras would pick me up. Fortunately, I made it to the campus with no one stopping me and I went to my son's office, phoned him, and said: "Jim, this is Dad, I'm in your office standing here in my fishing waders, come and get me and take me to my house." Being wakened out of a sound sleep his reply was, "You are what?" I replied, "I don't have time to explain it to you now other than I got locked out of my house, I'll explain it to you later...hurry down to the college, thanks." Well, when he arrived and I told him the story, he had a good laugh. How insensitive! I took a shower to try and warm up and went rather groggy to the breakfast meeting. As I reflected on the experience, I was reminded that even though we reached the Promised land, there still would be challenges to overcome, some of our own making, doors that would close and frustrate us, but God will provide the needed waders so that we can move forward to survive and thrive.

To prepare our college community for the move, we brought people to San Jose from the Rocklin Chamber of Commerce to talk to us about the city; realtors to talk about housing; some people to help us process the move psychologically as a number of families had lived in the San Jose area for many years, and it was going to be a tough move for them. These meetings were held frequently, and it helped our college family to deal with the transition issues and feel valued and cared for.

We made plans to have a "teach out" in San Jose for those students who could not make the move with us to Rocklin. This would be held at our degree completion facilities, our School of Professional Studies (SPS), on Saratoga Avenue in San Jose. There were around 40 students that we served in the "teach out" program once we moved to Rocklin and opened our main campus there.

Our last graduation at the San Jose campus was held on May 21, 2004. We thought we had the last graduation in San Jose three years earlier as we prepared to move into the former St. Louise Hospital in Morgan Hill, but God had a much better plan for us in Rocklin. Below is a picture of the graduating class and also of professor Al Hammond and some of his family. Al was our commencement speaker. He graduated from SJBC in 1952, served for many years as a missionary in Japan and came to teach at SJBC in 1971. Al retired from fulltime teaching at the 2004 graduation, though he continued to teach on a part-time basis at our San Jose extension site until his homegoing on July 21, 2011. He was a much appreciated teacher and friend, contributing to the molding of thousands of lives during his fruitful ministry.

2004 Graduating Class

Al Hammond, Curt & Sharon Lueck, Jim and Bill Hammond

As the school year progressed, we began to make plans for a final evening celebration on the San Jose campus at 12th and Virginia Streets. It was to be a time of reflection on all the good things God had done through the college family at that location. So the week following our May 2004, graduation ceremonies in San Jose, we had a final evening rally of celebration on Friday, May 28, 2004, concerning all that God had done in San Jose during our more than 65 years of ministry there. God had transformed and trained hundreds of Christ-followers and sent them forth globally to more than 50 countries around the world. Scores of churches were planted and hundreds of churches were served and are being served by those of us who received our training for ministry in San Jose. In addition, hundreds of people were sent into the market place to be a witness for our Lord. Around 500 people showed up to reflect on the contribution that the college had made in their lives there in San Jose. Songs were sung, former student singing groups blessed us, testimonies were given, and most of all we just thanked God for his grace and goodness to us through the years and for His magnificent provision of a new campus in Rocklin which would allow us to multiply the impact of the college many times over. It was a time of laughter, tears, hugs,

and anticipation of the future. Here are some pictures of our last time together on the San Jose campus. We had dinner on the lawn and then a program in the gym. Also, here is a picture of our last graduating class at 12th and Virginia Streets, and a view of the playing field below the campus.

Not everyone was thrilled with our leaving Santa Clara Valley. Some felt like we were running from one of the most needy areas in America. However, we felt God was in it and that He led us to the Promised Land. We would have loved to have stayed in San Jose, but all the doors that we tried to enter kept slamming shut on us, and we fully believed that God opened the door and provided the resources to get us to where He wanted us to be. Therefore, following the service, the new owners of the property, KB Homes, put up fences around the property and started tearing down the buildings to build houses. It was hard for me to go back to the campus to see what they were doing, as those buildings held for me so many treasured memories going back to my high school days. Here are some pictures of the fences and the buildings being torn down and replaced by more than 50 new homes that were built.

I thought KB Homes exercised tender compassion in leaving the women's restroom on campus as the last room they destroyed. Those who have been to our old campus will know exactly where this was located!

Well, we said goodbye to the 12th and Virginia Street campus and said hello to the marvelous new campus in Rocklin in the summer of 2004. Leaving with our hearts filled with gratitude for the thousands of lives that had been transformed in over 65 years of ministry in Santa Clara County. To Dad and all those who have gone before us: "We fall on our knees in deep appreciation for your vision and dedication to change the landscape of eternity through building a Christ-centered ministry equipping institution in San Jose. What a profound and powerful legacy you have given to us. To God be the glory!!"

Our official moving day for some of us just happened to be on my birthday, June 11, 2004, and it has proven to be the most wonderful birthday I ever celebrated! Over ninety people including their families made the transition to the new campus. This included all of our fulltime teachers and all but one fulltime administrator, and many staff workers joined with us in our move to Rocklin. Pretty amazing, but these felt God's call on their lives and that He had a bright and promising future awaiting us in the Promised Land. So they sold their homes and took the leap of faith in moving to Rocklin. Our faithful workers and their families were our bravest heroes!

Glen Basey, David Beavers, April Belles, Sabrina and David Blue, Cameron Caruthers, Les Christie, Merilyn Copland, Cameron and Erin Cox, Jim Crain, Emily Darlington, Gene De Young, Becky Gomes, Rex Gurney, Portia Hopkins, Jim Jessup, Rob Jones, Wayne Keller, Karen Lambrechtsen, Kay Llovio, Malia McCormick, Bill and Stephanie (Wight) Maus, Jon McFarland, Dan Miller, Fritz Moga, Aaron and Shelby Muhic, Tina Petersen, Lynn Roderiques, Tom Ruscica, Melinda Ryen, Roger Salstrom, Craig Sanborn, Ed Schmidt, Farnum Smith, Liz Stanley, Tom Stephens, Lee Wanak, Kim Whitt, Bev Wiens, Joe Womack, Nam Soo Woo, May Wu.

The community of Rocklin welcomed us with open arms. Though the city has its roots going back to the late 1800s, there was little growth until the 1990s when the area came alive and significant growth occurred. It is a friendly, family-oriented community of approximately 58,000 people. The churches, schools, businesses, Chamber of Commerce, and the political systems were all very eager to partner with us to see the first regionally accredited, private, residential, four-year university in the whole Sacramento region come to their city. Rocklin being one of the smaller cities in the region was proud to have us in their community. We quickly got to know most of the 'movers and shakers' in the region as they took the initiative to step up and welcome us.

The buildings were taking shape and would soon be completed for the opening day in August. Enthusiasm was running high! I loved the new sign at the entrance and the clarity of purpose: "CHRIST-CENTERED HIGHER EDUCATION". This is our most treasured value and the foundation upon which WJU has been built! Every person coming to the campus is greeted by this central purpose... putting Christ at the center and circumference of all that we are and do.

Following our move to Rocklin on June 11, our administrators, faculty and staff met on campus on Tuesdays and Thursdays for the "Promised Land Celebration." It was a time of prayer, unity and celebrating what God had done and was about to unfold in the near future. We focused on the biblical story of the children of Israel and their journey through the wilderness and into the Promised Land. The reflections embraced the whole of our journey from San Jose, to Morgan Hill, to Rocklin, as we had reflected on this story long before we got to Rocklin to provide direction and encouragement. Now in Rocklin, we walked around the facilities and prayed. It was a powerful time of igniting our hearts for the huge task that was just around the corner. School would start in August, and we needed God's direction and power in order for it to be a successful journey and to provide sustainability for the momentum that had been created. Our first meeting was on June 14, 2004, in the yet to be named Edrington room. I welcomed them to the Promised Land stating, "We have crossed the Jordon River…we have entered God's dream of building a premier Christian University in Northern California. You are pioneers, my heroes…God did it…God is Good!"

Then we read together *Joshua 1:6-11 (NIV)* and focused on our journey to the Promised Land.

> [6] *"Be strong and courageous, because you will lead these people to inherit the land I swore to their forefathers to give them.* [7] ***Be strong and very courageous.*** *Be careful to obey all the law my servant Moses gave you; do not turn from it to the right or to the left, that you may be successful wherever you go.* [8] ***Do not let this Book of the Law depart from your mouth; meditate on it day and night,*** *so that you may be careful to do everything written in it. Then you will be prosperous and successful.* [9] *Have I not commanded you? Be strong and courageous.* ***Do not be terrified; do not be discouraged, for the LORD your God will be with you wherever you***

go. *" ¹⁰ So Joshua ordered the officers of the people: ¹¹ "Go through the camp and tell the people, 'Get your supplies ready. Three days from now you will cross the Jordan here to* **go in and take possession of the land the LORD your God is giving you for your own.** *'"*

Below is an outline I passed out at our first meeting. It reflects some of the thoughts which emerged among us and guided our thinking during our summer 2004 meetings.

<u>*Things God Taught Us On Our Journey*</u>
<u>*To The Promised Land*</u>
Theme Verses Joshua 1:6-11

1. Expect the wilderness to last for awhile...be strong and courageous
2. The wilderness is not a straight road, but a round-about hiking trail
3. Keep moving in the direction that seems right... always keeping your eye on the end vision
4. Follow confidently your trail guide...He will be with you wherever you go
5. Decide to not complain or grow weary...do not be terrified or discouraged
6. Don't give up if what you thought was the "promised land" becomes an expensive mirage... the mirage may expand your vision of a better future (Morgan Hill)
7. God will show you His "promised land" if you will keep your eyes open...it may be much bigger than you imagined
8. If He shows you the "promised land"...take others with you to "spy it out"

9. As you journey toward the "promised land"... trust God to provide the resources to get you there...quail and manna and shoes that don't wear out

10. Put your foot in the Jordan River and watch God work upstream to stop the water so you can walk in on dry land

11. Having arrived...use the "promised land" to change the nations of the world

12. Expect to face numerous battles before the "promised land" is fully conquered...but remember...the Lord your God himself will fight for you

13. Give God glory both privately and publicly for every step of victory...The Lord has given you this land to take possession of it

14. Once you settle in...be careful that you do not forget the Lord who gave you the Promised Land...*Scriptures for further study:* Deuteronomy 8 & 31, Joshua 1-5, 14 & 21, Numbers 13-14

These principles helped empower us to keep moving forward and constantly reminded us of God's faithfulness. We were not in Rocklin by accident, or by human innovation. We were here because of God's faithfulness and His obvious desire to see a university center developed which would forever transform young people and send them forth globally to change the world. It was a miracle!

The "City on a Hill" was reaching its first stage of final development in preparation for the grand opening of school on August 30, 2004. The buildings were now completed, and we were ready to welcome our students with great anticipation and joy. We had hoped that 300 students would be enrolled, matching our enrollment in the previous year. We thought this to be an ambitious goal given all the transition issues and our being new to the community. We were ecstatic when we opened for the first day of classes on our brand new campus with a total of 436 students, including our students in San Jose "teach out" classes and our Degree Completion Program! We had 192 new students. Both of these were school records in our 65 year history!

In my October 14, 2004 board report I stated: "School opened with 436 students, with three more modules of our Degree Completion Program starting up this month. The spirit of our whole WJU community is still riding very high. There is an atmosphere of continued celebration, worship, and anticipation of what God is up to among us. I keep waiting for some of the initial excitement to begin to diminish, but it has not happened yet. What I read as excitement may in fact be God's presence and smile continuing to affirm the relocation of the University to Rocklin."

Our dorms were nearly full the first year with 157 students in our three new campus state-of-the-art residence halls. Our chapel services were held during our first year on campus in our lecture hall, but moved the following year to our warehouse because of the growing student body. Enthusiasm and high morale were evident throughout our campus community as we basked in God's goodness and planned for a certain and greatly expanded future. Gene DeYoung, our Vice President for Finance and Administration, put it well in the November 2004 Broadcaster.

Just In Time

By Gene DeYoung
Vice President for
Finance and Administration

Residences (above), Alice Mills teaching (below).

The Commons (above and right)

The reality that "we made it" is slowly sinking in as faculty, staff and students take up residency where welders, plumbers, and painters used to roam. These days are filled with putting the final pieces into place as the storm of relocating from San Jose to Rocklin passes by.

These past months were framed in the pressing reality of our circumstances. The migration of faculty and staff to Rocklin started even before the final graduation in San Jose. Houses were bought, apartments were rented and lives transplanted. The calendar loomed with dates of June 1, 2004—opening of the new Degree Completion campus in San Jose; June 14—all staff report to work in Rocklin; August 21—student student body arrives in Rocklin; and August 30—start of academic instruction. Awestruck visitors to the campus under construction would invariably ask, "Are you sure you'll make it?" or "What happens if you're not done?" The admission of our "no fail situation" provided little comfort.

Our strategy for success was mapped out in a master construction schedule. It hung on the wall for easy reference and delivered a constant reminder to the state of our progress. It included items like "pour concrete" and "paint walls" or "moving vans from San Jose" and "install library shelving." What it did not account for were delays in governmental approvals, winter storms or shortage of construction materials. These were continually at work to jeopardize the transition.

The odds seemed insurmountable at the start of this venture. Even mid-course, it was a challenge to see the finish. Yet here in mid-October it is clear how it all came together. Many companies today use a strategy called "Just In Time Manufacturing," where parts are provided for assembly right when they are needed. The success of the University is built on that concept, except that God was working right along side us for "Just In Time Delivery." For just in time, God delivered beams that were delayed due to the worldwide steel shortage. Just in time, God provided the crucial contact at the phone company to deliver service for our arriving staff. Just in time, God provided required city approvals to allow occupancy for dorms, offices and classes. Time and again, after we exhausted our human abilities, God showed His presence around us, through us, and sometimes in spite of us to assure the timely completion of William Jessup University.

Now, the new San Jose extension campus on Saratoga Avenue is open—on time. Faculty and staff made their pilgrimage to Rocklin—on time. Students arrived to new residence halls, classrooms and cafeteria—right in the nick of time! It is no wonder then that emotion was deep and eyes grew misty as we belted out "Great is Thy Faithfulness" at the building dedication service. The challenges and accomplishments of these past months and years serve as tangible proof of God's faithfulness to the University and those of us involved with it.

The building of Phase 1 is complete. The faculty and staff are moved. The students have arrived. Just think of what God has in store as He writes the next chapters for William Jessup University. Considering what He has done so far, we'll count on continued examples of timeliness and faithfulness as He uses WJU to further His kingdom.

It is interesting that three other colleges also had plans for building a university campus in the region, CSUS Branch Campus, De LaSalle University, and Drexel University. What is so remarkable about it is that the projected plans put two of them in our own backyard, just one or two miles from the campus that we were negotiating for and now occupied. See the picture below. To date, only WJU's plans materialized. The local newspaper, the Sacramento Bee printed the following article in their Sunday edition on August 29, 2004. This was the day before school opened on August 30th. Below is a portion of the article which was written.

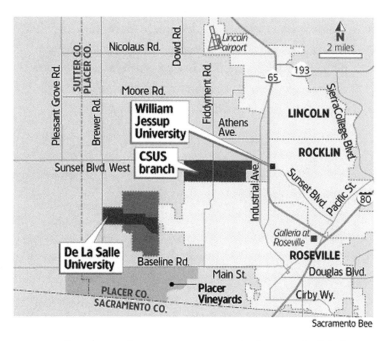

Developers last year announced plans to build the region's first religious college - a Catholic school to be called De La Salle University - on property west of Roseville, but since then, William Jessup University quietly has assumed that title.

"They were two different ideas happening at the same time," said Joe Womack, vice president of WJU. "The more Sacramento becomes a destination for private higher education, the better it will be for all of us."

Placer County officials continue to study a proposal to build De La Salle University on land west of Roseville, as well as a proposal to build a satellite campus of California State University, Sacramento, a few miles west of WJU. In both cases, the proposals involve developing agricultural land and building thousands of surrounding homes.

WJU, on the other hand, built its campus in an industrial area, pumping $20 million into renovating the former Herman Miller furniture warehouse at Highway 65 and Sunset Boulevard. The construction gave new life to a building the community took great pride in - the warehouse was designed by architect Frank Gehry.

CHAPTER ELEVEN

A New Era Begins...
City On A Hill *(2004-2010)*

In many ways, we are a 75-year-old start up! New location, new facilities, new workers, new programs, and abundant new opportunities. Our message is still the same; it is the message "once for all delivered unto the saints." Our mission is still the same; "Christ-Centered Higher Education." However, most of our methods or delivery systems are new. Why? Though our message and mission have not changed and will not change, we must always be changing the delivery systems to match the changing culture or we will no longer have an audience. Too frequently, human tradition becomes more important than divine mission. When that happens, colleges and churches go out of existence by holding onto programs that are no longer working instead of seeking God's direction in creating new local and global delivery systems for the timeless message and mission of scripture. What works in one generation may not work in the next generation. Those institutions which are unwilling to adapt their delivery systems to match a changing world soon become history!

We have moved from being a Bible College to being a Christian Liberal Arts university. Though we still have all of the church vocational degrees and required Bible classes, we now offer over 20 degrees and emphases that are focused on taking Christ to the marketplace. Technology has changed our world in so many ways. We have online delivery systems, and an adult School of Professional studies in the evening for working adults. Some have abandoned us for we are not like we used to be and thus from their perspective we are going down the slippery slope. One minister wrote me recently and said that he was heavy hearted because he was dying of cancer, but what hurt most is that his alma mater is dying faster than he is. He has since gone on to glory and I am saddened that we added to his pain. Other individuals and churches have withdrawn their fellowship and support of us because of similar perceptions. Some have given up on us because they perceive us as compromising to accommodate the broader Christian community for growth and survival purposes. I feel badly about that, but I believe that God has led us to where we are today. His desire is that we be Christ-centered, biblically focused, and have a passion for touching a hurting world with God's love.

He is calling us to be a center for unity in the region and beyond. The roots of the college are in the Restoration Movement, which is a movement guided by the principle: "In essentials unity, in opinions liberty, and in all things love." I believe we are getting back to the restoration principles that guide us. The principle of joining hearts with all those who are authentic Christ- followers to reach a hurting and dying world expresses the unity for which Christ prayed. We will never have unity based upon our interpretations of scripture, for our unity is not to be found in something our minds create, but in something God created in a personal relationship with Christ alone! There is a shared, emerging hunger for this among most of the evangelical communities today as never before in recent history. I think much of it is born of the desperation of our times and an awareness that much of what we used to fight over needs to be replaced with deeper values. We will continue to partner with all Christ-centered churches for we are here as an extension of the church's ministry until Christ returns. The church gave birth to the University and we exist to serve the church's mission of turning on light in a dark world.

WJU Welcomes Over 400 Students

When we made plans to move to Rocklin, we were hoping that our enrollment in Fall 2004 might be around 300 students. We felt many students would not make the move with us. We were pleasantly surprised when our three dorms were nearly filled to capacity with 161 students, and our enrollment exceeded our expectations with 441 students enrolled for Fall Semester on our beautiful new campus. 192 were new students, a school record for an incoming class!

So, as a start up in Rocklin, a new era begins! We have the freedom to create all kinds of new systems to impact our world for Christ, and it is an exciting opportunity that we dare not miss. As I sat in chapel week after week looking over the hundreds of young people that God had brought to us, my gratitude cup overflowed and I found myself drinking from my saucer as I saw them worshipping our Lord. The potential for world change is dramatic through these who are becoming equipped to be warriors for our Lord. It just may be that revival will someday break out from among our students to impact the region and beyond, for most great revivals had their beginnings on a college campus.

I wrote in the Fall 2004 issue of the Broadcaster these words: "God saw and planned for something we did not see and could not have planned. We stumbled into the opportunity on the heels of a failed attempt to move the campus to Morgan Hill. Failed from the human perspective, but used by God to expand our vision and demonstrate that He is still the God of the impossible." I went on to say: "These are the greatest days of forward progress for the school in its 65 year history, and we are just beginning...I am so grateful to God for His provision. The momentum continues to build and we will pedal as fast as we can to keep up with where He is leading us. We are full of energy, joy, life, and a certain hope for the future. Thank you so much for being with us in the journey. We have reached our *destination* – The Promised Land. Now, from The Promised Land we follow God to achieve our *destiny!*"

As our campus community began to settle into their new roles in Rocklin, the momentum and morale continued high, though some of our students from San Jose expressed that they missed the more intimate atmosphere of the smaller campus. On Thursday, October 10, 2004, instead of chapel, our campus community, Church and individual partners came together to dedicate our new facilities to the glory of God. It was a rousing time of enthusiasm and deep gratitude to God for all that He had done, and a setting aside of the facilities for the purpose of student transformation and preparation for church and market-place ministries.

I had written in my prayer journal in July of 2003, and then again in 2004 my earnest and frequent desire and prayer which is reflected in the dedication of Solomon's Temple and my prayer response in bold type.

"The trumpeters and singers joined in unison, as with one voice, to give praise and thanks to the Lord. Accompanied by trumpets, cymbals and other instruments, they raised their voices in praise to the Lord and sang: He is good; his love endures forever. Then the temple of the Lord was filled with a cloud, [14] and the priests could not perform their service because of the cloud, for the glory of the Lord filled the temple of God. **Dear God, I so look forward to watching the glory of the Lord come down at our dedication service...what a blessing that will be...make it memorable Lord!"** - 2 Chron. 5:1314

It was memorable indeed! I yearned for this day, salivating with anticipation, and I was not disappointed. It seemed this was the "something" for which I was created and called to do with my life on planet earth and the day had arrived. The choir sang, local dignitaries spoke, our board and campus community shared; it was a grand celebration to dedicate the new buildings to transforming young people. The following article appeared in our Fall 2004 Broadcaster.

"WJU is the Biggest Thing to Happen to Placer County in 20 Years."

During the chapel hour Thursday, October 14, the WJU community gathered in the Academic Square to dedicate the new campus as a place for students to be equipped for significant contributions to the church and society for years to come.

Worship, prayer, and thanksgiving were lifted up in humble gratitude for the wonderful provision of the new campus and the extraordinary opportunities God has given to the University.

Several dignitaries (whose photos line the right of this page) offered words of congratulations to the students, faculty, staff, and guests in attendance. From top to bottom they were: **Brett Storey** (Mayor, City of Rocklin), **Doug Crozier** (President, Church Development Fund), **Mark Luster** (Community Relations Manager, Sierra Pacific Industries), **Jonathan Brown** (President, Association of Independent California Colleges & Universities), **John T. Doolittle** (Congressman, US House of Representatives), **Patricia Cureton** (Director of Human Resources, Oracle Corporation), **Greg Jamison** (President/CEO, San Jose Sharks), **Ted Gaines** (Supervisor, Placer County Board of Supervisors), **F. C. "Rocky" Rockholm** (Mayor, City of Roseville), **Rick Stedman** (Pastor, Adventure Christian Church & WJU Board Chair), and **Kevin Ramirez** (President, Sierra College).

Assemblyman Tim Leslie, while presenting a State Assembly Resolution honoring the opening of WJU in Rocklin, *"WJU is the biggest thing to happen to Placer County in 20 years."*

Just four days following the dedication of the facilities, we celebrated on a Sunday afternoon the official opening of WJU. Below is the Broadcaster article:

WJU Grand Opening

**Sunday,
October 17, 2004**

William Jessup University
President Bryce Jessup speaking
at the Grand Opening ribbon
cutting ceremonies (right).
Behind Mr. Jessup (from left to
right) Sandy Harris, Ed Harris,
Josiah Gelsinger, Norma
Crawford and Frank Bergandi.

Over 1500 friends, old and new, crowded the front walk of William Jessup University to join the ribbon cutting celebration to officially open the University on Sunday, October 17.

Special guests selected to assist President Bryce Jessup in the ceremony included Jack and Mary Kendrick, two students in the first class at San Jose Bible College in 1939. The Kendricks held the two ends of the ribbon while Josiah Gelsinger of Beaverton, Oregon, the first student to move into the new residence halls on the WJU campus, cut the center of the ribbon officially opening the new campus in Rocklin.

Long time supporters Veltie & Eilene Jessup, Jack & Nancy Horton, Norma Crawford, Ed & Sandy Harris, Ed & Janeen Kellar, and Frank Bergandi were on hand to help cut the ribbon. "The whole of our history was represented today," said President Jessup. "It was a special afternoon here in Rocklin to have the Kendricks, students from the first class in 1939, partner with Josiah, a student from this first class at WJU."

Following the brief opening ceremony those in attendance flooded the new campus to view the facilities and visit with current students and faculty.

Mary Kendrick with family, friends and guests.

Jack Kendrick preparing to cut ribbon.

8

BROADCASTER November 2004

Grand Opening Day guests at William Jessup University Rocklin Campus (above).

Pictured from left to right: Frank Bergandi, Nancy Horton, Jack Horton, Janeen Kellar, Ed Kellar, Eileen Jessup and Veltie Jessup (right photo)

Students preparing to disburse balloons at the Grand Opening ceremonies (left).

As a new freshman student at WJU and the first to move into our new dorms, Josiah Gelsinger cut the ribbon. He represented the strong partnership of his family with WJU, and the thousands of students who would in the future be walking up the ramp to enter WJU. What a glorious day of celebration, hugs, laughter, and tears of gratitude to our God who successfully led us to the Promised Land. This will be the launching pad for global kingdom impact for many years to come.

The first year on the Rocklin campus, 2004-05, was a time of continued celebration at meetings and events. Gratitude, joy and planning for the future growth of WJU occupied much of our time. The Centennial Time Capsule was buried on January 18, 2005, and it will be opened in September 2039 on the 100-year anniversary of the University. In the time capsule are tee shirts, pictures, DVDs of the University, and many different memorabelia items from the past and present. I also wrote a letter to the President who will be serving at that time to encourage him/her in their journey and to predict what I think WJU will look like when the capsule is opened. I would love to be around to see if I am a true or false prophet. If I am still around I will be 104, not impossible, but highly improbable! Below are pictures of some of our first year events.

All Personnel Meeting   *Christmas Quartet*

Centennial Time Capsule Plaque

Burying of the Time Capsule

First Graduating Class on Our New Campus May 2005

We invited Chris Dancy, former West Coast Director of Operations of Herman Miller Office Furniture Manufacturing plant, that we now own and occupy, to be our commencement speaker for the 101 graduates of our first graduating class in Rocklin. Chris had shared with us that he and a couple of his workers had walked around the facilities on the day it was opened in 1988 and prayed that someday God might use these facilities for a higher purpose than manufacturing furniture. It was obvious to him and us that God had answered their prayers, for which we were extremely grateful!

Half Dome Headstands!

In the summer of 2005, the time had come for me to participate in a family tradition which dated back to my Dad. He had a childhood dream of standing on top of his head on top of Half Dome in Yosemite National park on his 70th birthday. Such a spiritual goal! So a number of us family members took the trip up the dome with him on his 70th birthday in 1975 as he exibited his gymnastic skills. It was a fun time of hiking and celebration of God's goodness to our family. My brother Veltie did the same thing on his 70th, and of course I was obligated to continue the traditon. So in June of 2005, a number of our family members made the climb up Half Dome. It is a rather challenging hike as the floor of Yosemite Valley is around 3,500 ft. and the top of Half Dome is over 8,800 ft. We started our climb around 7:00 a.m. and we got down to the floor of the valley around 6:00 p.m.

The local newspaper, The Placer Herald, picked up on the story and wrote an article entitled "One Half Dome Meets Another." So complimentary! The third picture is what one local pastor, Ray Johnston, showed to his congregation. He did not believe that I could do all that was needed without some outside help and so he said he got the original picture from my wife! Right!!

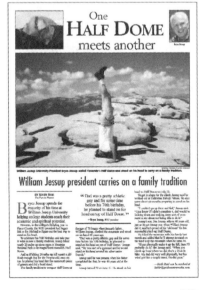

My plan is to do it again on June 11, 2015 on my 80th birthday. I am looking forward to seeing Dad in heaven, pulling him off to the side and telling him the story. I have an idea he will interrupt me and say something like, "Son, there is no bragging in heaven. I saw what you did and I am proud of you, but you better keep it to yourself or they just might kick you out of here." Given his fun loving spirit, his response is rather predictable, and I am looking forward to having a good laugh with him.

Record Enrollment in 2005

As we headed toward Fall, God continued to bless us with good growth projections and we opened for classes with a record 532 students. Our program offerings and curriculum continued to expand to meet the increased enrollment numbers and to provide majors that would meet student needs as we continued to build Christ-Centered Higher Education for both the church and the marketplace ministries. At the October 2005 Board Meeting I shared with the Board our newly developed five year plan which would be completed in 2010. Here is the outline for the plan which consisted of many pages reflecting the details of the plan and the many hours of research, meetings, etc., The statement below is from the Board minutes. As you will notice, there was a lot of planning and work that needed to be done to get out ahead of the wave of growth that God was bringing to WJU, and we wanted to be good stewards of God's provision in Rocklin.

Five Year Plan
(presented to the Board in October 2005)

Bryce talked about the process in developing the five-year plan. It took over a year and involved numerous strategic planning meetings and two strategic planning retreats. He discussed the Overall Purpose, University Mission, University Vision (new), and University Relationships.

Challenges
- Program Development
- Facility Expansion
- Personnel Additions (over 100 employees)
- Accreditation Reviews (self review in 2 years)
- Financial Health
- Enrollment Uncertainties
- Mission Stability
- Constituency Engagement
- Employee Competency
- Institutional Identity

Bryce stated: The development of our Five Year Plan will become an important tool to guide us in the forward movement of WJU. We continue to face an enormous opportunity for growth. In our growth we want to do it right so the future can be powerful. The church, business, education, and political communities continue to welcome and support us. Add to this the blessing of God, and we are confident that the goal of becoming the premier Christian University of Northern California will one day be a reality.

I am encouraged by the newly organized WJU Foundation Board. In a recent conference call among the members, they made the choice to employ a local fundraising company out of the four which had been interviewed. The agency will do a feasibility study to see if the goal of $35 Million dollars is a doable one. Then we will launch into the campaign using the names which were generated during the feasibility study. The Lester Group will provide professional, yet personal leadership to take us successfully through the campaign.

Following our feasibility study, we determined that by combining our previous Genesis One campaign, which had not been completed due to the failed attempt to move to the hospital in Morgan Hill, and the projected Genesis Two campaign for Rocklin, a reasonable goal would be $25 Million. Many visits were made with churches and individuals both on and off campus over a three year period of time to achieve the goal, and thus give us the needed resources to move forward. What an exciting part of the journey to see the way the Lord provided through the generosity of so many who caught the vision and wanted to partner with us.

A Foundation was formed out of our Dream Team to provide additional opportunities for partnerships and to strengthen our leadership DNA. The Foundation played a major role in the campaign, connecting the University with people of resource. Following the completion of the campaign, the Foundation was merged into our Board of Trustees, giving us additional leadership strength to move us into the future that God was opening up before us.

The WJU Executive Leadership team that God had led us to develop was very effective in producing the growth that was occurring on our Rocklin campus. My primary role was the caster and keeper of the mission and vision of WJU, building confidence that God has a powerful and impactful future for us, the connecting of individuals and churches as partners, and empowering our team to lead WJU internally. All of our Executive Administrators were bright, well-qualified, committed to the Lord and His mission, each other, and their area of responsibility. They functioned well as a team, willing to confront tough issues, supportive of each other, and my leadership. I loved them like family, trusted them, and stood back at times and marveled at how God was working in and through their lives. WJU owes a huge debt of gratitude to these four men for what they meant to the early years of growth on our Rocklin campus. I will forever be personally indebted to each of them for what they contributed to my life and the future of WJU. Joe Womack was our VP for Advancement, Paul Blezien our VP for Student Development, David Nystrom our VP for Academic Affairs, and Gene DeYoung our VP for Finance and Administration.

Dr. Joe Womack   Dr. Paul Blezien   Dr. David Nystrom   Gene DeYoung
Dr. Bryce Jessup

Our evening adult School of Professional Studies has been growing as we have expanded the majors and made the program more visible to the region and beyond. Sam Heinrich, Director of the Program, has led us effectively into new areas of growth, impact, and record enrollment. The program is also available at our extension site in San Jose on Saratoga Avenue. We look for this to continue to expand and grow along with our online programs.

Along with the growth have been the many increased opportunities for service both locally and globally. Through our Campus Ministries program approximately 20,000 hours of community service are given to the region annually by our students and staff. This is done through food drives, city cleaning projects, care centers for the elderly, disabled and youth, The Salvation Army, Christmas gift programs for the needy, and in a multiplicity of other ways. This does not include the thousands of hours that are given to church ministries in the region by the WJU community.

We host many regional business and educational institutions on campus as they see our campus as a comfortable and welcoming place to meet. I recall one gathering of local school teachers on campus for a conference. At the break time the lines outside our restrooms were rather long. My capable assistant during my Presidency in Rocklin, Myrna Smith, was carrying some supplies to the women's restroom. One of the ladies in line yelled out to her, "What is your title?" She said, "I am the assistant to the president." The lady replied, "How demeaning, you are the assistant to the president and you are carrying towels." When Myrna told me the story I was reminded of something I had read a number of years ago. "It seems the insecure are into titles and the secure are into towels." We tell our students to pick up their towels and go forth and serve others by washing dirty feet wherever they find them as did Jesus.

Every year in the summer and during winter and spring breaks, mission teams are sent out globally to do mission projects. Our students are willing to go on student mission trips more readily than in the past. Perhaps due in part to the greater availability of transportation and with technology our world has become a lot smaller in recent years. However, many believe that it is born of the desperation of our world, the failure of building our own Kingdoms to produce a fulfilled and fruitful life, and our youth realizing that the deeper values of knowing and sharing God's love with a hurting world is what is needed as never before. As many as 100 students have participated each year since our move to our new campus. Here are a few pictures of some of their mission work in recent years.

Cambodia...Amsterdam...Ethiopia... Tanzania...Thailand...Malaysia Belize...Mexico...Romania...Brazil... Honduras...Kenya...and more!

The growth of the student body is reflected in the pictures below. The pictures reveal the wonderful growth that has occurred since we welcomed our first class of students to our new Rocklin campus in 2004. Only God knew what the future was going to look like in Rocklin, and we believe He has great things in store for WJU in the years which lie ahead.

Our music program has grown significantly in Rocklin under the capable leadership of Tom Ruscica and Liz Stanley. In addition to their teaching in the classroom, they have developed choirs, ensembles, orchestras, and select corral groups. They take these high quality groups to bless churches on the west coast, produce CD's, perform on campus in Fall, Winter, and Spring Concerts, and for many special campus events. We are indeed blessed by their ministry!

Our athletic teams have done well from our Rocklin campus under the dedicated leadership of our Athletic Director, Farnum Smith, who served faithfully in San Jose and in Rocklin. His wife, Myrna, was my capable Administrative Assistant during my Presidency in Rocklin. As members of the

Cal-Pac Conference our teams have won a number of league championships. Below are a few pictures of our teams and their achievements.

Basketball Champs

Cross Country Champs

Soccer Champs 2010

Basketball Champs

Soccer Champs 2011

Cross Country Champs 2011

Softball 2013

Jerry and Renette Manuel and Dusty Baker

The last picture is of Jerry Manuel, former manager of the New York Mets, and Dusty Baker, former manager of the Cincinnati Reds. They have been very special to the development of our baseball program which will have its first playing season in the 2014-2015 school year. I connected with Jerry at an area prayer breakfast back in 2006, and he and Renette consulted with us and raised funds from major league baseball players. The Manuels and the Bakers live in the region and have raised hundreds of thousands of dollars to renovate a local baseball stadium for our baseball team. These dedicated Christian partners have been a huge blessing to WJU.

Other sports such as women's basketball, golf, track and men's soccer, have done well from the Rocklin campus. Due to a shrinking number of NAIA colleges in Northern California, we will be joining with the GSAC conference in Southern California in 2014-2015. The conference is made up of many of the strong Christian colleges to the south, such as Biola, Azusa, Westmont and Hope International, so we will be facing stronger competition.

We are grateful for the growth and changes which have been documented with WASC in annual reports. The information below reflects the magnitude of change from 2002 – 2007.

- A 1500% larger campus (from 8 to 126 acres)
- Award-winning remodeling of an award-winning original facility
- State-of-the-art technology supported classrooms
- Relocation of 88% of the regular employees to a site 150 miles away
- Recruitment and hiring of 108 new employees
- Retention of 75% of students during the move
- Enrollment growth of 67% in the traditional program and 27% in the degree completion program
- Program offerings increased by four new majors
- Adoption of new student learning outcomes and general education requirements compatible with a Christian liberal arts program

It has been exciting to see growth occurring with each successive year on the Rocklin Campus. Each year with the exception of two, have been record enrollment years on our new campus. The pictures below reflect some of the growth which has occurred. Chapel was held in the Lecture Hall only during the first year on our Rocklin campus. Following this it was moved into our Academic Warehouse where we are able to seat a thousand or more. It has become a meeting place in the community for teachers associations, athletic conferences, city and county gatherings, etc.

Student Body 2004   *First Chapel in Lecture Hall 2004*

Student Body 2011   *Chapel in Academic Warehouse 2011*

Student Body 2013

Chapel in Academic Warehouse 2013

It has been interesting to look at the growth of WJU since its beginning in 1939. As has been stated earlier, there were periods in our history when we wondered if the time had come to shut down the school. Thank God for what He had done through it to build His church, and move on to what He had for us in the next season of our ministry as God's family. However, it is obvious that God was not finished with the school, for the greatest days in its history are taking place right now, and the days which lie ahead promise to be even better. The growth chart certainly reflects that perspective.

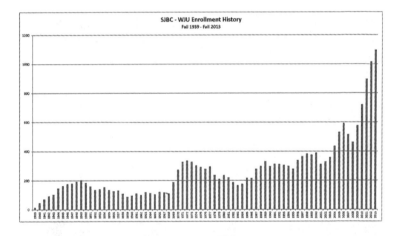

It is interesting to note that we took a downturn in the years 2007 and 2008. I am not sure we ever figured out the major contributing factors, certainly the economy was an issue, and also our having focused so much on relocation that program development lagged behind. Therefore, we upped our marketing program, became more aggressive in our recruitment strategy, and focused on expanding our majors and class offerings.

We also did something that was unique in American higher education. In 2008, we lowered our tuition by 2%, unheard of in higher education. The message we wanted to send was that we wanted to do all that we could to make Christian higher education affordable to those who want to receive it and attend WJU. The decision was so unique that it made CNN TV National news as the only institution they knew of in higher education in America which did this in order to make a bold statement about accessibility for students who want to attend a Christian University. Since that time we have had to raise tuition, but we still are more affordable than most other comparable Christian Liberal Arts Universities.

Our student enrollment has tripled since our move to Rocklin, and the number of graduates has more than doubled. We had 101 graduates in our first graduating class in May of 2005, and 215 graduates in May of 2013.

Below are pictures of some of our graduating classes from Rocklin.

Graduation is an inspiring time as we send our graduates forth to become world changers. One of the traditions that we have practiced since the early 1990s has been giving our graduates not only a diploma, but a towel. We like to say, WJU exists to give each student something for their heart, head, and hands. The purpose of this is that we have attempted to give them Christ's character for their *hearts*, integration of faith and learning for their *heads*, and now we send them forth with a towel for their *hands* to duplicate the serving ministry of our Lord. The towel has embroidered on it "Prepared to Serve". Pictured below receiving his diploma and towel is Josiah Gelsinger, our first student to move into the dorm in Rocklin, who graduated in 2008 while his Dad, Pat Gelsinger, brought the commencement address and was awarded an honorary doctorate degree from WJU. Josiah's brother Nathan graduated from WJU the following year.

It was around 2008 that it seemed right for me to begin to get serious about passing the leadership baton to another. I had considered it many times previously, but it seemed God kept saying "not yet." Pat Gelsinger, my long time friend, mentor, and Board chair, kept saying to me with a smirk on his face when I would bring it up, "Moses didn't start his ministry until he was 80, so what's your problem?" Well, it just seemed right this time that God was nudging me to step down so that there could be fresh leadership and a different skill set to take WJU forward.

So I submitted my letter of resignation to the Board of Trustees in May of 2009 announcing that I would be completing my 26 years of service in May of 2010. It had been a great ride and my joy and gratitude cup was full and running over, but it was time to pass the baton. I continued to serve as President during the 2009-2010 school year. The board appointed a search committee to work with the Search firm that had been secured to begin the process of finding a new President for WJU.

My last chapel message as President was given on May 5, 2010. In that message I challenged the students to become all that God had planned for them, to make great choices, and to achieve great things for our Lord for they are destined to greatness in God's Kingdom. At the conclusion I told them I wanted to do something I had not done before in chapel. I had brought with me my fishing waders and a pool of water. I knew of a number of students who had made decisions for Christ during this past school year and I wanted to provide an opportunity for them to be baptized. So while Daniel Gluck, our campus pastor was leading us in a song, I was putting on my waders. I told them I would be happy to baptize anyone who felt led of the Lord to do so. As I pulled back the curtain, there stood more than 20 students who stepped forward to be baptized in their street clothes. What a thrilling morning it was!

A week later on May 13th, the Board of Trustees put together a retirement dinner for Jo and me. It was a sweet time of memory as a number of very special friends shared stories about our friendship, ministry and family. So many came representing the history of the school, our Board, ministers, community leaders, etc. The board totally surprised us as Pat Gelsinger, Board Chair and MC for the evening, showed a slide of the prayer chapel now named "Bryce & Jo Jessup Prayer Chapel." We were honored, as the College was given birth to by Dad's prayers and those of many other prayer warriors. I love that the prayer chapel is right in the center of the campus and is run by our students. Then Pat gave my wife and me a set of keys to a brand new Chevrolet Tahoe that was hidden behind a curtain. It was amazing! I had about worn our old one out in the many travels for the school, and so the marvelous gift could not have been more deeply appreciated. Here are a few pictures of the Retirement Celebration activities.

Our Heroes…Some Current and Past Board Members in Attendance

Introducing Our 20 Family Members

Our Reaction to Seeing The Tahoe   *Getting Acquainted with The Gift*

Don Hinkle Leading Great is Thy Faithfulness

It was indeed a blessed evening that Jo and I will always remember and cherish in our hearts. The Board, WJU community, friends, churches and beyond outdid themselves. The evening closed with Don Hinkle, my cherished buddy in ministry for more than 30 years, leading us in my favorite song, Great is Thy Faithfulness. I stood looking out at the audience, brushing away a tear or two, and thanking God for His Faithfulness to us and SJBC/SJCC/WJU through the years. He is worthy of all praise for what He has done!

The Search Committee, under the able leadership of Board Member Holly Tiche, continued getting the word out, collecting names, reading resumes, conducting interviews, etc.

Over 200 candidates applied, so the process was going to take some time. It was ultimately narrowed down to about eight viable candidates. During the 2010-2011 school year, Paul Blezien and Gene DeYoung served as the interim Office of the President. Mike West, my compassionate personal encourager, Board member and consultant to many Silicon Valley CEOs, served with them to help process the issues and keep WJU moving forward. The three of them did an excellent job of providing leadership during the interim period. I enjoyed visiting campus, attending chapel, mentoring students, doing some teaching, speaking at churches, and being available to help in any way that was appropriate without getting in the way. As Dad always said, "There ain't no retirement in God's Kingdom."

Around January of 2011, Dr. John Jackson started coming on campus some. His daughter Rachel was a student and he wanted to poke around a bit and check things out to make sure that things were still going well at WJU without a President. The more questions he asked, the more intrigued he became with WJU, its current ministry and future. At that time he was the Executive Pastor at Bayside Church in Granite Bay and President of Thriving Churches International. It wasn't long until God started a work in his heart to draw him closer and closer to WJU. Soon the Search Team heard about him as he wanted to meet with them to see what kind of President they were pursuing and how it was going.

The first meeting with the Search Committee, John took on a rather disengaged relationship with the team, probing to find out where they were headed in their process. However, he requested a second meeting as his heart was beginning to be shaped with a greater desire to learn more. Long story short...after many meetings with every portion of the WJU community including the Board, staff, and students, Dr. John

Jackson was hired to become the sixth President of WJU. I have asked John to write the concluding chapter of this book wherein he will describe his coming to Jessup in greater detail and share his vision for the future at WJU.

John hired me back as a part time private contractor soon after his assuming the Presidency in Fall 2011. He has asked me to assist in introductions, development work, the Capital Campaign, the writing of this book, speaking in churches, and helping in whatever ways are most useful in continuing to move WJU forward. It is a delight to still be serving at WJU as it has been my home since Dad started it in 1939. John loves the Lord, has a big vision for the future, possesses high energy, and I believe with God's help he will take us up huge mountains that God wants us to climb. He is uniquely prepared and qualified to lead us into significant, global impact for the Kingdom of God. I stand on tip toe to watch it all unfold.

To conclude my portion of the book, I stand amazed and overwhelmed with gratitude for what God has done. In a time when many colleges and universities are struggling or folding, WJU is thriving. I have no clear explanation for this other than God has blessed WJU for the purpose of making a major impact to change the very landscape of eternity. So many people stepped up to be our faithful partners. I thank each of you for your generous support, prayer, encouragement, and love. I wish there was room in this book to thank all of you by name, but our partners through the years literally number in the thousands. As WJU continues to be faithful in following the leadership of our Lord, I believe that we are only seeing the tip of the iceberg of what one day we will see. There will be a day when thousands of young people will be calling WJU their home and then going forth to transform the world from the corridors of WJU. May the statement on our entry sign to the campus always be our most important core value: Christ-Centered Higher Education. To Him be the glory! Thanks, Dad, for your legacy!!

"Now to Him who is able to do immeasurably more than all we ask or imagine, according to His power that is at work within us, to him be glory in the church and in Christ Jesus throughout all generations, for ever and ever! Amen." ~ Ephesians 3:20-21 (NIV)

CHAPTER TWELEVE

The Story of Jessup Continues... Seeing and Seizing the Future

The story of William Jessup University is one of God's continued faithfulness. Our story intersected with the Jessup family in such a way that we personally feel "grafted on" to a wonderful family tree. But the grafting operation was not something I planned for! In early 2004 I had visited the new campus of Jessup; at the time I was pastoring a church we

had planted in Northern Nevada and Jim Jessup invited me to join with a few hundred other pastors and tour the facility. Our own daughter Rachel attended Jessup starting in 2009. Over time God began to intertwine our lives with the Jessup story by placing me as the co-founder of Thriving Churches International and as one of the senior leaders of Bayside

Church. In late 2010, I met with the Jessup Search Committee to challenge them not to "settle" for 1000 students and simply surviving. I had heard rumor of this and was willing to meet with the search committee to challenge them that Northern California deserved a first rate Christ centered Liberal Arts University that would be thriving. Little did I know that in God's economy I would end up being selected as the 6th President of William Jessup University and begin my service in March of 2011.

While I had never served as a University President before, the leadership task soon became clear as I spent two months transitioning from Bayside Church to the University. I was able to interview about 30 College Presidents in my first year on the job, networked with other Christian universities in California and across the nation, and became as much of a "quick study" as I could be about Academics and Student Life arenas in particular (I felt comfortable with the Operations and Development aspects of the University from the beginning). God provided many gracious teachers in the Jessup family as faculty, staff, students, and the community surrounded my wife Pam and I during those first months. We felt richly received; Bryce and Jo Jessup in particular were and are very helpful. In fact, very early on I decided to ask Bryce to come back in his role as President Emeritus and help me do development work: working with our local seniors group, and networking with churches. It has been a great partnership and I deeply appreciate what God has been doing among us. The Board of Trustees of the University, under the stellar leadership of Pat Gelsinger, and supported by an increasing number of richly capable people, have been and are a supportive team.

At my inauguration in October of 2011, I had established a clear enough framework for the future, in conversation with our Jessup community, to outline a vision that sounded like this:

In his book, The Outrageous Idea of Christian Scholarship, historian George Marsden observes that the "contemporary university culture is hollow at its core." Or as a Harvard Law School professor once expressed, many professors have become like "priests who have lost their faith, and kept their jobs." [p. 63] I am here to tell you today that WJU is NOT hollow at its core! Our scholars, staff, and students have remained faithful to the vision of this University that was present at its founding. In 1939, Eugene Sanderson invited William Jessup from the Central Valley to establish what was then named San Jose Bible College. Over 74 years of fantastic history have produced close to 3,000 graduates that now serve in vocational ministry, global missions, and in the marketplace as ambassadors of Jesus Christ. The visionary fire that burned brightly 74 years ago, and was served so faithfully by so many and for the past quarter century by Bryce Jessup is still burning hot, clear, and strong!

In just the few short minutes that remain of my time, I'd like to sketch a broad vision of why I believe that WJU is standing at a kairos moment in our history: a Kingdom opportunity that we must not and will not allow to pass us by. ***We are not content to simply be yet one more option in the field of Christian Higher Education. We want to make a profound difference in the world for the cause of Christ.*** *We are passionate and committed to this challenge; we live it out in an integrated fashion through connecting head, heart, and hands in all we do. Through the power of the gospel and for the sake of Christ, we partner with the church to make an impact in ways we are just now beginning to dream.*

Our vision is that WJU be a Premier Christ Centered University equipping scholars, students,

and staff to be agents of transformation for people, communities, and culture.

For the past 6 months, everywhere I speak I have been declaring that our passion is for our students to be spiritually thriving, receive quality liberal arts education, and be exceptionally employable. Rather than accept the notion that we have to be either a liberal arts or a vocational school, WJU is uniquely positioned in that *we provide an integrated educational experience* with particular strength in spiritual formation, critical thinking skills, and vocational exposure through our soon to be award winning internship model. WJU has the opportunity to build a new Christian higher education model for this century.

We are unashamed about our commitments. We believe that students can and should become more spiritually thriving during college. We believe that students can and should receive a quality liberal arts education that equips them to think and behave well as followers of Christ. We believe that our students can and will be exceptionally employable...that a season of learning should be followed by a lifetime of earning!

In the years ahead, WJU will lead the way in a number of specific dimensions:

- Our faculty will be recognized as thought and transformation leaders in their respective disciplines.

- Our Arts and Athletic programs will become known across the region and the West Coast as excellent and of the highest quality.

- Partnerships in the areas of ministry, business, education, health care, and public policy will position WJU as a community leader, partner, and strategic resource.

- Transformational Leadership will bleed through everything we do. Our business is transformation and student transformation leads the list of everything else we do. Our business is the transformation of people, communities, and culture for the glory of God. If WJU is doing it, it is because we believe it has transformative power.

- We will innovate new methodologies for delivering higher education while retaining the best of our commitments to the Lordship of Jesus Christ, the Authority of Scripture, and the Unity of the Church.

- WJU is committed to reaching the lost, the last, and the least. We will not only be a diverse community, we will be a global community. As such, our graduates will be impacting the world around them WHILE they are in school AND when they graduate.

We are a Great Commission University in that we love our Lord and we are deeply devoted disciples of Jesus Christ. We are a Great Commandment University in that we are committed to loving God and loving the world around us for His glory.

The prophet Micah said: "And what does the LORD require of you? To act justly and to love mercy and to walk humbly with your God." (Micah 6:8). With the help of our Lord, we pledge to do just that here at WJU as we are about the business of TRANSFORMING TOMORROW... TODAY

Early on in my leadership at Jessup, we established three themes and four priorities. The four priorities came out of a strategic planning exercise with about 20 staff, faculty, administrators, and students. Our three themes are "Thriving Spiritually, Quality Liberal Arts, and Exceptionally Employable. I'll elaborate on those themes later. Our four priorities that have served us since December of 2011 include Raising our Profile, Expanding Educational Programs with Quality, Securing our Financial Future, and Growing our People. Those four themes have served us well; in fact we have established a number of strategic goals related to them. I think the early framing of our three themes and four priorities helped us to dream some BHAG (Big Holy Audacious Goals) that have galvanized our lives together.

A WASC (Western Association of Schools and Colleges; our accreditation agency) reviewer who visited our campus in 2012 said, "Jessup University is moving from a single-celled family organism to a complex multi-celled learning organization." That change has come with some difficulty. However, in the main we have been so excited to see faculty, staff, and administrators all embrace the new move of God in building His future for Jessup.

We have repeatedly commented through the last few years about the people that God has brought to Jessup. Dennis Jameson, our Provost, previously served at a much larger University and has been so helpful in shaping our faculty and curricular framework. Eric Hogue came to Jessup after 31 years in media and has led the enormous effort of transforming our development department to reach three times the number of donors in three years from what it was in 2011. Other members of the Executive Team for our 75th Birthday include Rhonda Capron (stellar business professor and trusted Strategic Management and Academic Budgeting liaison), Todd Erickson

(Enrollment Management and Strategic Initiatives who is leading our charge into distributed education), and Judy Rentz (amazing Chief Information Officer who has transformed our IT department into a customer service operation).

In addition, we were blessed to celebrate the Grand Opening of our beautiful new cafeteria and gymnasium in August of 2012.

As our facilities have grown, our programs have also been strengthened as we have continually watched God bring new faculty, staff, and administrators to join with our already committed team. In search process after search process we have marveled at the quality of people that God calls to Jessup. We know that He is preparing us for a journey that we can scarcely imagine in this present hour.

Our three themes of Thriving Spiritually, Quality Liberal Arts, and Exceptionally Employable have become an essential part of our conversation at the Jessup Community. Our prayer is that students will experience, receive, and become each one of those dimensions.

Thriving Spiritually

So…what does it mean to be *Thriving Spiritually*?

When I speak about it publicly, I often will say that we believe that college is a time when your faith should be built up not torn down. As a Christ-Centered Higher Education University, Jessup is making a commitment to be about Jesus, about His Word, and about His work in the world. The mission statement for Jessup that I am hoping to have the Board endorse is a slight editing of our existing statement…"In partnership with the church, Jessup University exists to equip students to transform their world for the glory of God."

I believe that transformation stands at the center of all we do; personal, organizational, and cultural. Romans 12:1-2 tells us that transformation happens when we present ourselves to God as an act of worship, and it occurs through the renewing of our minds by the power of His Spirit. God's will gets lived out and proved by us when we are in submission to Him. What does that look like for us at Jessup? Here are a few "markers" that I look for:

We are men and women who are passionately in love with Jesus. We are devoted to Him more than any tradition, denomination, or tribe. We are His. He is Lord of our lives.

We are deeply committed to Biblical Authority. Jesus is the Word incarnate, Scripture is the Word given by inspiration of God for us (see 2 Timothy 3:16). We recognize that Jesus-loving and Bible-believing Christians disagree on some matters of interpretation, but the core of the faith is unquestioned. We believe in absolute truth and proclaim it boldly.

We are in partnership with the Church. We recognize that the Church is the Bride of Christ and because of that we are unashamedly pro-church. We also recognize the local church, made up of people like us, is fundamentally flawed. Therefore, we live in humility and grace with one another and are committed to a local body of believers where we can love, grow, serve, and manifest the life of Christ in our local communities.

We are committed to transformation, to leadership, and to Biblical justice. As such, we recognize that there is a constant call for us to be servant leaders and learners in our covenant community. As faculty and staff, we are entrusted with the stewardship of the lives of our student learners. We are committed to serving one another and our world in a way that models Christlikeness for the world around us.

The heart of God is redemption. Therefore, we live and work as redemptive people. We are always looking to share the life giving message of hope in Christ and are consistently seeking to walk as Jesus did; full of grace and truth. We think the order of those words; "grace and truth" is significant. There is no diminishing of truth among us, but we lead with grace. We are seeking to point people to Jesus, and not to us.

When I share the vision of William Jessup University, it is a great joy to point people to our amazing heritage. The Restoration Movement itself historically, the founding of San Jose Bible College in 1939, the move to Rocklin in 2004, and our present experience all powerfully speak to the working of God in our midst. It is my prayer that the Jessup community will *Thrive Spiritually* as we continue to walk humbly and faithfully with our God.

Quality Liberal Arts Education

I am a firm believer in the liberal arts. Long ago, I came to understand that all truth is God's Truth. That all beauty is a (poor) reflection of the ultimate beauty of the Creator, and all art is a (poor) symbol of the ultimate Artist. I was fortunate to learn at an early age that God is infinite and we are finite. Our conceptions of God are always necessarily limited by our finite understandings. At the same time, I learned early that we did not suffer alone in a world where the Creator would choose to remain mysterious and unknowable. Instead, we live in a world in which the Creator has revealed Himself. Our Creator has revealed Himself in the created world, in the written Word of God, and in Jesus — the Living Word of God. This general, special, and incarnate revelation of God means that He wants to be known and that He has made Truth available to us. In fact, Jesus tells us to love Him with all our "heart, soul, mind, and strength" (Matthew 22:37). This understanding of God as the one who reveals Himself, and as the source of all Truth, is at the heart of the liberal arts.

There is no branch of knowledge that does not have its source in Him, nor is there any discipline of study about which God does not loudly proclaim "MINE!" (a riff on a line from a Dutch reformed theologian, Abraham Kuyper). Here at Jessup University, we have articulated our University Learning Goals in a very helpful way that is, I think, at the core of the study of the liberal arts in a Christ-centered university.

Our students will be able to:

Articulate the relevance of Jesus Christ, His teachings, and a Biblical worldview to their personal and professional lives

Communicate effectively across cultures

Demonstrate critical, analytical, and creative thinking

Exhibit competence in their chosen disciplines

Engage in a lifelong pursuit of knowledge, character formation, and service to their local and global communities

Here at Jessup, a quality liberal arts education will equip you to have a grounded Biblical worldview; think, read, and write well; and communicate effectively across cultures and contexts. Those are the goals of our University's liberal arts education, and I think they speak well to preparing Christ followers to be personally transformed and be transformational agents for their families, organizations, and culture.

I continue to be excited at the fantastic growth we are experiencing here at Jessup. But I'm not just excited about numerical growth and reaching more people. I'm excited that we are fulfilling the "why" of William Jessup. I think we are seeing progress in our University Learning Goals and students are receiving a *Quality Liberal Arts Education*. That education equips students to face an ever changing world with an unchanging worldview anchored in the Truth of God's Word and able to relate truth across the spectrum of their personal and vocational pursuits.

Exceptionally Employable

I am well aware of the conversation and debate regarding the difference between education and training. Many who have heard me speak about exceptionally employable have gently suggested that maybe exceptionally employable is not a good aspiration for a liberal arts university. You know the old stories about liberal arts graduates having to find work in the fast food or retail industries because they are not employable elsewhere. You know the other side of the argument, where the university is always resistant to change and prepares students for the world that passed two decades ago when its professors were graduating from college. I have opinions about both thoughts. I think they are both wrong.

You likely know that I have spent more than 30 years in some form of pastoral ministry. People would regularly ask me the question, "In the Great Commission, which is more important—evangelism or discipleship?" My answer was always yes! BOTH are absolutely vital. You can't have discipleship without evangelism, and evangelism without discipleship violates the John 16 exhortation to bear fruit that remains. I think the same way about university education. University education equips students with the ability to think, read, write, and speak well, among other disciplines. Here at Jessup, our University Learning Goals (http://www.jessup. edu/departments-and-programs/educational-philosophy-goals-and-objectives) spell out clearly our desire to integrate faith and learning. HOWEVER, here at Jessup we are also deeply devoted to the notion that as a Christ-centered University, our mandate is to be servant leaders engaged in the work of transformation. That transformative work happens in us personally, in organizations we lead and serve, and in our culture.

So, I do NOT see any conflict between having a quality liberal arts education and being exceptionally employable; in fact, quite the opposite. Many employers already trust Jessup and its graduates to be moral, trustworthy, and prepared to think and lead well. I had the privilege to attend a WASC (our accreditation agency) briefing in the fall of 2011 where research was shared from 2010 regarding what employers are looking for; I think you'll be surprised at this list of what employers are looking for...I think our Jessup education can and should prepare our students for this:

Critical thinking and analytic reasoning	81%
Complex problem solving	75%
Teamwork skills in diverse groups	71%
Creativity and innovation	70%
Information literacy	68%
Quantitative reasoning	63%

So...if I could script it for our students, here is what I would call the "triple braided cord" for them to be exceptionally employable:

1) Engage their academic pursuits fully; progressively grasp general studies and major focus across the span of their four years.

2) Engage in a series of increasingly challenging and focused "real world" internships, work experience, and practical settings over their four years.

3) Engage with a Christ following community of relationships where they are mentored, encouraged, held accountable, and growing in and over time.

If our students do those three things, they will not only be exceptionally employable at graduation, but will have multiple options to pursue. Employers are looking for people who can think and communicate well, collaborate with others well, and integrate head, heart, and hands. Jessup wants its students to have all that, for the glory of God.

And the Story Continues....

I cannot predict what will happen in the future of William Jessup University. As was often said in my childhood, "We do not know what the future holds, but we do know who holds the future." I know that the road ahead likely will include many leadership challenges. We may be facing many cultural pressures in California and the United States, so our goal of financial independence is a critical aspect of our life going forward (in 2013 about 50% of our tuition revenue comes through students receiving state and federal grants and federal loans). Our Board is clear that we will not compromise our core mission and must be prepared to maintain that mission even if we someday are unable to receive students with state and federal grants and loans. Providing access to Christ-centered education, with or without receiving students with state and federal funding, is a critical and challenging component of the transformative future I see in front of us.

Perhaps the best way to close this chapter is to share the heartbeat of our Rising Capital Campaign. This campaign will help to shape the Jessup community for the next season. Thank you for being part of the journey. My wife Pamela and I are grateful to have been grafted on the Jessup tree.

Rising: A Comprehensive Campaign for William Jessup University

William Jessup University is positioned at the epicenter of the largest and most influential State in the Nation. Our geographic focus of the Capitol Region, the Bay Area, and the Central Valley of California are the hubs of legislative, technological, and agricultural influence in California. After a period of record growth in enrollment, a substantial expansion in the number of degrees offered, and increasing demand for the Christ-centered distinctive of a Jessup education, our University has many opportunities to keep pace with the innovation and expansion required of our facilities, faculty and program delivery. We are leading and experiencing an unparalleled disruptive environment for Christ-centered leadership development. **For our time and beyond, in partnership with the Church, Jessup University is equipping transformational leaders for the glory of God.**

The William Jessup Board of Trustees has approved *Rising - A Comprehensive Campaign for Jessup.* This campaign is named Rising as a metaphor for the upward path of the University, for the transformational growth we see in our students' lives, and for the expanded impact we believe God is calling us to in our world. Though ambitious, we view **Rising** with the same level of faith and vision that empowered William Jessup University's early pioneers more than 75 years ago.

Rising will strengthen and build upon both the roots of our great foundation and our recent achievements. *We are committed to helping students at Jessup to Thrive Spiritually, Receive a Quality Liberal Arts Education, and to become Exceptionally Employable upon graduation.* In that regard, we are partnering with families and the church to equip transformational servant leaders for global influence in business, education, health care, government, arts/media and entertainment.

At the writing of this book, the story of Rising has not been completed, but we believe that God will continue to be faithful beyond our wildest dreams. And that, my friends, is really the "rest of the story" as Paul Harvey would say. We do not know the specifics of the future story of Jessup but we know the theme: God is faithful beyond our wildest dreams and the best is yet to be…